Perspectives on Developm and North Africa (MENA

C000046328

Series Editor

Almas Heshmati, Jönköping University, Jönköping, Sweden

This book series publishes monographs and edited volumes devoted to studies on the political, economic and social developments of the Middle East and North Africa (MENA). Volumes cover in-depth analyses of individual countries, regions, cases and comparative studies, and they include both a specific and a general focus on the latest advances of the various aspects of development. It provides a platform for researchers globally to carry out rigorous economic, social and political analyses, to promote, share, and discuss current quantitative and analytical work on issues, findings and perspectives in various areas of economics and development of the MENA region. Perspectives on Development in the Middle East and North Africa (MENA) Region allows for a deeper appreciation of the various past, present, and future issues around MENA's development with high quality, peer reviewed contributions. The topics may include, but not limited to: economics and business, natural resources, governance, politics, security and international relations, gender, culture, religion and society, economics and social development, reconstruction, and Jewish, Islamic, Arab, Iranian, Israeli, Kurdish and Turkish studies. Volumes published in the series will be important reading offering an original approach along theoretical lines supported empirically for researchers and students, as well as consultants and policy makers, interested in the development of the MENA region.

More information about this series at http://www.springer.com/series/13870

Mohamed Sami Ben Ali
Editor

Economic Development in the MENA Region

New Perspectives

 Springer

Editor
Mohamed Sami Ben Ali Ⓘ
College of Business and Economics
Qatar University
Doha, Qatar

ISSN 2520-1239   ISSN 2520-1247 (electronic)
Perspectives on Development in the Middle East and North Africa (MENA) Region
ISBN 978-3-030-66382-7   ISBN 978-3-030-66380-3 (eBook)
https://doi.org/10.1007/978-3-030-66380-3

This Springer imprint is published by the registered company Springer Nature Switzerland AG
The registered company address is: Gewerbestrasse 11, 6330 Cham, Switzerland

Contents

About the Editor

Dr. Mohamed Sami Ben Ali is a professor of Economics at Qatar University. Previously, he was head of the economics department and member of the scientific board at HEC Business School, Tunisia. He holds a H.D.R. degree, the highest European qualification for research. Previously, he received a Ph.D. in Economics with high honors from the University of Lille, France, an M.Phil. (D.E.A.) in International Finance and International Trade, and a B.A. in Business Economics. Dr. Ben Ali is serving as associate editor for Springer and De Gruyter journals and editor for Palgrave and Springer books series. He has been teaching for the past years at graduate and undergraduate levels in Tunisia, Qatar, and France where he was a visiting professor. He has published numerous articles in French and in English in international refereed academic journals. His research and publications focus mainly on economic development and international monetary macroeconomics. He is actively participating and chairing in numerous international conferences.

Chapter 1
Introduction

Mohamed Sami Ben Ali

The Middle East and North Africa region is composed of a number of countries representing diverse political, economic, and social features. This region is of a strategic importance as it holds a huge part of the oil reserves of the world. While oil represents the major source in many countries in this region, some of them are trying to diversify the source of their income sources. The region is also presenting several development issues and perspectives. This volume is a compilation of studies dealing with numerous economic development issues that the MENA region is facing such as economic growth, pollution, military spending, foreign aid, international migration, the resource curse, the circular economy, unemployment, oil prices, and tourism.

The first chapter introduces the volume and discusses the main features and outcomes of each chapter.

The second chapter investigates the reasons for the established disappointing performance of the Arab education system as compared to the rest of the world and focuses on the role of the quality of informal and formal institutions. The analysis shows that the region exhibits the lowest quality of institutions in many instances and that its performance in terms of growth is disappointing. A part of the explanation to the established disappointing performance of the Arab countries' education system is to be found in the low quality of their institutions.

The third chapter investigates the impact of remittances on economic growth while distinguishing between the short- and long-run effects of remittances and the channels through which they may impact growth. The investigation shows that while remittances contribute to promote growth in the long run, they may impede growth in the short run as an important time-lapse is required for the growth-generating transmission channels to produce the expected positive effects. The short-run effect

M. S. Ben Ali (⊠)
Department of Finance and Economics College of Business & Economics, Qatar University, Doha, Qatar
e-mail: msbenali@qu.edu.qa

© The Author(s), under exclusive license to Springer Nature Switzerland AG 2021
M. S. Ben Ali (ed.), *Economic Development in the MENA Region*, Perspectives on Development in the Middle East and North Africa (MENA) Region, https://doi.org/10.1007/978-3-030-66380-3_1

is explained by the share of remittances devoted to consumption, which may reduce labor supply within the recipient population. Besides remittances, investment and human capital contribute to promote long-run growth. The short-run dynamics and mainly the speed of adjustment toward the long-run path vary considerably from one country to another. The causality tests confirm that investment, human capital, and financial development are the main channels through which remittances produce their long-term positive effect on growth.

The fourth chapter examines the oil price asymmetric and how it influences tourism. The findings document the existence of a long-run relationship among tourism receipts and the positive and negative changes in the oil price for some MENA countries. When testing for the long-run asymmetric influence, evidence was found just for some countries while other countries exhibit a short-run asymmetry.

The Middle East and North Africa region has the highest rate of youth unemployment. High records of youth unemployment have increased the risk of political instability and other social concerns. Chapter 5 aims to investigate the role of quality of education in explaining the within-country variation of youth unemployment in the region. The results find a highly significant and robust negative effect of poor quality of education system on youth unemployment rate.

In the empirical literature, there is evidence of both a negative and a positive impact of military spending on countries' performances. The Middle East and North Africa region is composed of a group of countries with high military spending. Chapter 6 examines the relationship between military expenditure in these countries and some economic indicators. The findings highlight a possible link between military spending, natural resources, human capital, and economic development.

A large literature has emerged to explore the relationship between foreign aid and emigration from aid-recipient countries. Scholars suggest that aid affects international migration from these countries through its impacts on economic growth, civil conflict, and political institutions. Chapter 7 builds on this literature with specific attention to the Middle East and North Africa by reviewing the relevant literatures on aid, development, and international migration, describes the volume and composition of aid to MENA countries, and reflects on how aid is affecting migration patterns.

Chapter 8 discusses whether the Middle East and North African countries are prone to be cursed or blessed by their natural resources. It reviews the literature on the resource curse theory and discusses the transmission channels. This chapter also presents to what extent MENA countries are affected by the curse and show how the curse could be turned into a blessing through institutional improvements.

The water–food nexus in the Middle East and Northern African region is characterized by resource depletion, import dependence, and environmental degradation. Chapter 9 proposes that consumption awareness and resource circularity can be seen as a pathway to alleviate environmental problems and achieve long-term supply security in the water and food sectors. The chapter introduces wastewater recycling as a salient and highly relevant development in the MENA region. Current directions in using treated wastewater are analyzed. Furthermore, forerunner countries from different MENA sub-regions are briefly introduced with the focus on the particular characteristics and policy challenges in each of presented cases of wastewater reuse. Furthermore, crosscutting issues are presented. These include the need for addressing the large consumption footprints in MENA countries, the existence of distorting subsidies for agricultural water, the lack of communities' participation, the inadequacy of existing strategies, and the suboptimal coordination mechanisms between water and food sectors.

Chapter 10 conducts both descriptive and empirical analyses for environmental deterioration and globalization level in the MENA region by giving a snapshot of the current globalization level of MENA countries, including economic, social, and political aspects. Besides, it discusses environmental issues in the region, such as forest area, internal freshwater resources, and environmental degradation level. This study utilizes the Pearson's Correlation Coefficient analysis between ecological footprint and types of globalization indices. According to the findings, not only economic globalization but also social and political globalization has a major impact on the environmental problems in the MENA region.

The last chapter assesses the impact of information and communication technologies on growth for a sample of 14 MENA countries and investigates various transmission channels of this effect using the difference GMM estimator to control for endogeneity. The results show that Internet use contributes significantly to promote growth. Investment and human capital are the main involved transmission channels. The positive relationship between ICT and growth is however nonlinear. The intensity of this relationship is higher in countries investing massively in ICT infrastructure. The results also suggest that ICT substitutes for control of corruption in the MENA countries.

Chapter 2
Quality of Institutions and the Macro-Return to Education: The Case of Middle East and North Africa (MENA)

Khalid Sekkat

Abstract The paper investigates the reasons for the established disappointing performance of the Arab education system as compared to the rest of the world. We focus on the role of the quality of informal institutions as measured by the World Value Survey (WVS) and formal institutions as measured by the International Country Risk Guide (ICRG) and the World Governance Indicators (WGI). We consider a Barro's type production function where we condition the impact of education on growth by the quality of institutions. The resulting specification is estimated on a sample of 74 developed and developing countries over the period 1984–2017. The analysis shows that the region exhibits the lowest quality of institutions in many instances and that its performance in terms of growth is disappointing. Since our econometric investigation shows that the impact of education on growth increases with the quality of institutions, we conclude that a part of the explanation to the established disappointing performance of the Arab countries' education system is to be found in the low quality of their institution. The conclusion provides some policy recommendations.

Keywords Education · Institutions · MENA · Developing countries

2.1 Introduction

The performance of the education system is much lower in Arab countries than in the rest of the world while it has been convincingly established that education has positive impacts on many facets of the society. Through its contribution to human capital building, education is one of the most important drivers of growth and development (McMahon 2000). It also puts citizens in a better position to voice opinions and monitor politicians which can foster the development of democracy and trust in the country's institutions (Milligan et al. 2004). These last factors also contribute

K. Sekkat (✉)
University of Brussels and Economic Research Forum, Brussels, Belgium
e-mail: ksekkat@ulb.ac.be

to growth and development. Moreover, educational institutions play an important role in professional certification, which aims at ensuring good health and safety. Only competent doctors, teachers, and other professionals graduate and perform their important tasks (Cumberland et al. 2018). The evidence suggests, however, that the economic return to education is much lower in Arab world countries than elsewhere. Moreover, educated Arabs seem much less emancipated by their education on political and social values compared to their global peers (Diwan 2016).

The assessment of the economic gain from education can be conducted for individuals by comparing their investment in learning to the return they get from this activity. One way to this assessment is comparing the time devoted to education and the individual's wage profile. The return to education can also be conducted at the macro-level, for a whole country for example. Here, one can use Solow's growth accounting approach or the macro-growth regressions based on the "new growth theories." This framework simply extends the basic production function by allowing an extra input, human capital, to enter the function. This way, the estimation at the economy-wide level takes into account human capital externalities which increase the level of output. An early survey of the above approaches is provided by Sianesi and Van Reenen (2002). Acikgoz and Ben Ali (2019) provide evidence for the MENA (see below).

Researches focusing on the MENA are very few. The micro-approach was used recently by Tzannatos et al. (2016) to assess the rate of return to education in some countries and compare the MENA to other regions of the world. The analysis leads to important conclusion that the rate of return to education in the region is the lowest compared to other regions. The macro-approach has been adopted by Makdisi et al. (2006) and Acikgoz and Ben Ali (2019). Makdisi et al. (2006) show that human capital contributes to the under-performance of the MENA's Total Factor Productivity (TFP) as compared to East Asia and Latin America. Illiteracy ratios remain very high in the region and the educational attainment of the labor force is very low in comparison with other regions in the world. Acikgoz and Ben Ali (2019) find that economic growth in MENA countries arises from capital accumulation rather than from human capital and/or from TFP. These results confirm the findings by El-Erian et al. (1998) who have found that the rapid expansion in education in the MENA did not result in higher productivity or more rapid economic growth. A number of explanations to this situation have been advanced (El-Erian et al. 1998; Ridha 1998 and Pritchett 1996). Some authors suggest such weak link between education and growth can be attributed to the low quality of education and to the labor market conditions which have distorted educational choices in the region. Another argument relates to the over politicization of the education system which deviates education from the objectives it is supposed to achieve. In the same vein, it has been argued that in a perverse institutional environment, such as the one prevailing in many MENA countries, education and human capital could be used in wasteful and counterproductive activities.

The institutional environment of a country is key to its economics performance. Such environment consists of formal rules, informal constraints, norms of behavior, conventions, and self-imposed codes of conduct and their enforcement characteristics. From an economic point of view, institutions aim at organizing and supporting market transactions (North 1991). Empirically, the quality of institutions has been found to affect growth through its impact on the protection of property rights and transaction costs which affect the incentives faced by private agents. There is now extensive empirical evidence supporting the above claim. Some analyses focus directly on growth while others examine the impact of institutions on the determinants of growth. For instance, Rodrik et al. (2004) investigated the impact of institutions on per capita income. Their results supported the primacy of institution over trade and geography as a determinant of growth. Mauro (1995) examined the impact of the quality of institutions on growth and investment. He found that when such quality is low, growth and investment are low. Similarly, two studies related to the GCC countries document the existence of a negative relationship between corruption and economic growth (Ben Mim and Ben Ali 2020; Apergis and Ben Ali 2020). Wei (2000) showed that corruption, bureaucratic delays, and imperfect contract enforcement are associated with lower FDI to GDP ratios. Besides investment, other studies focus on productivity growth (Olson et al. 2000) or international trade (Anderson and Marcouiller 2002). We are not aware, however, of a publication dealing with the relationship between institutions and the macro-return to education in the MENA except Shrabani and Ben Ali (2017) which focuses on the nexus between corruption and economic development in the region.

Our objective in this paper is to examine whether the quality of institutions explains the low macro-return to education in the MENA. To this end, we estimate a Barro's type production function (i.e., including human capital-related variables on the right-hand side of the equation) and test whether the coefficient of human capital is influenced by the quality of institutions in the country. The next section analyzes the data that will be used for the study. Section 2.3 presents the econometric approach. Section 2.4 examines and discusses the estimation results while Sect. 2.5 concludes and suggests some policy recommendations.

2.2 Data and Measurement Issues

Since the seminal works by Barro (1991) and Mankiw et al. (1992), the modern growth literature, although quite dense, has focused on a common specification. The specification, which has become standard, considers a set of countries and expresses their average rate of per capita growth of a given period as a function of GDP per capita in the initial year of the period under study, average population growth, school completion, investment ratio, and a measure of openness to trade. Depending on the purpose of the empirical analysis, additional explanatory variables (e.g., war, ethnicity, corruption) are incorporated. Likewise, the studies of the impact of institutions have widely used the same approach by adding indicators of the quality of institutions as explanatory variables.

The objective of the present study is to examine how the quality of institutions affects the impact of schooling on growth. Hence, additional explanatory variables are considered. They refer to the quality of institutions in each country. In econometric terms, our analysis implies testing how the quality of institutions affects the coefficient of schooling in the growth equation. Hence, the usual set of explanatory variables in the growth regression is complemented by a quality of institutions index and an interaction term defined as the product of that index with school completion. This specification is estimated on a sample of 74 developed and developing countries over the period 1984–2017. The sample is determined by the availability of the data. For instance, the year 1984 is the first year for which the quality of institution index is available. We tried to use the largest available sample of countries and time coverage. However, for the results to be meaningful, we decided to retain only those countries having at least three successive observations pertaining to institutions. We end-up with 293 observations. Appendix 1.A presents the list of countries in the sample.

2.2.1   Economic Data

Economic data are from the World Development Indicators database except school completion which comes from Barr-Lee[1]. The variables are averaged over 5-year periods. As pointed out by Easterly et al. (1993), it is not sure that the yearly variation over time of country characteristics adds much explanation to the regressions. It can indeed be argued that institutions are a long-term issue that evolves slowly. For instance, Paldam (2002) suggests that those indices are typically based on surveys and it is likely that respondents—who may be experts, firm managers, or general citizens—found their answers on their past experience that is typically built over several years.

2.2.2   Institutional Data

Past decades witnessed flurry of theoretical and empirical research examining, among other issues, the institutional determinants of economic growth. These findings give support to North's (1991) view that secure property rights over capital and profits are necessary to give an incentive to accumulate capital and, hence, push economic growth. It is thus tempting to jump to the conclusion that a set of institutional reforms would guarantee capital accumulation and should be uniformly adopted. However, yielding to that temptation would be ill-advised. Indeed, as Rodrik (2007) points out, attempts at importing the same set of good practices everywhere may prove futile, if not counterproductive, if they do not take their environment into account. As Dixit (2009) points out, the informal institutional environment, which chiefly includes

---

[1]http://www.barrolee.com/.

trust, matters as much as the formal environment. Williamson (2009) summarizes the distinction between formal and informal institutions by defining the former as those that are government defined and enforced, while the latter are private constraints.

Evidence supports the view that formal and informal rules are both important. This paper, therefore, examines the effects of both informal and formal institutions on the impact of school completion on growth. The most relevant indicator of informal institutions in our context is the extent of trust in different components of the societies. We will, therefore, examine the role of informal institutions based on the World Values Surveys (WVS). The most widely used indicators of formal institutions are the World Governance Indicators (WGI) of the World Bank and the International Country Risk Guide (ICRG).

2.2.2.1   WGI

The dataset contains six indicators of the quality of institutions. They are available from 1996 to 2002 every two years and yearly since 2003 (Kaufmann et al. 1999).

Control of Corruption: This captures perceptions of the extent to which public power is exercised for private gain, including both petty and grand corruption, as well as "capture" of the state by elites and private interests.

Government Effectiveness: This captures perceptions of the quality of public services, the quality of the civil service, and the degree of its independence from political pressures, the quality of policy formulation and implementation, and the credibility of the government's commitment to such policies.

Political Stability and Absence of Violence/Terrorism: This measures perceptions of the likelihood of political instability and/or politically motivated violence, including terrorism.

Regulatory Quality: This captures perceptions of the ability of the government to formulate and implement sound policies and regulations that permit and promote private sector development.

Rule of Law: This captures perceptions of the extent to which agents have confidence in and abide by the rules of society, and in particular the quality of contract enforcement, property rights, the police, and the courts, as well as the likelihood of crime and violence.

Voice and Accountability: This captures perceptions of the extent to which a country's citizens are able to participate in selecting their government, as well as freedom of expression, freedom of association, and a free media.

The indicators vary between −2.5 and 2.5. The higher is the score the better is the situation

2.2.2.2   ICRG

This provides twelve indicators yearly since 1984 (PRS Group 1999). Those indicators assess the following dimensions:

Stability of the government: This is an assessment of both the government's ability to carry out its declared program(s) and its ability to stay in office.

Socioeconomic conditions: This is an assessment of the socioeconomic pressures at work in society that could constrain government action or fuel social dissatisfaction.

Investment profile: This is an assessment of factors affecting the risk to investment that are not covered by other political, economic, and financial risk components.

Internal conflict: This is an assessment of political violence in the country and its actual or potential impact on governance.

External conflict: This is an assessment of the risk to the domestic government of both non-violent external pressure (diplomatic pressures, withholding of aid, trade restrictions, territorial disputes, sanctions, etc.) and violent external pressure (cross-border conflicts to all-out war).

Corruption: This is an assessment of corruption within the political system.

Military in politics: When military is not elected by anyone, its involvement in politics, even at a peripheral level, is a diminution of democratic accountability.

Religious Tensions: These tensions may stem from the domination of a single religious group that seeks to replace civil law by religious law and to exclude other religions from the political process. It also includes the suppression of religious freedom or, the desire of a religious group to express its own identity, separate from the country as a whole.

Law and order: This concerns both the strength and impartiality of the legal system and the popular observance of the law.

Ethnic tensions: This component is an assessment of the degree of tension within a country attributable to racial, nationality, or language divisions.

Government's democratic accountability: This is a measure of how responsive government is to its people.

Quality of the bureaucracy: The institutional strength and quality of the bureaucracy tend to minimize revisions of policy following change of governments.

The indicators have different scales between 4 and 12 and the higher is the score the better is the situation.[2]

2.2.2.3   WVS

This is a global research project started in 1981 as a part of the European Values Study and quickly became one of the most widely used cross-national and time-series surveys covering almost 100 societies (nearly 90% of the world's population). The project explores people's values and beliefs, their stability or change over time, and their impact on social and political development of the societies in different countries of the world. It covers a very large number of aspects. The project is implemented

---

[2]Government Stability 12, Socioeconomic Conditions 12, Investment Profile 12, Internal Conflict 12, External Conflict 12, Corruption 6, Military in Politics 6, Religious Tensions 6, Law and Order 6, Ethnic Tensions 6, Democratic Accountability 6, Bureaucracy Quality 4.

in waves spanning around 4 years each. Here, we limit ourselves to some aspects of trust and confidence. These are responses to questions:
"In general, do you think most people can be trusted?"

"Are you confident in the following institutions: government, justice, family, education etc.?"

The percentage of person responding yes is used as an indicator of informal institutions.

2.2.3 Descriptive Analysis

The performance of the MENA in terms of growth is disappointing over the period 1990–2017 as shown in Fig. 2.1. The five-year average growth rate of real per capita GDP in the MENA is among the lowest compared to the non-OECD regions presented in Fig. 2.1. From 1990 to 2005, the region occupies either the second or the third-lowest rate among non-OECDs depending on the sub-periods. After 2005, the rate is the lowest among non-OECDs. This occurred before the Arab Spring which explains the important drop between the 2010 and 2015 sub-period.

Figures 2.2, 2.3 and 2.4 give the completion ratio with respect to the relevant cohorts in the primary, secondary, and tertiary school completion, respectively. Interestingly, the region shows better achievements with respect to school completion than with respect to growth. Focusing on primary, the region shows the lowest score or the one just above the lowest score among non-OECDs. However, the MENA ratio is steadily increasing over the whole period of observation. A similar picture emerges for the secondary and tertiary completion ratios. Starting from the last position in 1990–1995 the MENA's ratio steadily increased to reach one of the good performers.

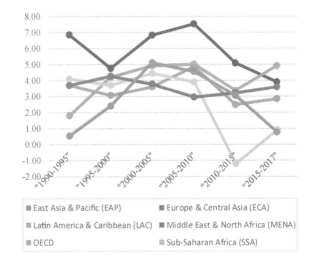

Fig. 2.1 Growth rate of real per capita GDP by world regions

Fig. 2.2 Schools completion ratio by world regions (primary)

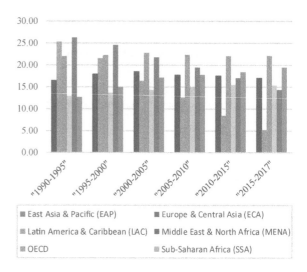

Fig. 2.3 Schools completion ratio by world regions (secondary)

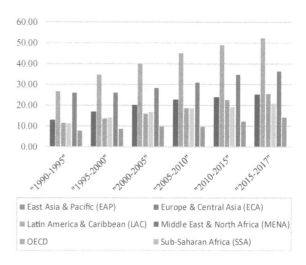

Some catch-up of the MENA seems to take place with respect to non-OECDs but it is insufficient to make it highly ranked.

Table 2.1 presents a sort of combination of the above figures. It concerns estimates of macro-returns to education by world region. We borrow this from Montenegro and Patrinos (2014). The table shows that returns to additional year of schooling are highest in sub-Saharan Africa (12.4%), significantly above the global average (9.7%). Returns are lowest in the Middle East/North Africa region (7.3%). Good returns are experienced in East Asia (9.4%) and Latin America (9.2%). The returns are below average in the Eastern European economies (7.4%) and in South Asia (7.7%).

Fig. 2.4 Schools completion ratio by world regions (tertiatry)

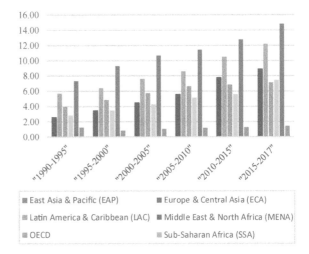

■ East Asia & Pacific (EAP)   ■ Europe & Central Asia (ECA)
■ Latin America & Caribbean (LAC)   ■ Middle East & North Africa (MENA)
■ OECD   ■ Sub-Saharan Africa (SSA)

Table 2.1 Comparable estimates of the macro-return to education

	Average return to schooling			Average years of schooling		
	Total	Male	Female	Total	Male	Female
High-income economies	10	9.5	11.1	12.9	12.7	13.1
East Asia and Pacific	9.4	9.2	10.1	10.4	10.2	10.7
Europe and Central Asia	7.4	6.9	9.4	12.4	12.2	12.7
Latin America and Caribbean	9.2	8.8	10.7	10.1	9.5	10.9
Middle East and North Africa	7.3	6.5	11.1	9.4	9.2	11
South Asia	7.7	6.9	10.2	6.5	6.5	6.4
Sub-Saharan Africa	12.4	11.3	14.5	8	8.1	8.1
All economies	9.7	9.1	11.4	10.4	10.2	10.8

Source Montenegro and Patrinos (2014)

Figure 2.5 compares the indicators of the quality of formal and informal institutions by world regions for the period 2015–2017.[3] The position of the MENA is highly variable depending on the indicator under consideration. Reminding that highest score is associated with better quality of institution, the region exhibits the best rank among the non-OECDs regarding the quality of the bureaucracy, confidence in family, and confidence in justice. It occupies a good position regarding corruption, religious tensions, and ethnic tensions. The region is badly ranked for socioeconomic conditions, government effectiveness, government's democratic accountability, government's attitude toward investment, external conflict, political stability, and internal conflict.

---

[3]For a recent review of the institutional background of countries in the Middle East and North Africa (MENA), see Ben Ali and Krammer (2016).

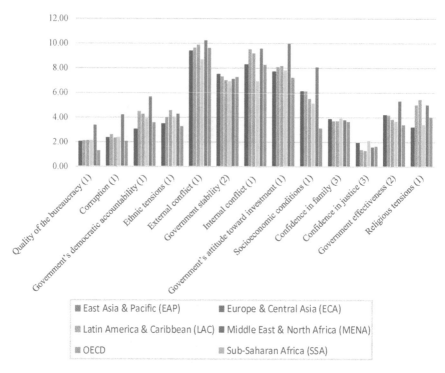

Fig. 2.5 Indicators of the quality of formal and informal institutions by world regions. The sources of the indicators are between parentheses: (1) = ICRG, (2) = WGI, (3) = WVS

2.3 The Econometric Analysis

2.3.1 The Model

Based on the discussion in Sect. 2.2, we will estimate the following equation:

$$\ln(y_{i,t}) = \beta_0 + \beta_1 \ln(y_{i,t-1}) + \beta_2 \ln(SK_{i,t}) + \beta_3 \ln(SH_{i,t})$$
$$+ \beta_4 \ln(\delta + g^* + n_{i,t}) + \beta_5 \ln(SH_{i,t}) * \ln(Instit_{i,t})$$
$$+ \beta_6 \ln(Instit_{i,t}) + \varepsilon_{i,t} \quad (2.1)$$

where

y	is the average national real per capita income
SK	is the rate of savings in physical capital,
SH	is the rate of saving in human capital,
Instit	is the indicator of institution under consideration,
g^*	is the rate of exogenous technical progress,
n	is the population growth rate,

δ is the depreciation rate of physical capital,
$\varepsilon_{i,t}$ is the error term,
indices i and t refer to the country and time, respectively, and Δ is the first difference
                 operator.

Equation (2.1) is standard in the literature (e.g., Barro 1991; Mankiw et al. 1992). The only novelty here is to take institution into account. The lagged per capita income $y_{i,\,t-1}$ captures the possible conditional convergence of income. The variable SK is the investment in physical capital which is expected to have a positive impact on the growth rate ($\beta_2 > 0$). The variable SH is the rate of saving in human capital which should have a positive impact on growth ($\beta_3 > 0$). The parameters β_6 give the direct effects of institutions on growth. This effect has been extensively studied in the literature and it is expected that $\beta_6 > 0$. The indirect effect of institutions on growth through education is assessed by the coefficients β_5. Following our hypothesis, $\beta_5 > 0$.

The rate of saving in physical capital and the rate of saving in human capital are measured by the ratio of investment to GDP and the secondary school completion ratio, respectively. Following Mankiw et al. (1992), we assume that $\delta + g^*$ equals to 0.05. All these variables are readily available from the World Development Indicators (WDI). The descriptive statistics of the variables are presented in Appendices B.

2.3.2 Econometric Consideration

Equation (2.1) can be estimated using a fixed effect model which is a common choice among macroeconomists. It is generally more appropriate than a random effect model for many macro-datasets (see, Beck and Katz 2011). The model includes, however, the lagged dependent variable as a repressor. In this case, the least square dummy variable estimator (LSDV) generates biased estimates. Among the several solutions that have been proposed to cope with this problem, the one put forward by Kiviet (1995) is very popular: he derived a formula of the bias, which should be subtracted from the estimated LSDV coefficient. Beck and Katz (2011) and Judson and Owen (1999) conducted Monte Carlo analyses to investigate the best choice between LSDV, LSDV-Kiviet, Generalized Method of Moments (GMM), and the GMM-system estimators in a context similar to ours. They used two criteria to evaluate the proposed estimator: bias and efficiency. Their results show that with any of these methods, the bias of the coefficient of the lagged dependent variable is very severe, whereas the bias of the coefficient of the independent variables is not. Recall that the latter is precisely the parameter of interest in our analysis. Another result is that, for typical panel data with fixed effects, the GMM-system estimator with the adequate set of instruments performs better than the other estimates, including the much more complicated Kiviet estimator.

Based on these results, we choose to use the GMM-system. We include all lagged independent variables as instruments, in addition to others inspired by the findings in the literature. To ensure that our choice of instruments is appropriate and, hence, that the GMM-system estimation is reliable, the instruments must be both highly correlated ("strong instruments") with the explanatory variables and uncorrelated ("valid instruments") with the disturbance term in Eq. (2.1). The strength of instruments requires that the first-stage F-statistics of the regression, of the variables to be instrumented on the instruments, is above 10 (Staiger and Stock 1997). The validity of the instruments is assessed using the test of over-identifying restrictions (Sargan 1958).

2.4 Results and Discussions

2.4.1 Preliminary Estimation: Regional Difference in the Return to Education

Table 2.2 presents the estimates of a slightly modified version of Eq. (2.1). We remove the explanatory variables related to institutions and interact education with regional dummies. The motivation is to investigate whether the return to education is different across regions. As the ordinary least squares (OLS) is often used as a benchmark, the table gives the OLS estimates in the first column and those of the GMM-system in the second. The estimated coefficients of interest are those corresponding to the interaction terms. With the OLS estimates, the coefficient of interest corresponding to SSA is the only significant meaning that the return to education is different in this region. The GMM-system estimates are reliable since the value of the F-Statistics pertaining to the strength of the instruments is above 10, and the P-values of the test of over-identifying restrictions are all higher than 10%. The estimated coefficients of interest are of different magnitude and are all significantly negative at the 5% or the 1% levels. These estimates mean that the return to education is different across regions and always lower than the OCDEs which lend stronger support to our expectation than the OLS.

2.4.2 Results with Institutional Indicators

Tables 2.3 presents the GMM-system estimates of Eq. (2.1) with institutional indicators.[4] It shows that the tests for the strength and validity of the instruments always support the econometric validity of the results. The coefficients corresponding to the lagged level of per capita income, β_1, are in general significantly negative suggesting

---

[4] Here, we report only the results of those specifications for which at least one coefficient involving institutions is significant. The others are available from the author.

Table 2.2 Estimation results of Eq. (2.1) using interaction with regional dummies

Estimator	OLS	GMM
Lagged real per capita income	−0.036	−0.128
	(5.049)*	(3.056)***
Openness	−0.029	0.022
	(1.761)*	(0.977)
School completion	0.019	0.180
	(1.342)	(2.766)***
Investment rate	0.165	0.077
	(7.856)***	(1.703)*
Population growth	−0.35	0.332
	(2.044)**	(0.536)
Asia * school completion	0.007	−0.079
	(1.169)	(2.222)**
LAC * school completion	−0.006	−0.092
	(1.291)	(2.659)***
MENA * school completion	−0.007	−0.08
	(1.173)	(2.770)***
SSA * school completion	−0.015	−0.127
	(2.016)**	(2.894)***
Adjusted R^2	0.46	
P-value: test of over-identifying restrictions		0.56
Value of F-statistics: strength of instruments		1372.19
Number of observations	293	282

Reference region: OECD countries. t-statistics are in parentheses and are heteroscedastic-consistent. ***, ** and * mean respectively significant at 1%, 5%, and 10%

the existence of a catch-up process in per capita income across countries. The coefficients pertaining to investment, β_2, are almost always significantly positive at the 1% level. Accumulation of physical capital significantly boosts growth. The estimates of β_4 almost always exhibit the expected negative sign and significant at the 1% level meaning that population growth reduces per capita growth. This is not surprising. For a given level of GDP (i.e., once the drivers of growth have been controlled for), larger population means lower share for each individual. The estimates of the impact of the quality of institutions on growth, β_6, when significant, are positive which is in line with the literature showing that better quality of institutions increases growth. This is the case of government effectiveness and external conflict. The coefficients of openness are never significant. Finally, out of 13 estimated coefficient of education, only 3 are significant at the 5% and 4 at the 10%. In all these cases, the coefficient is positive. Education has a positive impact on growth but such impact is not always significant. However, this does not mean that education is not a driver of growth because, as shown below, we should take account of the impact the quality of institutions on the effect of education.

In Eq. (2.1), we allow the effect of education to be a function of the quality of institutions. The effect is captured by the parameters β_5. Formally, the whole marginal effect of education on economic growth in country i over sub-period t can be computed by differentiating Eq. (2.1) with respect to the log of education. It reads:

Table 2.3 Estimation results of Eq. (2.1) using interaction with institutional indicators (GMM-system estimators)

(a)

Lagged real per capita income	−0.134	−0.051	−0.096	−0.161	−0.081
	(2.709)***	(1.244)	(3.067)***	(3.884)***	(2.212)**
Openness	0.024	−0.015	0.002	0.002	0.002
	(1.056)	(0.905)	(0.151)	(0.086)	(0.126)
School completion	0.073	−0.007	0.042	0.109	0.007
	(2.013)**	(0.213)	(1.863)*	(2.754)***	(0.236)
Investment rate	0.131	0.139	0.123	0.051	0.12
	(3.762)***	(4.142)***	(4.443)***	(1.226)	(4.314)***
Population growth	−1.338	−1.748	−1.232	−1.651	−2.111
	(3.345)***	(2.950***)	(2.173)**	(2.467)**	(3.947)***
Bureaucracy quality * school completion	0.011				
	(1.841)*				
Bureaucracy quality	0.071				
	(0.876)				
Corruption * school completion		0.009			
		(1.881)*			
Corruption		0.062			
		(0.925)			
Investment profile * school completion			0.006		
			(2.378)**		
Investment profile			0.022		
			(0.494)		
Government effectiveness * school completion				0.002	
				(0.276)	
Government effectiveness				0.708	
				(3.417)***	
Religious tensions * school completion					0.010
					(2.760)***
Religious tensions					−0.003
					(0.092)

(continued)

Table 2.3 (continued)

(a)

P-value: test of over-identifying restrictions	0.49	0.43	0.37	0.29	0.65
Value of F-statistics: strength of instruments	1372.19				
Number of observations	270	217	217	112	217

(b)

Lagged real per capita income	−0.167	−0.078	−0.044	−0.02	−0.135	−0.131
	(2.823)***	(2.313)**	(0.714)	(0.941)	(2.567)**	(2.342)**
Openness	0.035	−0.004	−0.007	−0.019	0.023	0.009
	(1.214)	(0.365)	(0.242)	(1.306)	(0.953)	(0.370)
School completion	0.107	0.03	0.034	0.022	0.082	0.083
	(2.190)**	(1.230)	(0.631)	(0.676)	(1.776)*	(1.700)*
Investment rate	0.182	0.149	0.157	0.182	0.166	0.151
	(4.157)***	(5.192)***	(2.419)**	(5.197)***	(4.199)***	(3.625)***
Population growth	−1.853	−0.888	−0.894	−0.724	−1.843	−1.535
	(2.916)***	(3.466)***	(1.380)	(1.124)	(3.676)***	(2.698)***
Democratic accountability * completion	0.011					
	(1.971)**					
Democratic accountability	0.062					
	(0.895)					
Socioeconomic conditions * completion		0.006				
		(1.815)*				
Socioeconomic conditions		0.065				
		(0.808)				
Trust family * school completion			0.010			
			(1.838)*			
Trust family			−0.024			
			(0.080)			
Trust justice system/courts * school completion				0.020		
				(2.108)**		
Trust justice system/courts				0.020		
				(0.269)		
Government stability * school completion					0.008	
					(2.348)**	
Government					0.083	
					(1.446)	

(continued)

Table 2.3 (continued)

(b)

External conflict * school completion						0.004
						(1.337)
External conflict						0.232
						(1.893)*
P-value: test of over-identifying restrictions	0.87	0.25	0.24	0.61	0.73	0.58
Value of F-statistics: strength of instruments	1372.19					
Number of observations	270	270	147	155	270	270

(a) Regional dummies are included in each regression but, for space, these estimates are not reported. *t*-statistics are in parentheses and are heteroscedastic-consistent. ***, **, and * mean, respectively, significant at 1%, 5%, and 10%

(b) Regional dummies are included in each regression but, for space, these estimates are not reported. *t*-statistics are in parentheses and are heteroscedastic-consistent. ***, **, and * mean, respectively, significant at 1%, 5%, and 10%

$$\frac{\partial\left(\Delta \ln\left(y_{i,t}\right)\right)}{\partial\left(\ln(SH_{i,t})\right)} = \beta_6 + \beta_5 \ln\left(Instit_{i,t}\right) \qquad (2.2)$$

Under the hypothesis we follow in this paper, the whole marginal effect of education on growth should increase with institutional quality. Since the institutional indicator *Instit* increases with institutional quality, our assumption implies that β_5 is positive.

The estimated coefficients of the interaction terms appear to be significantly positive at the 10% or 5% levels depending on the indicator of the quality of institutions. The estimated coefficients of bureaucratic quality, corruption, socioeconomic conditions, and trust in family are significant at the 10% level. Those of investment profile, democratic accountability, trust in justice, government stability, and religious tensions are significant at the 5% level. In these cases, the marginal effect of education increases with the quality of institutions. In other words, the higher is the quality of institutions the more a given level of education induces higher growth.

Combining the discussion in the descriptive section and the results in Table 2.3 leads to the following conclusion. On the one hand, the region exhibits the lowest quality of institutions for investment profile, democratic accountability, and government stability. On the other hand, these indicators have significant and positive estimated interaction coefficients at the 5% level. As a consequence, their lower quality implies that the region does not reap all the growth benefit is could from education.

Using Eq. (2.2), Table 2.4 reports the point estimates and *t*-statistics of the whole marginal effect of education on growth at the lowest, the median, and the highest levels of some institutional indicators. We focus only on the indicators which have a significant estimated interaction term at 5%. The whole marginal effect of education

Table 2.4 Estimation of the whole marginal effects of education on growth at different levels of the quality of institutions

	Government stability	Democratic accountability	Religious tensions	Attitude toward investment	Trust in justice
Minimum	0.096	0.107	0.007	0.048	0.033
	(2.053)**	(2.19)**	(0.242)	(2.184)**	(1.104)
Median	0.099	0.125	0.026	0.055	0.040
	(2.112)**	(2.379)**	(0.904)	(2.514)**	(1.393)
Maximum	0.101	0.128	0.027	0.058	0.052
	(2.150)**	(2.402)**	(0.962)	(2.609)***	(1.820)*

t-statistics are in parentheses and are heteroscedastic-consistent. ***, **, and * mean, respectively, significant at 1%, 5%, and 10%

on growth is significantly positive at different probability levels (from 1% to 10%) depending on the level of the indicator.[5] At the minimum level of the quality of institution, as it is the case for the MENA in many instances, the whole marginal effect of education is the lowest. In these cases, the macro-return to education in the region is lower than it could be if the quality of its institutions was higher.

2.5   Conclusion and Policy Implications

While it has been convincingly established that education has positive impacts on many facets of the society, the performance of the education system in Arab countries is much lower than in the rest of the world. Surprisingly, researches focusing on this issue are very few. In this paper, we seek to fill this gap by investigating the reasons of such Arab failure. We draw on prominent authors who argue that in a perverse institutional environment education and capital accumulation could be used in wasteful and counterproductive activities. Hence, we seek to determine whether the quality of institutions in the Middle East and North Africa (MENA) explains the low macro-return to education. To this end, we estimate a Barro's type production function and test whether the coefficient of human capital is influenced by the quality of institution. This test consists in adding an interaction term between the quality of institutions and education in the initial specification. We consider both informal and formal institutions as measured, respectively, by the World Values Surveys and World Governance Indicators and the International Country Risk Guide (ICRG).

Preliminary analysis confirms that the performance of the MENA in terms of growth is disappointing over the period 1990–2017. Interestingly, the region shows better achievements with respect to school completion. The comparison of the MENA

---

[5]The whole marginal effect of education on growth is never significant with religious tensions.

to the rest of the world's non-OECD regions shows that in terms of both formal and informal institutions, the performances are, in general, disappointing.

The econometric investigation shows that the estimated coefficients of the interaction term are significantly positive for a number of indicators of the quality of institutions. This means that the marginal effect of education on growth increases with these measures of the quality of institutions. However, the Region exhibits the lowest quality in these cases. The return to education is, therefore, the lowest implying a loss in terms of growth in the Region.

A strand of the literature points to the quality of the education system as one cause of the lost growth. Our analysis shows that another mechanism is in play. Actually, families and their children seek the maximum return of their investment in education. This is achieved in large part through good jobs. Following the reforms in many countries, the opportunity of employment in the public sector has been drastically reduced. This means that the private sector should be dynamic enough to offer jobs and, hence, motivate youth to invest in, useful and may-be difficult, learning. As discussed above, the low quality of institutions hampers the development of a dynamic private sector. One possibility to improve such quality is to enact and implement certain laws and regulations. Experiences around the world suggest, however, that this is a very long process with uncertain outcomes. The example of the failure of anti-corruption policies around the world is instructive in this respect. Many interest groups do their best to block the enactment of the law or its application. Therefore, the legal reforms should be complemented by an improvement of the business environment through the development of competition, removal of barriers to trade and investment, and more flexibility of the labor and capital markets. The resulting enhancement of market incentives should more efficiently induce an improvement of the quality of institutions. However, for these reforms to succeed, participation of different actors such as ministries, agencies, employers' and workers' associations, and so forth is important. This way, the marketfriendly policies have more chance to succeed than only the law-based reforms.

Appendix 1: Countries in the Sample

Albania	Kazakhstan
Algeria	Kosovo
Argentina	Kyrgyz Rep.
Armenia	Latvia
Australia	Lebanon
Azerbaijan	Lithuania
Belarus	Malaysia
Belgium	Mexico

(continued)

(continued)

Albania	Kazakhstan
Bolivia	Moldova
Bosnia and Herz.	Mongolia
Brazil	Montenegro
Cambodia	Morocco
Chile	Myanmar
China	Netherlands
Colombia	Nicaragua
Costa Rica	Pakistan
Cyprus	Panama
Czech Rep.	Paraguay
Dominican Republic	Peru
Ecuador	Poland
Egypt	Portugal
El Salvador	Romania
Estonia	Russia
France	Slovak Rep.
FYR Macedonia	Slovenia
Georgia	Spain
Germany	Sri Lanka
Greece	Sweden
Honduras	Switzerland
Hong Kong	Thailand
Hungary	Tunisia
India	Turkey
Indonesia	UK
Italy	Ukraine
Jamaica	Uruguay
Jordan	USA
	Venezuela
	Vietnam

Appendix 2: Statistics

See Tables 2.5 and 2.6.

Table 2.5 Descriptive statistics

	Mean	Std. Dev.	Minimum	Maximum
Growth rate	0.121	0.118	−0.592	0.498
Lagged real per capita income	9.289	1.167	6.494	11.253
Openness	4.204	0.537	2.848	5.326
School completion	3.902	0.333	2.684	4.489
Investment rate	3.156	0.233	2.502	3.858
Population growth	0.037	0.041	−0.050	0.192
Government effectiveness	1.713	0.140	1.442	1.953
Democratic accountability	1.685	0.370	0.000	1.946
Political stability	1.631	0.163	1.082	1.881
Bureaucracy quality	1.249	0.323	0.000	1.609
Investment profile	2.263	0.207	1.613	2.565
Corruption	1.382	0.271	0.693	1.946
Socioeconomic conditions	1.954	0.308	0.916	2.473
Religious tensions	1.766	0.234	0.693	1.946
External conflict	2.409	0.115	1.941	2.565
Ethnic tensions	1.611	0.242	0.773	1.946
Internal conflict	2.351	0.148	1.672	2.565
Trust in family	1.556	0.034	1.414	1.601
Trust in justice	0.930	0.135	0.571	1.258

Table 2.6 Correlations

	(1)	(2)	(3)	(4)	(5)	(6)	(7)	(8)	(9)	(10)	(11)	(12)	(13)	(14)	(15)	(16)	(17)	(18)
Lagged real per capita income (1)	1.000																	
Openness (2)	-0.052	1.000																
School completion (3)	0.436	0.322	1.000															
Investment rate (4)	-0.310	0.105	-0.078	1.000														
Population growth (5)	-0.318	-0.102	-0.397	0.196	1.000													
Government effectiveness (6)	0.850	0.086	0.382	-0.131	-0.082	1.000												
Democratic accountability (7)	0.355	-0.034	0.236	-0.376	-0.151	0.302	1.000											
Political stability (8)	0.603	0.248	0.522	-0.081	-0.255	0.691	0.242	1.000										
Bureaucracy quality (9)	0.446	0.008	0.168	-0.253	0.067	0.585	0.662	0.436	1.000									
Investment profile (10)	0.509	0.139	0.337	-0.200	-0.150	0.568	0.557	0.456	0.607	1.000								
Corruption (11)	0.574	-0.014	0.229	-0.193	0.028	0.703	0.580	0.585	0.746	0.551	1.000							
Socioeconomic conditions (12)	0.533	0.083	0.215	-0.130	-0.065	0.600	0.473	0.460	0.760	0.656	0.641	1.000						

(continued)

Table 2.6 (continued)

	(1)	(2)	(3)	(4)	(5)	(6)	(7)	(8)	(9)	(10)	(11)	(12)	(13)	(14)	(15)	(16)	(17)	(18)
Religious tensions (13)	0.304	-0.119	0.269	-0.252	-0.172	0.211	-0.028	0.424	0.029	0.085	0.175	0.064	1.000					
External conflict (14)	0.075	0.170	0.212	-0.079	0.017	0.147	0.340	0.426	0.373	0.183	0.356	0.237	0.103	1.000				
Ethnic tensions (15)	0.240	-0.068	0.148	-0.057	-0.157	0.271	-0.120	0.470	0.015	0.058	0.203	0.009	0.464	0.149	1.000			
Internal conflict (16)	0.362	0.274	0.415	-0.028	-0.208	0.458	0.136	0.851	0.290	0.270	0.438	0.331	0.327	0.448	0.422	1		
Trust in family (17)	-0.025	0.073	-0.079	0.201	0.170	0.127	-0.018	0.047	0.143	-018	0.103	0.037	-0.129	-0.115	0.073	0.049	1	
Trust in justice (18)	-0.201	0.165	-0.257	0.376	0.454	0.076	-0.311	0.002	0.072	-0.049	0.030	0.121	-0.284	-0.088	0.040	0.080	0.366	1

References

Acikgoz S, Ben Ali MS (2019) Where does economic growth in the Middle Eastern and North African countries come from? Q Rev Econ Finance 73:172–183

Anderson JE, Marcouiller D (2002) Insecurity and the pattern of trade: an empirical investigation. Rev Econ Stat 84(2):342–352

Apergis N, Ben Ali MS (2020) Corruption, rentier states and economic growth: where do the GCC countries stand? In: Miniaoui H (ed) Economic development in the gulf cooperation council countries: from rentier states to diversified economies. Springer, Berlin

Barro RJ (1991) Economic growth in a cross section of countries. Q J Econ 106:407–443

Beck N, Katz JN (2011) Modeling dynamics in time-series–cross-section political economy data. Annu Rev Polit Sci 14:331–352

Ben Ali MS, Krammer SMS (2016) The role of institutions in economic development. In: Ben Ali MB, (ed) Economic development in the Middle East and North Africa: challenges and prospects. Springer, Berlin

Ben Mim S., Ben Ali MS (2020) Natural resources curse and economic diversification in GCC countries. In: Miniaoui H (ed) Economic development in the Gulf cooperation council countries: from rentier states to diversified economies. Springer, Berlin

Cumberland DM, Petrosko JM, Jones GD (2018) Motivations for pursuing professional certification. Perform Improv Q 31(1):57–82

Diwan I (2016) Low social and political returns to education in the Arab world. Econ Res Forum Policy Briefs 17

Dixit A (2009) Governance institutions and economic activity. Am Econ Rev 99(1):3–24

Easterly W, Kremer M, Pritchett L, Summers L (1993) Good policy or good luck? Country growth performance and temporary shocks. J Monetary Econ 32:459–483

El-Erian M, Helbling T, Page J (1998) Education, human capital development and growth in the Arab economies. Paper presented in the Joint Arab Monetary Fund, Arab Fund for Economic and Social Development Seminar on "Human Resource Development and Economic Growth", Abu Dhabi, United Arab Emirates, 17–18 May 1998

Judson RA, Owen AL (1999) Estimating dynamic panel data models: a guide for macroeconomists. Econ Lett 65(1):9–15

Kaufmann D, Kraay A, Zoido P (1999) Governance matters. World Bank Policy Research Working Paper 2196

Kiviet JF (1995) On bias, inconsistency, and efficiency of various estimators in dynamic panel models. J Econometrics 68:53–78

Makdisi S, Fattah Z, Limam I (2006) Determinants of growth in the MENA countries. Contrib Econ Anal 278:31–60

Mankiw NG, Romer D, Weil DN (1992) A contribution to the empirics of economic growth. Quart J Econ 107:407–437

Mauro P (1995) Corruption and growth. Quart J Econ 110:681–712

McMahon WW (2000) Education and development: measuring the social benefits. Clarendon Press

Milligan K, Moretti E, Oreopoulos P (2004) Does education improve citizenship? Evidence from the United States and the United Kingdom. J Pub Econ 88(9):1667–1695

Montenegro CE, Patrinos HA (2014) Comparable estimates of returns to schooling around the world. World Bank Policy Research Working Paper 7020

North DC (1991) Institutions. J Econ Perspect 5(1):97–112

Olson M, Sarna N, Svamy AV (2000) Governance and growth: a simple hypothesis explaining cross-country differences in productivity growth. Public Choice 102(3–4):341–364

Paldam M (2002) The cross-country pattern of corruption: economics, culture and the seesaw dynamics. Eur J Polit Econ 18:215–240

Pritchett L (1996) Where has all the education gone? World Bank Policy Research working paper # 1581

PRS Group (1999) International country risk guide (ICRG). https://www.prsgroup.com/explore-our-products/international-country-risk-guide/

Ridha MJ (1998) Charting the future education and change in the Arab countries: a platform for the 21st century. Paper presented in the Joint Arab Monetary Fund, Arab Fund for Economic and Social Development Seminar on "Human Resource Development and Economic Growth," Abu Dhabi, United Arab Emirates, 17–18 May

Rodrik D (2007) One economics, many recipes: globalization, institutions and economic growth. Princeton University Press, Princeton

Rodrik D, Subramanian A, Trebbi F (2004) Institutions rule: the primacy of institutions over geography and integration in economic development. J Econ Growth 9(2):131–165

Sargan JD (1958) The estimation of economic relationships with instrumental variables. Econometrica 26(3):393–415

Shrabani S, Ben Ali MS (2017) Corruption and economic development: new evidence from the middle eastern and North African countries. Econ Anal Policy 54:83–95

Sianesi B, Van Reenen J (2002) The returns to education: a review of the empirical macro-economic literature. J Econ Surv 17(2):157–200

Staiger D, Stock JH (1997) Instrumental variables regression with weak instruments. Econometrica 65(3):557–586

Tzannatos Z, Diwan I, Abdel Ahad J (2016) Rates of return to education in twenty-two Arab countries: an update and comparison between MENA and The Rest of the World, Economic Research Forum Working Paper 1007

Wei SJ (2000) How taxing is corruption on international investors? Rev Econ Stat 82(1):1–11

Williamson CR (2009) Informal institutions rule: institutional arrangements and economic performance. Pub Choice 139(3–4):371–387

Chapter 3
Short- and Long-Run Causality Between Remittances and Economic Growth in MENA Countries: A Panel ARDL Approach

Sami Ben Mim and Mohamed Sami Ben Ali

Abstract This paper assesses the impact of remittances on economic growth for a selected sample of MENA countries over the 1987–2018 period. Using an ARDL model, we investigate the short- and long-run effects of remittances and the channels through which they may impact growth. Estimation outcomes show that while remittances contribute to promote growth on the long run, they may impede growth on the short run, as an important time lapses is required for the growth-generating transmission channels to produce the expected positive effects. Our findings show that besides remittances, investment and human capital contribute to promote long-run growth while the credit to GDP ratio fails to produce any significant effect on growth because of the limited access to the financial system in MENA countries. We also note that the short-run dynamics and the speed of adjustment toward the long-run path vary considerably from one country to another. Finally, the causality tests confirm that investment, human capital, and financial development are the main channels through which remittances may produce their long-term positive effect on growth. Based on these results, we provide numerous policy recommendations for the MENA countries.

Keywords Remittances · Economic growth · ARDL · Panel causality

3.1 Introduction

Remittances can be defined as the money that international migrants send to their home countries. For example, in 2017 these flows recorded an amount of around 466 billion dollars to low- and middle-income countries with an increase of 8.5%

S. Ben Mim
University of Sousse, IHEC, LaREMFiQ, PB 40-4054 Sousse, Tunisia
e-mail: sbenmim@yahoo.fr

M. S. Ben Ali (✉)
College of Business & Economics, Qatar University, P.O. Box: 2713, Doha, Qatar
e-mail: msbenali@qu.edu.qa

M. S. Ben Ali (ed.), *Economic Development in the MENA Region*, Perspectives on Development in the Middle East and North Africa (MENA) Region, https://doi.org/10.1007/978-3-030-66380-3_3

as compared with 2016. Although there is a consensus on the importance of these flows, international institutions failed to assess their exact amount. This stems from the fact that a major part of these resources is transferred through illegal and parallel channels rather than official ones.

These flows witnessed a surge during the last decades both in per capita and absolute terms. An important feature that can explain this surge is that, compared to other types of financial flows, these capital transfers increase during periods of crisis and economic downturn (Ben Mim and Ben Ali 2012). According to a recent study by the World Bank (2018), international official remittances represent the second most important source of funding in developing countries after the foreign direct investment. This is particularly important for countries lacking financial resources to fund small and medium enterprises which represent the major part of their local industries and therefore a primary source of national income. International remittances are usually driven by two main motives. First, altruism: Remittances are sent to cover the expenses of family members which are usually among the poorest households. Second, self-interest: Emigrants send funds for investment purposes to take advantage from high return rates in their home countries.

Economic growth is a central issue for all countries. Assessing the sources and the potential determinants of economic growth is of paramount importance for developing countries and specifically for the Middle East and North Africa region. Two main streams of research can be distinguished in the literature regarding the sources and factors driving economic growth (Feng et al. 2017; Acikgoz and Ben Ali 2019; Acikgoz et al. 2016). The first strand of literature, based on the seminal paper of Solow (1956), tries to assess the sources of economic growth by discussing the role of factor accumulation or productivity in the growth process. The second strand, instigated by the endogenous growth theory, discusses the factors that could impact economic growth such as education, public spending, trade openness, financial development, and foreign direct investment.

Literature dealing with remittances revealed that they can impact economic growth directly or indirectly through various channels. Empirical studies investigated the impact of remittances on various economic variables. A study by Adelman and Taylor (1990) found that every dollar Mexico received from migrants working abroad increased its gross national product by $2.69–$3.17. Similarly, Fayissa and Nsiah (2008) proved that a 10% increase in the remittances of a typical African migrant would result in about 0.4% increase in average per capita income. Adams and Page found that a 10% increase in per capita official international remittances will induce a 3.5% decline in poverty. Combes and Ebeke (2011) highlighted the stabilizing effect of remittances and showed that they may improve macroeconomic stability for the recipient country by up to 6%.

The national account approach argues that remittances may negatively impact economic performance through the balance of payment, trade deficit, exchange rate, and inflation. Oppositely, a study by Giuliano and Ruiz-Arranz (2009a, b) showed that these flows can relieve credit constraints and spur investment and therefore contribute to economic growth. In this vein, Lucas argued that remittances contributed to accelerate investment in Morocco, Pakistan, and India. Similarly, Glytsos (2002) found that investment rises with remittances in six out of the seven Mediterranean countries considered in his sample. According to Ratha and Riedberg (2005), if remittances are invested they will contribute directly to increasing output, but if they are allocated to consumption they will induce a positive multiplier effect (Maiga et al. 2016).

By relaxing the budget constraints, remittances allow households to allocate further resources to education and health expenditure (Azizi, 2018). In that way they may contribute to improve labor productivity and produce a positive impact on economic growth (Mamun et al. 2015). It has also been documented that these inflows can have a boosting effect on consumption by increasing the disposable income during periods of depressed demand (Yang and Choi 2007). A more recent paper by Ben Mim and Ben Ali (2012) reported the positive impact of remittances on economic growth through human capital accumulation for the Middle East and North Africa during the 1980–2009 period. Beyond their effect on economic growth, some recent studies showed that remittances can help reducing poverty (Anyanwu and Erhijakpor 2010) and inequality in high recipient countries (Bang et al. 2016). Remittances may also contribute to foster financial development (Fromentin 2017). Indeed, to benefit from workers' remittances developing countries are called to improve their financial systems so that they can attract and allocate funds efficiently into the local economy. A recent study by Sobiech (2019) assessed the impact of remittances on economic growth while considering the interfering effect of financial development for a panel of developing countries. Results suggest that remittances boost economic growth during the early stages of financial development. The empirical findings showed also that the more developed the financial systems, the lower is the impact of remittances on economic growth. According to the same study, financial systems substitute for remittances as they gain in complexity and development. Substitution effect between financial development and remittances has been already highlighted by Giuliano and Ruiz-Arranz (2009a, b) for a large sample of developing countries.

While most of the studies documented an obvious positive impact of remittances on economic growth, some studies reported the existence of a negative impact. In line with this idea, Rao and Hassan (2011) showed some skepticism about the potential significant positive impact of remittances on economic growth. Remittances can for example negatively impact economic growth by inducing a Dutch disease effect or by decreasing the demand for labor supply in the recipient countries (Acosta et al. 2009). Barajas et al. (2009) found that decades of remittances hindered long-run economic growth in receiving economies. This negative effect is mainly attributed to the fact that remittances are affected to consumption rather than to investment, and serve as an implicit insurance to help family members cover their basic needs. Other studies documented that remittances may exacerbate capital volatility and lead to the emergence of a sizable informal sector in the recipient countries (Opperman and Adjasi 2019).

Although a copious literature has been devoted to the growth-remittances nexus, there is no clear-cut consensus on the transmission channels involved in this relationship. Moreover, little attention has been given to the differentiation between the short-run and the long-run effects of remittances on growth. The empirical literature suggests also that the intensity of these effects may differ from one region to another.

The Middle East and North Africa region is unique by its diversity, location, and natural resources endowments (Saha and Ben Ali 2017; Ben Ali and Saha 2016). This study takes a step toward assessing this impact on a sample of MENA countries over the 1987–2018 period. We stand apart from the existing literature by highlighting the difference between the short-run and the long-run dynamics of the remittances-growth relationship. The remainder of this chapter is structured as follows: Sect. 3.2 develops the empirical framework of our study. Section 3.3 discusses the main results. The last section concludes and provides some policy implications.

3.2 Model, Data, and Methodology

The main objective of this paper is to assess the effect of remittances on growth and to highlight the main transmission channels in operation. It aims also to distinguish between the short-run and the long-run effects of remittances on growth. As documented in the empirical literature, remittances contribute to promote growth by accelerating investment and by fostering human capital accumulation and financial inclusion (Ben Mim and Ben Ali 2012). Nevertheless, an important span of time is needed for the involved transmission channels to produce their expected effects on growth. Consequently, the remittances' effect on growth is more likely to arise on the long run rather than on the short run.

Multivariate error correction models (ECM), initiated by Johansen (1988, 1991, 1995), are the most used approach to capture the interaction between the long-run and the short-run dynamics. The idea consists to test for the existence of a long-run relationship between non-stationary series. The residuals of the long-run equation, called the error correction term, are then introduced as an independent variable in the short-run equation, which is estimated using stationary differenced series. The error correction term acts as a restoring force which prevents a durable divergence between the short-run and the long-run relationships. The coefficient associated with this term, which is necessarily negative, indicates the speed of adjustment toward the long-term path.

A major drawback of the error correction model is that it requires all series to have the same order of integration. To overcome this restrictive condition, Pesaran et al. (2001) developed a cointegration test among series of different order of integration, namely I(0) and I(1) series. The so-called bounds cointegration test relies on an Auto Regressive Distributed Lag (ARDL) model including the dependant and independent variables as well as their lagged differences. In our case, an ARDL (p, q) model can be defined as follows:

$$\Delta Y_{i,t} = \lambda_0 Y_{i,t-1} + \sum_{k=1}^{4} \lambda_k X_{i,t-1}^k + \sum_{j=1}^{p-1} \beta_j \Delta Y_{i,t-j} + \sum_{k=1}^{4} \sum_{j=1}^{q-1} \alpha_j \Delta X_{i,t-j}^k + \gamma_0 + \varepsilon_{it}$$

$$(3.1)$$

where the dependent variable, Y_{it}, corresponds to per capita GDP growth, while X_{it}^1, X_{it}^2, X_{it}^3, and X_{it}^4 represent, respectively, the investment rate, human capital, financial development, and remittances. The information criteria are generally used to determine the optimal lags (p and q) to introduce in the model. Based on this model, testing for cointegration corresponds simply to test the following hypothesis:

H0: $\lambda_0 = \lambda_1 = \lambda_2 = \lambda_3 = \lambda_4 = 0$ while H1: $\lambda_0 \neq \lambda_1 \neq \lambda_2 \neq \lambda_3 \neq \lambda_4 \neq 0$

Pesaran et al. (2001) simulated a set of critical values for various specifications (including or not a constant and a trend) and for different significance levels. Two critical values, or bounds, denoted I(0) and I(1), are associated with each significance level. The test leads to three possible outcomes:

The calculated statistics is higher than the upper bound, I(1): The null hypothesis is then rejected indicating the existence of a long-run relationship.

The calculated statistics is smaller than the lower bound I(0): The null hypothesis cannot be rejected and no cointegration equation is detected.

The calculated statistics lies between the two bounds: The test is inconclusive.

Equation 3.1 can be written similarly to an ECM equation which highlights the interaction between the short-run and long-run dynamics:

$$\Delta Y_{i,t} = \sum_{j=1}^{p-1} \beta_j \Delta Y_{i,t-j} + \sum_{k=1}^{4} \sum_{j=1}^{q-1} \alpha_j \Delta X_{i,t-j}^k$$
$$+ \delta \left(Y_{i,t-1} - \left(\theta_0 + \sum_{k=1}^{4} \theta_k X_{i,t-1}^k \right) \right) + \varepsilon_{it}$$
$$= \sum_{j=1}^{p-1} \beta_j \Delta Y_{i,t-j} + \sum_{k=1}^{4} \sum_{j=1}^{q-1} \alpha_j \Delta X_{i,t-j}^k + \delta u_{it} + \varepsilon_{it} \qquad (3.2)$$

where u_{it} is the residual of the cointegration equation and δ is the adjustment coefficient which captures the speed of convergence toward the long-run path.

The long-run and short-run equations can be estimated simultaneously by applying the Pooled Mean Group (PMG) estimator developed by Pesaran et al. (1999). Moreover, this estimator is consistent to endogeneity and autocorrelation, as the model includes lagged terms of the dependent and independent variables. Including the appropriate lag structure should whiten the residuals and provide valid instruments to control for endogeneity. Another advantage of panel ARDL models is that they control for heterogeneity across countries by affecting to each country its own error correction coefficient, "δ", and a specific short-run equation. The ARDL model taking into consideration such heterogeneities can be written as follows:

$$\Delta Y_{i,t} = \sum_{j=1}^{p-1} \beta_j^i \Delta Y_{i,t-j} + \sum_{k=1}^{4} \sum_{j=1}^{q-1} \alpha_j^i \Delta X_{i,t-j}^k$$

$$+ \delta^i \left(Y_{i,t-1} - \left(\theta_0 + \sum_{k=1}^{4} \theta_k X_{i,t-1}^k \right) \right) + \varepsilon_{it} \qquad (3.3)$$

In this study, we consider a sample of 8 MENA countries which are highly concerned by international migration and benefit therefore from important amounts of remittances, namely Algeria, Egypt, Iran, Jordan, Morocco, Tunisia, Turkey, and Palestine. We excluded oil producing countries, which are sources of remittances rather than recipient countries. Syria and Lebanon were also dropped because of data unavailability. Annual data cover the period from 1987 to 2018.

The descriptive statistics are summarized in Table 3.1 in the appendix. We first notice that the remittances to GDP ratio are high for the whole panel (6.33% on average over the sample period), but the average level differs significantly from one country to another. Figure 3.1 shows that we can distinguish three groups of countries: Palestine and Jordan where remittances are generally above 10% with peaks exceeding 20%; Tunisia, Morocco, and Egypt for which remittances range between 4 and 10%; and finally, Iran, Algeria, and Turkey where remittances represent less than 2% of GDP (Table 3.2).

The average growth rate is quite high over the sample period (3.89%), with the lowest and highest average rates registered, respectively, by Algeria (2.61%) and Turkey (4.66%). However, the high standard deviation (4,14) suggests that the growth path was far from being steady. Figure 3.2 confirms this intuition and highlights the volatility of the growth rate, compared to remittances which are much more stable.

Table 3.1 Definition and sources of the variables

Variable	Abbreviation	Definition
Growth of real per capita GDP	pcGrowth	Log difference of per capita GDP in constant US dollars. Source: World Development Indicators, World Bank
Investment rate	Investment	Fixed capital formation as a percentage of GDP. Source: World Development Indicators, World Bank
Human capital	School	Secondary school gross enrollment ratio. Source: World Development Indicators, World Bank
Financial development	Credit	Domestic credits provided by the banking sector as a share of GDP. Source: World Development Indicators, World Bank
Remittances received	Remittances	Personal transfers and compensation of employees received as a percentage of GDP. Source: World Development Indicators, World Bank

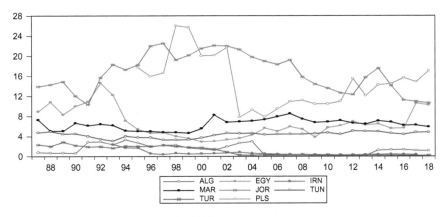

Fig. 3.1 Remittances by country, 1987–2018

Table 3.2 Descriptive statistics by country, 1987–2018

	Remittances (% GDP)		GDP growth		Investment (% GDP)		School enrollment		Domestic credit (% GDP)	
	Mean	Std. Dev.	Mean	Std. Dev.	Mean	Std. Dev.	Mean	Std. Dev.	Mean	Std. Dev.
ALG	1285	1030	2606	2187	29,331	6435	68,844	13,499	19,758	18,907
EGY	6572	2969	4418	1540	20,345	5339	75,825	7648	36,403	11,386
IRN	0583	0527	3441	4799	28,549	4070	74,843	10,891	34,037	15,201
JOR	16,566	3827	3867	4728	23,797	4279	77,762	6774	70,651	8196
MAR	6386	1044	3946	3838	27,326	3325	47,736	13,876	46,539	18,238
PLS	14,796	5169	4536	7410	26,550	5981	83,605	6357	26,327	9314
TUN	4271	0549	3782	2294	23,055	2331	70,880	18,840	54,294	6516
TUR	1062	0906	4660	4533	25,235	3203	77,310	18,903	30,386	18,175
All	6333	6188	3889	4143	25,483	5304	71,780	16,614	40,264	21,006

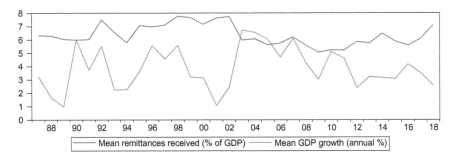

Fig. 3.2 Remittances and GDP growth mean levels, Full Sample 1987–2018

Such stability stems from the fact that remittances are partly motivated by altruism which moderates their decrease during recession periods. We can also note the countercyclical behavior of remittances: Following the subprime crisis, the growth rate showed a clear downward trend, while remittances experienced a moderate increase. Such a countercyclical behavior confirms the altruistic aspect of remittances.

For the control variables, we note the low volatility of the investment rate which lies between 20.3 and 29% over the sample period. All countries show high secondary school enrollment rates, with the exception of Morocco where access to secondary education is still limited. Finally, the credits to GDP ratio is relatively low for all countries, except for Jordan. It seems to the financial system, and particularly to the banking systems, is highly restricted in MENA countries.

Surprisingly, Table 3.3 reveals a negative correlation between growth, investment, and school enrollment on the one hand and remittances on the other hand. For remittances, the only positive correlation coefficient is associated with the credits ratio. We also notice that correlation among the control variables is relatively weak which excludes any multicollinearity problem.

3.3   Results and Discussion

Results relative to the unit root tests are reported in Table 3.4 in the appendix.[1] Tests assuming a common unit root, such as the Levin, Lin, and Chu test, are run in parallel with those assuming country-specific unit roots, like the Im, Pesaran, and Shin, the Augmented Dickey–Fuller and the Phillips–Perron tests. We notice that among the five series, only per capita GDP growth is stationary in levels.[2] Furthermore, results in Table 3.5 reported in the appendix show that the remaining series are difference stationary.

According to the unit root tests results we cannot rely on the ECM approach because our series do not have the same order of integration. In this case, The ARDL model represents the appropriate alternative to test for cointegration and to study the interaction between the long- and the short-run dynamics. We first identify the optimal lag structure, the one that minimizes the information criteria. Results in Table 3.6 in the appendix indicate that an ARDL (1, 2, 2, 2, 2) is the specification that best fits our data. Table 3.7 reports the PMG estimator results for the full ARDL model, while Table 3.8 provides the Pesaran et al. (2001) cointegration test results. We notice that the test statistic is greater than the upper bound I(1) for the three significance levels, attesting to the validity of the estimated cointegration equation.

---

[1]The reported results are relative to the specification including only a constant. The specification including a constant and a trend leads to similar results for all the series.

[2]For the school enrollment rate, we opt for the tests assuming individual unit roots, which fail to reject the unit root hypothesis, even though the Levin, Lin, and Chu test concludes that the series is stationary in levels.

Table 3.3 Correlation matrix

	GROWTHPC	LNINVESTMENT	LNSCHOOL	LNCREDIT	LNREMITTANCES
GROWTHPC	1.000				
LNINVESTMENT	0.059	1.000			
LNSCHOOL	0.056	−0.080	1.000		
LNCREDIT	0.022	c0.035	0.161**	1.000	
LNREMITTANCES	−0.132*	−0.259***	−0.193***	0.220***	1.000

***, and ** indicate significance levels at 1, 5%, respectively

Table 3.4 Unit root tests, level series

	Pcgrowth	LnInvestment	LnSchool	LnCredit	LnRemittances
Tests assuming common unit root process					
Levin, Lin and Chu test	−3.491***	−1.174	−2.067**	−0.156	−0.692
Tests assuming individual unit root process					
Im, Pesaran and Shin test	−6.443***	−0.691	0.530	0.949	−0.871
ADF test	73.989***	15.672	20.336	11.629	17.704
PP test	120.144***	12.353	24.002*	12.284	18.849

***, and ** indicate significance levels at 1, 5%, respectively

Table 3.5 Unit root tests, differenced series

	LnInvestment	LnSchool	LnCredit	LnRemittances
Tests assuming common unit root process				
Levin, Lin, and Chu test	−6.022***	−3.558***	−4.451***	−8.568***
Tests assuming individual unit root process				
Im, Pesaran, and Shin test	−7.125***	−3.532***	−5.132***	−7.679***
ADF test	80.190***	44.209***	56.481***	87.702***
PP test	134.445***	58.465***	100.366***	129.306***

***, and ** indicate significance levels at 1, 5%, respectively

Table 3.6 Selection criteria

Specification	LogL	AIC*	BIC	HQ
ARDL (1, 2, 2, 2, 2)	417,765	−4392	−2721	−3713
ARDL (2, 2, 2, 2, 2)	420,714	−4325	−2495	−3582
ARDL (1, 1, 1, 1, 1)	366,151	−4134	−3099	−3713
ARDL (2, 1, 1, 1, 1)	371,052	−4093	−2899	−3608

The first part of Table 3.7 is relative to the long-run equation. Results reveal that remittances produce a positive and significant effect on long-run growth. In line with theoretical expectations, investment and school enrollment contribute to enhance growth on the long run. However, the credits to GDP ratio do not produce any significant effect on long-run growth. Such a result may be attributed to the fact that MENA countries are characterized by limited access to the financial system, as shown by the descriptive statistics in Table 3.2. In such a context, Giuliano and Ruiz-Arranz (2009a, b) argued that remittances act as a substitute for the inefficient financial systems in the recipient countries. Using the System-GMM estimates they proved that the remittances promote growth in countries with shallower financial systems.

Table 3.7 Full ARDL model, PMG estimates

LNINVESTMENT	0.011** (0.005)
LNSCHOOL	0.025** (0.011)
LNCREDIT	0.007 (0.004)
LNREMITTANCES	0.009** (0.003)
Short-run equation	
COINTEQ 01	−0.932*** (0.140)
D(LNINVESTMENT)	0.122 (0.093)
D(LNINVESTMENT(−1)	0.043 (0.061)
D(LNSCHOOL)	0.023 (0.401)
D(LNSCHOOL(−1)	−0.095 (0.335)
D(LNCREDIT)	−0.038 (0.042)
D(LNCREDIT(−1)	−0.018 (0.020)
D(LNREMITTANCES)	−0.024 (0.017)
D(LNREMITTANCES(−1)	−0.0002 (0.019)
C	−0.140*** (0.020)
R^2	0.814
Nb Obs	157
Breusch-Godfrey prob.	2.822
Breusch-Godfrey stat.	0.244
Breusch-Pagan stat.	13.873
Breusch-Pagan prob.	0.383

***, and ** indicate significance levels at 1, 5%, respectively

Table 3.8 Pesaran et al. (2001) bounds test

Test statistic	Value	df	
Chi-square	15.23572	4	
Critical value bounds			
Significance	I0 bound	I1 bound	
10%	3.03	4.06	
5%	3.47	4.57	
2.5%	3.89	5.07	
1%	4.4	5.72	

For countries with well-developed financial systems, the impact of remittances on growth turned out to be non-significant or even negative.

The second part of Table 3.7 provides the short-run estimates. We notice that only the error correction term and the constant are significant. The non-significance of the lagged differences of the independent variables is likely to be due to the heterogeneity of the short-term dynamics across country, which prevents to obtain any significant results out from the pooled data. The high coefficient associated with the error correction term (-0.93) implies that any deviation from the long-run path is recovered within a period which barely exceeds one year. Finally, the post-estimation tests confirm that the residuals are free from autocorrelation and heteroscedasticity.

Table 3.9 describes the short-term dynamics by country. Results indicate that the speed of adjustment toward the long-run path differs significantly from one country to another: While the delay is less than one year for countries like Egypt, Morocco, Iran, and Turkey, it takes approximately four years for the Jordanian economy to recover deviations from the long-run equilibrium. Secondly, we notice that the determinants of short-run growth differ dramatically across countries. While investment stimulates growth in Egypt, Jordan, Tunisia, Turkey, and Palestine, it has a negative short-term effect on growth in Morocco and Iran. Similarly, school enrollment and financial development contribute to promote short-term growth in Algeria and Turkey, while they produce negative effects on growth in countries like Egypt or Tunisia. As mentioned previously, if all the independent variables revealed non-significant for the whole panel (Table 3.7), this is mainly due to the heterogeneity of the short-term determinants of growth across countries.

A major finding of this study is that remittances can produce a short-run negative effect on growth. Four countries are concerned by such a negative effect (Algeria, Iran, Turkey, and Palestine), while no significant effect is detected for the two other countries (Morocco and Jordan). A positive short-run effect is detected only for Egypt and Tunisia. In fact, remittances contribute to promote growth through various channels such as investment, human capital, and financial development. However, an important span of time is needed to activate these channels and to generate the expected effects on growth. Consequently, the remittances' positive effect on growth is more likely to arise on the long run rather than on the short run. The short-term effect stems mainly from the share of remittances devoted to consumption. Allocating remittances to unproductive activities, such as consumption, will not generate any effect on growth as asserted by Barajas et al. (2009). Moreover, Chami et al. (2005) argued that such an irrelevant use of remittances may produce negative effects on growth by reducing labor participation. According to Acosta et al. (2007) remittances inflows lead to an appreciation of the real exchange rate which may result in a Dutch disease effect in the receiving countries.

To confirm the validity of the transmission channels discussed previously, we implemented panel Granger causality tests between remittances and the variables through which they may act on long-run growth. Results reported in Table 3.10 offer evidence for causality running from remittances to investment and school enrollment, confirming the role of both variables as transmission channels of the remittances' effect on growth. Such results are in line with those of Giulliano and Ruiz-Arranz (2009) and Ben Mim and Ben Ali (2012) which confirmed the effectiveness of both transmission channels for panel data sets. Ben Mim and Mabrouk (2014) prove that the effectiveness of the human capital channel depends on the level of public spending on education in the receiving country.

Results reveal also a two-way causality between remittances and the credits to GDP ratio. Several studies have pointed out that a developed financial system helps

Table 3.9 Short-run dynamics by country

	Algeria	Egypt	Iran	Morocco	Jordan	Tunisia	Turkey	Palestine
COINTEQ 01	-0.692*** (0.015)	-1.025*** (0.010)	-1.186*** (0.116)	-1.484*** (0.049)	-0.249** (0.064)	-0.885*** (0.037)	-1.281*** (0.031)	-0.652*** (0.035)
D(LNINVESTMENT)	0.0005 (0.001)	0.081*** (0.0002)	-0.159*** (0.018)	-0.258*** (0.018)	0.188*** (0.014)	0.204*** (0.004)	0.426*** (0.003)	0.494*** (0.048)
D(LNINVESTMENT(-1))	0.042*** (0.001)	0.067*** (0.0002)	-0.170*** (0.015)	0.183*** (0.016)	-0.162*** (0.026)	-0.094*** (0.005)	0.175*** (0.006)	0.304*** (0.028)
D(LNSCHOOL)	0.031*** (0.002)	-0.008*** (0.0005)	-0.377 (0.461)	-0.164 (0.154)	2.434 (1.782)	-0.047* (0.015)	0.019** (0.006)	-1.705 (1.292)
D(LNSCHOOL(-1))	-0.072*** (0.003)	-0.142*** (0.0008)	-0.556 (0.276)	0.087 (0.062)	-1.898 (1.800)	0.209*** (0.013)	0.072*** (0.007)	1.541 (1.055)
D(LNCREDIT)	0.008*** (0.00007)	-0.019*** (0.0009)	-0.049* (0.019)	0.005 (0.004)	-0.138* (0.055)	-0.177*** (0.003)	0.203*** (0.004)	-0.134*** (0.012)
D(LNCREDIT(-1))	0.0351*** (0.00004)	-0.071*** (0.0007)	0.053** (0.009)	-0.006 (0.005)	0.047 (0.056)	-0.043*** (0.004)	-0.075*** (0.003)	-0.086*** (0.013)
D(LNREMITTANCES)	-0.017*** (0.00002)	0.004*** (0.00006)	-0.075*** (0.006)	-0.003 (0.002)	0.007 (0.007)	0.027*** (0.001)	-0.022*** (0.0002)	-0.116*** (0.003)
D(LNREMITTANCES(-1))	0.007*** (0.00002)	-0.038*** (0.00006)	0.051*** (0.004)	0.073*** (0.002)	-0.079*** (0.008)	-0.019*** (0.002)	0.052*** (0.0002)	-0.048*** (0.003)
C	-0.100*** (0.002)	-0.164*** (0.004)	-0.173*** (0.007)	-0.220*** (0.006)	-0.046*** (0.003)	-0.142*** (0.004)	-0.184*** (0.005)	-0.092*** (0.002)

***, and ** indicate significance levels at 1, 5%, respectively

Table 3.10 Panel causality tests

Null Hypothesis		F-Statistic	Prob.
LNINVESTMENT does not Granger Cause LNREMITTANCES		1.07229	0.3618
LNREMITTANCES does not Granger Cause LNINVESTMENT	4.58886	0.0039	
LNSCHOOL does not Granger Cause LNREMITTANCES		0.48105	0.6960
LNREMITTANCES does not Granger Cause LNSCHOOL	3.12991	0.0278	
LNCREDIT does not Granger Cause LNREMITTANCES		2.24998	0.0837
LNREMITTANCES does not Granger Cause LNCREDIT	5.98527	0.0006	

to attract more remittances, and that at the same time remittances promote financial inclusion, which in turn fosters financial development (Aggarwal et al. 2011; Toxopeus and Lensink 2007).

3.3.1 Conclusions and Recommendations

The main objective of this study is to assess the impact of remittances on growth in the MENA countries. We also distinguish between the short- and long-run effects of remittances and to identify the main transmission channels through which they may act on growth.

The empirical investigation led to some interesting conclusions. We first highlighted the importance of distinguishing between the long-run and short-run effects of remittances on growth. While they contribute to promote growth on the long run, remittances may impede growth on the short run. An important time lapses is required for the growth-generating transmission channels to produce the expected positive effects. The short-run effect is explained by the share of remittances devoted to consumption, which may reduce labor supply within the recipient population. Besides remittances, investment and human capital contribute to promote long-run growth. However, the credit to GDP ratio fails to produce any significant effect on growth. This is likely to be the result of the limited access to the financial system in MENA countries. We also note that the short-run dynamics vary considerably from one country to another, particularly the speed of adjustment toward the long-run path. Finally, the causality tests confirm that investment, human capital, and financial development are the main channels through which remittances produce their long-term positive effect on growth.

Two important recommendations arise from these conclusions. Firstly, governments should implement policies aiming to encourage growth-promoting uses of remittances. Fiscal and legal incentives may play a major role in encouraging the recipient population to affect remittances to investment. Developing the schooling infrastructure and providing the appropriate learning materiel should help remittances to promote and facilitate the access to the education system. Secondly, an important growth-promoting reform should concern the financial system, and particularly the banking system. Besides the allocational efficiency, financial inclusion seems to be a crucial concern for MENA countries. Financial development should amplify the effect of remittances on growth by accelerating the capital transfers and by allowing a more efficient use of the collected resources.

References

Acikgoz S, Ben Ali MS (2019) Where does economic growth in the Middle Eastern and North African countries come from? Q Rev Econ Finance 73:172–183

Acikgoz S, Ben Ali MS, Mert M (2016) Sources of economic growth in MENA countries: technological progress, physical or human capital accumulations? Economic development in the Middle East and North Africa. Springer/Palgrave Macmillan, New York, pp 27–69

Acosta PA, Lartey EK, Mandelman FS (2009) Remittances and the Dutch disease. J Int Econ 79(1):102–116

Acosta PA, Lartey EK, Mandelman F (2007) Remittances, exchange rate regimes, and the dutch disease: a panel data analysis. Federal Reserve Bank of Atlanta Working Paper No. 2008–12

Adelman, & Taylor (1990) Is structural adjustment with a human face possible? The case of Mexico. J Dev Stud 26:387–407

Aggarwal R, Demirguc-Kunt A, Martinez Peria M (2011) Do workers' remittances promote financial development? J Dev Econ 96(2):255–264

Anyanwu JC, Erhijakpor AEO (2010) Do international remittances affect poverty inafrica? Afr Dev Rev 22(1):51–91

Azizi S (2018) The impacts of workers' remittances on human capital and labor supply in developing countries. Econ Modell 75:377–396

Bang JT, Mitra A, Wunnava PV (2016) Do remittances improve income inequality? An instrumental variable quantile analysis of the Kenyan case. Econ Modell 58:394–402

Barajas A, Chami R, Fullenkamp C, Gapen MT, Montiel P (2009) Do workers' remittances promote economic growth? International Monetary Fund Working Papers 09/153

Ben Mim S, Ben Ali MS (2012) Through which channels can remittances spur economic growth in MENA countries? Economics 6(33):1–27

Ben MS, Mabrouk F (2014) A travers quels canaux les transferts des migrants promeuvent-ils le capital humain et la croissance? Mondes en Développement 42(167):131–147

Ben Ali MS, Saha S (2016) Corruption and economic development. Economic development in the Middle East and North Africa. Springer/Palgrave Macmillan, New York, pp 133–154

Chami R, Fullenkamp C, Jahjah S (2005) Are immigrant remittance flows a source of capital for development? Int Monetary Fund Staff Pap 52(1):48p

Combes J-L, Ebeke C (2011) Remittances and household consumption instability indeveloping countries. World Dev 39(7):1076–1089 (Special Section (pp 1204–1270): Foreign Technology and Indigenous Innovation in the Emerging Economies)

Fayissa B, Nsiah C (2008) The impact of remittances on economic growth and development in Africa. Department of Economics and Finance working paper series

Feng C, Wang M, Liu G-C, Huang J-B (2017) Green developmentperformance and its influencing factors: a global perspective. J Cleaner Prod 144:323–333

Fromentin V (2017) The long-run and short-run impacts of remittances on financial development in developing countries. Q Rev Econ Finance 66:192–201

Giuliano P, Ruiz-Arranz M (2009a) Remittances, financial development, and growth. J Dev Econ 90:144–152

Giuliano P, Ruiz-Arranz M (2009b) Remittances, financial development, and growth. J Dev Econ 90(1):144–152

Glytsos NP (2002) The role of migrant remittances in development: evidence from mediterranean countries. Int Migr 40(1):5–26

Johansen S (1991) Estimation and hypothesis testing of cointegration vectors in gaussian vector autoregressive models. Econometrica 59:1551–1580

Johansen S (1995) Likelihood based inference in cointegrated vector autoregressive models. Oxford University Press, OxfordUK; New York

Johansen S (1988) Statistical analysis of cointegrating vectors. J Econ Dyn Control 12:231–254

Mamun MA, Sohag K, Uddin GS, Shahbaz M (2015) Remittance and domestic labor productivity: evidence from remittance recipient countries. Econ Modell 47:207–218

Maiga EWM, Baliamoune-Lutz M, Ben Ali MS (2016) Workers remittances and economic development: which role for education? In: Ben Ali MS (ed) Economic development in the Middle East and North Africa—Challenges and prospects. Springer/Palgrave Macmillan, New York

Opperman P, Adjasi CKD (2019) Remittance volatility and financial sector development in sub-Saharan African countries. J Pol Model 41(2):336–351

Pesaran MH, Shin Y, Smith RJ (2001) Bounds testing approaches to the analysis of level relationships. J Appl Econometrics 16(3):289–326

Pesaran MH, Shin Y, Smith RP (1999) Pooled mean group estimation of dynamic heterogeneous panels. J Am Stat Assoc 94:621–634

Rao BB, Hassan GM (2011) A panel data analysis of the growth effects of remittances. Econ Modell 28(1):701–709

Ratha D, Riedberg J (2005) On reducing remittance costs. Unpublished paper. Development Research Group, World Bank, Washington, DC

Saha S, Ben Ali MS (2017) Corruption and economic development: new evidence from the Middle Eastern and North African countries. Econ Anal Policy 54:83–95

Sobiech I (2019) Remittances, finance and growth: does financial development foster the impact of remittances on economic growth? World Dev 113:44–59

Solow RM (1956) A contribution to the theory of economic growth. Q J Econ 70(1):65–94

Toxopeus H, Lensink R (2007) Remittances and financial inclusion in development. WIDER Working paper series No. 2007/49. World Institute for Development Economic Research (UNU-WIDER)

World Bank (2018) Migration and Remittances: Recent Developments and Outlook 2018. The World Bank, Washington D.C.

Yang D, Choi H (2007) Are remittances insurance? Evidence from rainfall shocks in the Philippines. World Bank Econ Rev 21(2):219–248 (Oxford University Press)

Chapter 4
Asymmetric Impact of Oil Price Shocks on Tourism: Evidence from Selected MENA Countries

Khalid M. Kisswani and Arezou Harraf

Abstract This study examines the oil price asymmetric influences on tourism (tourism receipts) for select MENA countries (namely: Egypt, Israel, Jordan, Lebanon, Morocco, Tunisia, and Turkey). Although annual sample data from 1995–2018 was collected, however, to be able to apply the asymmetric analysis, we transform the annual frequencies into quarterly series using the quadratic match-sum method that has been implemented in various empirical studies. The analysis employs the Shin et al. (2014) methodology known as the nonlinear autoregressive distributed lags (NARDL) model. The asymmetry is introduced via decomposing the oil price (P_t) to positive (P_t^+) and negative (P_t^-) changes. In addition, we take note of the data structural breaks, and incorporate the breaks within the NARDL model. The findings document evidence of long-run relationship (cointegration) among tourism receipts and the positive and negative changes of the oil price (P_t^+ and P_t^-) for all seven countries. However, when testing for the long-run asymmetric influence, evidence was found just for Lebanon and Tunisia. In addition, when we analyze the short-run asymmetry, the NARDL results show evidence of asymmetric impact for Jordan, Lebanon, and Tunisia only. These results imply that decision makers should pay attention to the asymmetric influence of oil prices at tourism in the MENA countries, provided that tourism is an important injection to their GDP and that tourism industry is a good source of jobs that can be very helpful in designing policies for reducing unemployment whether in terms of number or gender-workers.

Keywords Oil price · Tourism · MENA · NARDL · Asymmetry

K. M. Kisswani (✉)
Department of Economics and Finance, Gulf University for Science and Technology, P.O. Box 7207, Hawally 32093, Kuwait
e-mail: kisswani.k@gust.edu.kw

A. Harraf
Department of Business Administration, Box Hill College, Kuwait City, Kuwait
e-mail: a.harraf@bhck.edu.kw

© The Author(s), under exclusive license to Springer Nature Switzerland AG 2021
M. S. Ben Ali (ed.), *Economic Development in the MENA Region*, Perspectives on Development in the Middle East and North Africa (MENA) Region,
https://doi.org/10.1007/978-3-030-66380-3_4

4.1 Introduction

Economists recognized, over the last three decades, the vital impact of tourism in the economic growth. The literature also signifies the valuable importance of tourism in the economies around the world, since tourism is an engine for creating jobs, boosting GDP, and augmenting hosting countries' hard currency (see, e.g., Choi and Sirakaya 2006; Dwyer and Forsyth 2008). Numerous papers documented the positive effect of tourism on economic growth, where tourism is considered a key element in the total long-run economic growth (see, inter alia, Blackstock et al. 2008; Bernini 2009; Albalate and Bel 2010; Holzner 2011). Thus, the tourism sector has become a vital segment to all economies, including the MENA countries.

In general, the tourism sector's rapid growth in the last five decades has made the industry an integral economic engine for countries. World Tourism Organization's (UNWTO, henceforth) (2019) report estimated tourism arrivals at 1459.7 million dollars, while tourism receipts amounted to 1479.5 billion dollars, with 1732.8 billion dollars in international exports. Positioning tourism as an essential economic contributor in terms of GDP, employment opportunities, poverty elimination, source of foreign currency, increasing business activity through supporting the private sector and ultimately improving the living standards (Becken 2008; Habibi 2017; Jalil et al. 2013; Tang and Abosedra 2014). This economic contribution is further highlighted in UNWTO's 2019 report, which indicated that by the year 2050, tourism will be the most significant contributing industry worldwide in terms of GDP. This phenomenon has led governments, investors, and stakeholders to strive for strategies that allow them to maximize their share in global tourism (Meo et al. 2018). While investing in tourism and related activities are essential endeavors, given the economic importance of tourism, it is pertinent for stakeholders to understand factors that impact the industry and the ramification of this impact on the economic activity (Meo et al. 2018).

Research has posited different geopolitical and macroeconomic factors as impactful on the tourism industry. One of those factors is oil price, which is documented as an essential concern to levels of tourism and traveling (Becken 2008; Naccache 2010; Meo et al. 2018; Kisswani et al. 2020a, b). The tourism industry is mostly dependent upon oil prices, as oil is a direct driver for tourism supply and demand and affects it in both straightforward and covert channels (Meo et al. 2018). The increase in oil prices affects travelers' earnings and purchasing power through high inflation rates, which negatively impacts travelers' budgets and, therefore, limits their ability and choices in destinations to visit. Also, high oil prices result in higher fees for tourism-related activities in visited countries and thus serve as another hurdle for travelers. On the other hand, high oil prices cause a surge in the cost of air travel, which has a direct influence on the rate of tourism (Blake and Cortes-jiménez 2007; Naccache 2010; Katircioglu et al. 2015; Meo et al. 2018). Against this background, it is necessary for governments, policy-makers, and tourism sector stakeholders to develop a sound understanding of how oil prices affect tourism travel patterns and mitigate risks associated with higher oil prices and the tourism industry. Few empirical studies that have studied this phenomenon have focused on developed countries. Thus, this study aims on shedding light at the oil price influence on tourism in select MENA countries that heavily rely on tourism for their economic activities, where a couple of studies (Acikgoz and Ben Ali 2019; Acikgoz et al. 2016; Arezki and Nabli 2012) classify the MENA area into three major groups: (i) labor-abundant and resources-poor countries; (ii) labor-abundant and resources-rich countries; and (iii) labor-importing and resources-rich countries.

Interestingly, most of the studies that looked at the tourism-oil price nexus focused on the linear effect. That is, it was assuming symmetric effect. Symmetry implies that the influence of oil price increase will comprise the same magnitude (amount) as the price decrease, although this might not be the case in many relationships in which oil price effect is one of them (see, e.g., Donayre and Wilmot 2016; Moshiri 2015; Kisswani et al. 2020b). As such, in this study we aim on studying if the influence of oil price on tourism is asymmetric for the MENA countries. This is a significant addition to the literature as, to the best of our understanding, this was not done before. The asymmetry will be introduced via decaying the oil price variable to positive and negative shocks (as will be presented in the methodology part). Examining the nonlinear effect will be conducted by adopting the nonlinear autoregressive distributed lags model (NARDL) of Shin et al. (2014). The NARDL methodology surpasses other conventional methods because it can estimate the long- and short-run asymmetric impacts through one equation. Furthermore, the NARDL model can still function well even if the engaged variables are not all of order one of integration. As a matter of fact, the method allows variables to be of different integration orders, as long as it is not of order two (I(2)). On this basis, understanding the asymmetric relationship can lead to efforts to enhance tourism in the MENA countries in general.

The asymmetry of the oil price-tourism nexus was investigated for seven select MENA countries due to data availability, namely Egypt, Israel, Jordan, Lebanon, Morocco, Tunisia, and Turkey.[1] The sample data covered the period from 1995 to 2018, in annual frequency.

The rest of the study is organized as follows. Next section offers brief review of related papers. Section 4.3 discusses an overview of the data used and methodology employed. Section 4.4 produces the empirical outcomes, whereas conclusions and policy recommendations are suggested in Sect. 4.5.

4.2 A Brief Review of Previous Studies

Estimating tourism demand and efficiently using resources in accordance is vital for countries wishing to increase local and international tourism (Quayson and Var 1982). Therefore, it is pertinent for countries to develop a sound understanding of

---

[1] The selection of the seven countries was mainly due to the availability of the data.

factors that impact tourism demand, and establish adequate mechanisms to address any shortcomings in this regard.

Current literature posits factors such as inflation, exchange rates, political stability, and oil prices as factors that, among others, impact the demand for tourism (Meo et al. 2018). Song and Witt (2000) suggested that tourism prices are a substantial factor of tourism demand. In this vein, a rise in tourism prices lead to a negative effect on tourism demand, estimated by demand elasticity. Other studies, however, use different proxy variables for tourism prices. For examples, Hotel Price Index (HPI) and Service Price Index (SPI) as well as the average price of transport and entertainment accommodation are used in determining the demand for tourism (Dwyer et al. 2000; Cheung and Law 2001; Narayan 2004). Hanafiah and Harun (2010) posited a reduction in the volume of tourists visiting a given country as the rates of inflation increase. In the same line, Álvarez et al. (2011) established that shocks in oil prices have a substantial influence on inflation in Spain. Additionally, Shaeri et al. (2016) show that changes in oil prices notably impacted financial and nonfinancial subsectors. Yeoman et al.'s (2007) study of the nexus of tourism demand and oil prices indicated that as oil prices increase, tourism demand decreases. This finding is congruent with the findings of WTO (2006), which reported that high oil prices have negative influence on tourism. This said, research suggests different effects of this phenomenon in different countries. Becken and Lennox (2012) contended that increases in oil prices cause higher inflation rates, which in turn lowers the demand for tourism. The opposite may be true for oil-producing countries that economically benefit from higher oil prices. Additionally, studies have shown different dynamics regarding the influence of tourism on economic development in different countries. For example, Katircioglu conducted studies to confirm the role of tourism-led hypothesis on economic growth in different regions. While his findings in Turkey were indicative of no long-run association among international tourism and economic growth (Katircioglu 2009a), his findings in Malta and Singapore (Katircioglu 2009b; 2010) verified a long-run association among tourism and economic growth.

To better understand this phenomenon, numerous studies have used both quantitative and qualitative methods to determine the tourism demand. These methods have departed from the traditional approach of using regression techniques to leaning toward incorporating econometrics models using time series (Kisswani et al. 2020a). Lim and McAleer (2001), using cointegration methodology found that macroeconomic factors affecting tourist arrivals in Australia are impacted by the real income in the country of origin, cost of airfare, besides the bilateral exchange. A study conducted by Song and Wong (2003) incorporated time-varying parameters approach to comprehend all the shocks that impacted tourist arrivals in Hong Kong. Salleh et al. (2007) investigated the influence of cost of traveling, tourism price, incomes, and exchange rates on tourism demand in Malaysia utilizing a single cointegration technique. Their study results posited that both long- and short-term tourism demand is significantly related to most of the variables in their investigation. Kisswani et al. (2020a) utilized a cointegration with structural breaks methodology to examine the tourism receipts in 18 countries. Their findings suggested a long-run asymmetric effect in 11 countries of their sample study. In comparison, the remaining seven countries demonstrated symmetric long-run impact. Also, their results suggest the existence of a short-run asymmetric effect for 5 countries of the sample. On the whole, the asymmetry investigation in the literature still reveal mixed findings, and this requires continuation of more empirical analysis. In this regard, this paper pays attention to the asymmetric impact of oil prices at tourism in selected MENA countries.

4.3 Econometric Methodology

Several empirical investigations tested the relationship amid oil price shocks and tourism. However, considerable amount of these empirical investigations hypothesized a linear association. That is oil price increase and decrease both have the same magnitude effect and direction of association depending on the size and sign of the estimated coefficient of the association. Such strong assumption of symmetric effect offers less perception regarding the dynamics of the different shocks in the oil price. Accordingly, this study investigates the nonlinear relationship among tourism receipts and oil price shocks for seven select countries of the MENA region (Egypt, Israel, Jordan, Lebanon, Morocco, Tunisia, and Turkey) for the period 1995–2018.

The impact of oil price fluctuations on tourism receipts for the select MENA countries can be examined via proposing the following long-run relationship:

$$R_t = \beta_0 + \beta_1 P_t + \beta_2 N_t + \varepsilon_t \tag{4.1}$$

where in Eq. (4.1), tourism receipts in real terms is R_t, oil price in real terms is P_t, tourism arrivals is N_t, and ε_t represents the error term. However, the description of Eq. (4.1) exhibits symmetric impacts of oil prices at tourism receipts. The symmetric notion suggests that if the rise in oil price triggers a decline (or a rise) in tourism receipts, then a decrease should cause a rise (or a decline) in tourism receipts by the same amount, although this might not be the case. This also means that both the increase and the decrease of oil price (as the independent variable) will affect tourism receipts (dependent variable), which again might not be the case. As such, Shin et al. (2014) introduced an approach that helps in decomposing the independent variable (oil price here) to positive and negative shocks and afterward check if both do have the same effect or no (in terms of amount and sign of effect). This is known as asymmetric analysis. Shin et al. (2014) show that testing the asymmetric relationship and estimating long- and short-run influences can be done through a nonlinear autoregressive distributed lags (NARDL) methodology.

According to the NARDL method, the long-run association of Eq. (4.1) can be demonstrated as:

$$R_t = \beta_0 + \beta_1 P_t^+ + \beta_2 P_t^- + \beta_3 N_t + e_t \tag{4.2}$$

where β_1, β_2, and β_3 are the long-run effects that need to be estimated, along with P_t^+ and P_t^- being the partial sums of the positive and negative changes of oil price (P_t) that are computed as follows:

$$P_t^+ = \sum_{i=1}^{t} \Delta P_i^+ = \sum_{i=1}^{t} \max(\Delta P_i, 0) \tag{4.3}$$

and

$$P_t^- = \sum_{i=1}^{t} \Delta P_i^- = \sum_{i=1}^{t} \min(\Delta P_i, 0) \tag{4.4}$$

Indeed, Eq. (4.2) tests the asymmetric (nonlinear) influence of oil prices on the tourism receipts, given that β_1 shows the long-run influence of the oil price increase, meanwhile, β_2 shows the long-run influence of the oil price decrease. Theoretically, it is expected that $\beta_1 \neq \beta_2$, signifying that oil price increase could cause dissimilar long-run variations in tourism receipts when contrasted to oil price decrease, which implies asymmetric long-run pass through of oil price to tourism receipts.

The NARDL model is an expansion of the autoregressive distributed lags (ARDL) bounds testing approach of Pesaran et al. (2001), which allows, within a cointegration framework, estimating asymmetric long- and short-run coefficients. NARDL model, as a cointegration test, has a number of advantages over other conventional cointegration models, in that it evades some of the drawbacks encountered by a range of typical models. For instance, the NARDL model is applicable in testing cointegration (long-run relationship) irrespective of the order of integration of the variables involved in the analysis whether it is I(0), I(1) or combination, provided that none of the variables is integrated of order two (e.g., I(2)). Additionally, the NARDL model performs more efficiently than other conventional cointegration techniques when sample size suffers small number of observations (see: Romilly et al. 2001; Kisswani et al. 2020a, b; Kisswani et al. 2020b; Kisswani and Kisswani 2019; Kisswani 2019a, b; Kisswani et al. 2019; Kisswani 2017).

The NARDL approach estimates Eq. (4.2) through an unrestricted error correction model that can be described as:

$$\Delta R_t = \gamma + \alpha_0 R_{t-1} + \alpha_1 P_{t-1}^+ + \alpha_2 P_{t-1}^- + \alpha_3 N_{t-1} + \sum_{i=1}^{m} \delta_{1i} \Delta R_{t-i}$$

$$+ \sum_{i=0}^{n} \delta_{1i} \Delta N_{t-i} + \sum_{i=0}^{q} \left(\theta_i^+ \Delta P_{t-i}^+ + \theta_i^- \Delta P_{t-i}^- \right) + u_t \tag{4.5}$$

where Δ is the difference operator, m, n, and q are the lags length, and u_t is the serially uncorrelated error term. Furthermore, the NARDL structure allows each variable in Eq. (4.5) to take on a different number of lags. From Eq. (4.5), $-\frac{\alpha_1}{\alpha_0}$ is β_1 of Eq. (4.2), and $-\frac{\alpha_2}{\alpha_0}$ is β_2. As such, estimating $-\frac{\alpha_1}{\alpha_0}$ and $-\frac{\alpha_2}{\alpha_0}$ will show the long-run asymmetric impact of oil price at the tourism receipts. In addition, the asymmetric short-run impacts of oil price on tourism receipts are represented by $\sum_{i=0}^{q} \theta_i^+$ and $\sum_{i=0}^{q} \theta_i^-$ in Eq. (4.5).

Despite the fact that the NARDL methodology allows the involved variables to have different order of integration (I(1), I(0), or mix of both), yet variables are not allowed to be integrated of order two (I(2)), as this will nullify the cointegration test, and invalidates the outcome of the test. Hence, we test to check if any variable is I(2) or no as first step. This is done by utilizing the conventional Augmented Dickey–Fuller unit root test (ADF). Once evidence of no I(2) variable is established, then we can proceed with the NARDL methodology.

The NARDL estimation is implemented in three simple steps. First, Eq. (4.5) is estimated via the OLS method. Second, we test for long-run relationship (cointegration) through applying the F-test. This F-test examines if the lagged level variables $(R_{t-1}, P_{t-1}^+, P_{t-1}^-, \text{ and } N_{t-1})$ are jointly significant or no. The test involves a null hypothesis and assumes no cointegration ($\alpha_0 = \alpha_1 = \alpha_2 = \alpha_3 = 0$), against an alternative that assumes cointegration ($\alpha_0 \neq \alpha_1 \neq \alpha_2 \neq \alpha_3 \neq 0$). This test employs two settings of critical values (upper and lower bounds) produced by Pesaran et al. (2001). If the calculated F-statistic is bigger than the critical value of the upper bound, then this gives evidence of cointegration amid engaged variables. But, if the calculated F-statistic is smaller than the critical value of the lower bound, then we fail to reject the null (no cointegration). However, this test will be indeterminate if the calculated F-statistic value falls within the upper and lower bounds. Finally, once cointegration is verified, then we evaluate the asymmetric long- and short-run impacts.

Following the criteria applied by Kisswani et al. (2019, 2020b), Kisswani (2017, 2019a, b), Kisswani and Kisswani (2019), in addition to many others, the asymmetric long- and short-run impacts are investigated using the Wald test (distributed as χ^2 with one degree of freedom). For the long-run estimates of α_1 and α_2 [attached to P_t^+ and P_t^- variables in Eq. (4.5)] normalized on α_0, the asymmetry needs the coefficients to be significantly different, that is $-\frac{\alpha_1}{\alpha_0} \neq -\frac{\alpha_2}{\alpha_0}$. Likewise, the short-run asymmetry needs the sum of the short-run coefficients estimates of ΔP_{t-i}^+ and ΔP_{t-i}^-, in Eq. (4.5), to be statistically different, i.e., $\sum_{i=0}^{q} (\theta_i^+) \neq \sum_{i=0}^{q} (\theta_i^-)$. On the whole, the Wald test will be applied for examining $-\frac{\alpha_1}{\alpha_0} \neq -\frac{\alpha_2}{\alpha_0}$, and $\sum_{i=0}^{q} (\theta_i^+) \neq \sum_{i=0}^{q} (\theta_i^-)$.

In this study, structural breaks in the data is an issue we pay attention to, since it is considered an important element of the cointegration analysis. Gregory et al. (1996) illustrate that evidence of cointegration might not be found due to the unstable long-run relationship, as a result of the sudden shifts in the engaged variables (structural breaks). Usually structural breaks are connected to numerous extraordinary episodes such as the Asian financial crisis of 1997, the 1998 oil price crisis where oil exporters suffered from low market prices, the 2001 terrorist attacks on the USA, the 2008 US mortgage crisis that spread worldwide, the Arab Spring in the period 2011–2013 that lead to regime changes in some countries, besides, many other happenings around the world. For this reason, and following Kisswani (2017) among others, we examine if our sample data encounters structural breaks, by employing the multiple structural breaks test of Bai and Perron (1998). [2] Once the model shows confirmation of structural breaks, then a dummy variable for each break date will be designed and included in the model. This dummy variable will take a value of zero for all time periods before the break, and one since the break date and afterward. In accordance with Pesaran et al. (2001), incorporating dummy variables within the model will not influence the inferences drawn regarding the cointegration among the variables (Kisswani; 2017).

4.4   Empirical Findings and Discussion

In examining the asymmetric effect of oil prices on tourism receipts, we employ annual data from 1995 to 2018 for seven selected MENA countries, due to the availability of data as mentioned before. The selected countries are: Egypt, Israel, Jordan, Lebanon, Morocco, Tunisia, and Turkey. The variables included are: international tourism receipts in nominal values and priced in US dollars (World Bank data), international tourism arrivals (World Bank data), nominal Brent oil price in US dollars (International Financial Statistics (IMF) data), and US consumer price index (CPI), where 2010 is the base year (IMF data). To obtain the real values, we deflate the nominal US dollar values using the US consumer price index, and then variables are converted to logarithm values.

Since the sample data contains annual frequencies for the period 1995 to 2018, this will produce small number of observations which will create a challenge for decomposing the oil price variable to positive and negative shocks (P_t^+ and P_t^-). To overcome this problem, we follow Cheng et al. (2012), Hamdi et al. (2014), Kisswani et al. (2020b), among others, in transforming the annual values of the series into quarterly values by utilizing the quadratic match-sum approach. Such transformation will lead to a better assessment of the asymmetric nexus amid oil prices and tourism receipts. The quadratic match-sum method was implemented in various empirical studies (see, *inter alia*: Cheng et al. 2012; Hamdi et al. 2014; Kisswani et al. 2020b, among others).[3]

The first thing to do before proceeding with the NARDL is verifying that none of the variables is integrated of order two, i.e., I(2), since such issue would annul the results. Hence, we examine the stationarity of the first differences of the series by applying the ADF unit root with break test. The findings of the ADF test are illustrated in Table 4.1. The findings show that the first differences of all the series are stationary, implying that none of the variables is integrated of order two; I(2). The first difference of all the variables discards the null of unit root at the standard 5% significance level or lower, using Akaike Information Criterion, and allowing for maximum 11 lags. Overall, the findings from Table 4.1 noticeably suggest that we can carry on with the NARDL bounds test.

---

[2] See Bai and Perron (1998) for more details.

[3] For more information about the quadratic match-sum approach, see: Kisswani et al. (2020b).

Table 4.1 ADF unit root with break test

Country	Variable	Lags	1st difference
Egypt	R	0	−5.93***
	P^+	0	−6.355***
	P^-	0	−7.096***
	N	0	−5.690***
Israel	R	0	−4.838**
	P^+	0	−6.355***
	P^-	0	−7.096***
	N	11	−4.720**
Jordan	R	0	−5.801***
	P^+	0	−6.355***
	P^-	0	−7.096***
	N	11	−7.540***
Lebanon	R	11	−6.008***
	P^+	0	−6.355***
	P^-	0	−7.096***
	N	11	−6.214***
Morocco	R	0	−5.83***
	P^+	0	−6.355***
	P^-	0	−7.096***
	N	0	−5.844***
Tunisia	R	11	−4.852**
	P^+	0	−6.355***
	P^-	0	−7.096***
	N	11	−7.520***
Turkey	R	0	−5.205***
	P^+	0	−6.355***
	P^-	0	−7.096***
	N	0	−5.467***

Notes R is tourism receipts. P^+ is positive change of oil price, and P^- is negative change of oil price. N is tourism arrivals. Null Hypothesis: series has a unit root. AIC determined the lag length with maximum lags = 11. Significance at the 1% and 5% levels is denoted by *** and **, respectively

Before we move forward to apply the NARDL bounds test, we need primarily to check if the data suffers from structural breaksAs mentioned beforehand, we employ the multiple structural breaks test of Bai and Perron, and report the findings in Table 4.2. The summarized findings show that the 7 countries went through diverse number of breaks, along with being around dissimilar time periods. In the case of

Table 4.2 Bai and Perron (1998) structural breaks test

Country	Number of breaks	Break date
Egypt	3	1999: Q_3, 2003: Q_3, 2012: Q_4
Israel	4	1999: Q_1, 2003: Q_2, 2007: Q_1, 2015: Q_3
Jordan	3	1998: Q_3, 2008: Q_1, 2014: Q_3
Lebanon	2	1998: Q_3, 2002: Q_1
Morocco	3	2001: Q_2, 2005: Q_4, 2010: Q_1
Tunisia	3	2000: Q_1, 2011: Q_1, 2015: Q_2
Turkey	3	2001: Q_1, 2007: Q_1, 2015: Q_2

Egypt, 3 significant breaks were realized around: 1998: Q_3, 2003: Q_3, and 2012: Q_4. While for Israel, the test shows 4 significant breaks around: 1999: Q_1, 2003: Q_2, 2007: Q_1, and 2015: Q_3. For Jordan, the test reports 3 significant breaks around: 1998: Q_3, 2008: Q_1, and 2014: Q_3. As for Lebanon, the test shows 2 significant breaks around: 1998: Q_3, and 2002: Q_1. In the case of Morocco, 3 significant breaks were detected around: 2001: Q_2, 2005: Q_4, and 2010: Q_1. In the Tunisia case, 3 significant breaks were realized around: 2000: Q_1, 2011: Q_1, and 2015: Q_2. Finally, in the case of turkey, the test revealed 3 significant breaks around: 2001: Q_1, 2007: Q_1, and 2015: Q_2. Finding structural breaks in the data goes in line with episodes that have upset the oil market throughout the sample period. Remarkably, the oil market went through different shocks such as the 1973 oil embargo, the Iranian Revolution in 1979, the breakdown of oil prices through the 1980s due to the Iraq–Iran war, the aggression on Kuwait in 1990, the terrorist attacks during the 2001–2002 on the USA and UK, two wars on Iraq and Afghanistan during 2001–2003, the 2008 mortgage crisis that started in the USA and then extended all over, and a short time ago the so-called Arab Spring that triggered many regimes changes (see, for example, Kisswani 2017, 2019a, b; Kisswani and Kisswani 2019; Kisswani et al. 2019, 2020a). Now, since Table 4.2 gives support for the presence of the structural breaks, we will advance to estimate Eq. (4.5); the unrestricted error correction model, by incorporating the structural breaks as dummy variables, and then examine the asymmetric effects as explained earlier.

To start the NARDL analysis, we estimate Eq. (4.5), using OLS, and report the cointegration findings in Table 4.3 for each country. Table 3.3 describes, for each country, the F-statistic (revealing the significance of the test by analyzing the lagged levels of the variables), the selected number of lags for each NARDL model, and the cointegration decision, as elucidated before.

Table 4.3 reports the error correction coefficient (ECM_{t-1}) for each country. The ECM_{t-1} reflects the pace of adjustment on the way to the long-run equilibrium, once a shock in the short-run takes place, coupled with confirming cointegration if it is negatively significant, with absolute value less than one. The findings from Table 4.3 show that the F-statistics surpass the critical values (upper bounds) for all 7 countries, which provides evidence of a long-run relationship among tourism receipts and engaged variables (P_t^+, P_t^-, and N_t) for all countries. The findings go

Table 4.3 NARDL bounds cointegration test

Country	F-statistic	ECM$_{t-1}$	Conclusion	Selected model
Egypt	5.15***	−0.254(0.00)***	Cointegration	ARDL(4, 0, 0, 3)
Israel	4.82***	−0.260(0.00)***	Cointegration	ARDL(3, 0, 1, 3)
Jordan	3.95**	−0.089(0.00)***	Cointegration	ARDL(2, 3, 2, 2)
Lebanon	21.83***	−0.381(0.00)***	Cointegration	ARDL(3, 1, 0, 0)
Morocco	4.14**	−0.122(0.00)***	Cointegration	ARDL(3, 0, 1, 1)
Tunisia	10.47***	−0.305(0.00)***	Cointegration	ARDL(3, 1, 4, 3)
Turkey	6.02***	−0.276(0.00)***	Cointegration	ARDL(3, 0, 0, 3)

	Pesaran et al. (2001) critical values ($k = 3$)	
Significance	I(0) bound	I(1) bound
10%	2.37	3.20
5%	2.79	3.67
1%	3.65	4.66

Notes Null Hypothesis: No cointegration. AIC is employed to select of the model (lags). Bounds critical values are from Pesaran et al. (2001). Critical values: Case II restricted intercept and no trend. ECM$_{t-1}$ is the error-correction coefficient. p-value is reported in parentheses. Significance at 1% and 5% levels is denoted by *** and **, respectively

in line with many other studies (see, e.g., Kisswani et al. 2020a, b). The cointegration is established for Egypt, Israel, Lebanon, Tunisia, and Turkey at the 1% level, and for Jordan in addition to Morocco at the 5% level. In addition, the ECM$_{t-1}$, for all countries, confirms cointegration given that it is highly significant (at the 1% significance level) and negative, besides the absolute value is less than one as required.

Since cointegration was established for the 7 countries, at this point we analyze the long- together with the short-run coefficients to investigate if there is an asymmetric impact for each country. Long-run findings are described in Table 4.4, whereas short-run findings are described in Table 3.5.

Starting with the long-run estimates, Table 4.4 reveals that the positive and negative shocks in the oil price (P_t^+ and P_t^-) are not significant for Egypt, Morocco, and Turkey. That means oil price, for these countries, affect tourism receipts symmetrically. On the other hand, in the Lebanon case the impact of the oil price increase is significant while the oil price decrease is not significant. That indicates there is an asymmetric impact in the Lebanon case. The price increase shock significantly affects tourism receipts negatively. In addition, the effect of oil price increase and decrease is significant in the case of Israel, Jordan, and Tunisia. For Israel, both oil price change (P_t^+ and P_t^-) are significantly negative. Meanwhile in the case of Jordan and Tunisia both oil price change are positive. For this reason, we apply the Wald test for Israel, Jordan, and Tunisia to test if the positive and negative shocks in the oil price (P_t^+ and P_t^-) are affecting tourism receipts differently or no (asymmetric effect). Table 4.4 describes the Wald test statistic (χ^2) for the 3 countries: Israel, Jordan, and Tunisia. The Wald test reveals long-run asymmetric effect only for Tunisia, as

Table 4.4 NARDL long-run coefficients

Country	P^+	P^-	χ^2
Egypt	0.099	0.092	–
	(0.264)	(0.179)	–
Israel	−0.206***	−0.262***	1.099
	(0.008)	(0.003)	(0.295)
Jordan	0.424**	0.619**	0.887
	(0.020)	(0.029)	(0.346)
Lebanon	−0.155**	−0.043	–
	(0.013)	(0.504)	–
Morocco	−0.363	0.143	–
	(0.327)	(0.147)	–
Tunisia	0.169***	0.491***	19.542***
	(0.001)	(0.00)	(0.000)
Turkey	−0.045	0.011	–
	(0.306)	(0.807)	–

Notes P^+ is positive change of oil price, and P^- is negative change of oil price. χ^2 is the Wald test statistic. All variables in logarithmic format. Significance at 1% and 5% levels is denoted by *** and **, respectively

χ^2 is highly significant only in this case. Meanwhile, for Israel and Jordan the Wald test statistic (χ^2) is not significant, which means no long-run asymmetry exists. The Wald test findings show that the positive and negative shocks of the oil price (P_t^+ and P_t^-) are affecting tourism receipts differently (asymmetrically), in the case of Tunisia only. Both shocks have positive long-run effect but in dissimilar amounts. Overall, Table 4.4 shows that the asymmetric long-run effect is documented in two cases only: Lebanon (where P_t^+ is significant but P_t^- is not) and Tunisia (where χ^2 is significant).

Now, we examine the short-run asymmetry. Table 4.5 reports the short-run NARDL coefficients. The findings here show no short-run asymmetry for Egypt, Israel, and Turkey where the short-run changes in the positive and negative shocks of the oil price (ΔP_t^+ and ΔP_t^-) are not significant. As for Morocco, the short-run negative shocks of the oil price (ΔP_t^-) are significant, meanwhile the short-run positive shocks (ΔP_t^+) are not significant. However, the Wald test statistic (χ^2) is not significant. This means, there is no support for the short-run asymmetry in the case of Morocco. On the other hand, for Jordan the short-run changes in the positive and negative shocks of the oil price (ΔP_t^+ and ΔP_t^-) are significant. The Wald test statistic (χ^2) is significant as well. This means there is evidence of short-run asymmetry, but this asymmetry does not last in the long-run where no significant asymmetric impact was found for Jordan. Turning attention now to Lebanon, the short-run positive shocks (ΔP_t^+) are significant, but the short-run negative shocks of the oil price (ΔP_t^-) are not. Nonetheless, the Wald test statistic (χ^2) is significant for

Table 4.5 NARDL short-run coefficients

	Egypt	Israel	Jordan	Lebanon	Morocco	Tunisia	Turkey
ΔP^+	0.078	−0.107	0.174**	−0.432**	0.028	0.205***	0.001
	(0.425)	(0.307)	(0.011)	(0.023)	(0.761)	(0.002)	(0.986)
$\Delta P^+(-1)$	–	–	−0.160**	–	–	–	–
	–	–	(0.018)	–	–	–	–
$\Delta P^+(-2)$	–	–	−0.097	–	–	–	–
	–	–	(0.134)	–	–	–	–
ΔP^-	0.028	0.093	0.400***	0.063	0.146**	0.185***	−0.029
	(0.684)	(0.131)	(0.000)	(0.629)	(0.021)	(0.000)	(0.387)
$\Delta P^-(-1)$	–	–	−0.100*	–	–	−0.15***	–
	–	–	(0.091)	–	–	(0.003)	–
$\Delta P^-(-2)$	–	–	–	–	–	−0.133**	–
	–	–	–	–	–	(0.011)	–
$\Delta P^-(-3)$	–	–	–	–	–	−0.116**	–
	–	–	–	–	–	(0.014)	–
χ^2	–	–	8.893***	3.741*	0.924	9.350***	–
	–	–	(0.003)	(0.053)	(0.336)	(0.002)	–

Notes P^+ is positive change in oil price, and P^- is negative change in oil price. χ^2 is the Wald test statistic. All variables in logarithmic format. *p*-value is reported in parentheses. Significance at 1%, 5%, and 10% levels is denoted by ***, ** and *, respectively

Lebanon. This signifies that there is support for the short-run asymmetry in the case of Lebanon, and this asymmetry lasts in the long-run where significant asymmetric effect was found. Finally, for Tunisia, Table 4.5 shows that the short-run changes in the positive and negative shocks in the oil price (ΔP_t^+ and ΔP_t^-) are significant. The Wald test statistic (χ^2) is significant as well. This supports short-run asymmetry, which clearly lasts in the long run, where the asymmetric long-run impact was found significant. To sum up, the short-run asymmetric impact was confirmed for Jordan, Lebanon, and Tunisia.

To conclude the analysis of the asymmetric impact of oil prices on tourism receipts, we examine if the established long-run asymmetries for Lebanon and Tunisia are stable and consistent or not. This is done through particular diagnostic tools that evaluate the efficiency of the model. The tools are: (1) the Lagrange Multiplier (LM) statistic, which tests if the residuals are serially correlated (has a χ^2 distribution with two degrees of freedom). (2) Ramsey Regression Equation Specification Error Test (Ramsey's RESET), which tests the misspecification of the model (has a χ^2 distribution with one degree of freedom). (3) The cumulative sum of recursive residuals (CUSUM) and the cumulative sum of squares of recursive residuals (CUSUMSQ) tests of Brown et al. (1975), which evaluate the stability of the model (the CUSUM and CUSUMSQ tests are reported as "S" for stable, "NS" for not stable). The diagnostic tools are reported in Table 4.6. Besides, the graphs of the CUSUM

Table 4.6 NARDL long-run diagnostic tests

	LM (2)	RESET test	CUSUM	CUSUMSQ
Lebanon	15.16***(0.00)	6.306**(0.012)	NS	NS
Tunisia	1.465 (0.481)	0.682(0.409)	S	S

Notes LM (2) is the LM statistics for autocorrelation up to order 2. RESET test is Ramsey's test (null hypothesis: functional form is correctly specified). CUSUM is the cumulative sum of recursive residuals (S: stable, NS: not stable). CUSUMSQ is the cumulative sum of squares of recursive residuals (S: stable, NS: not stable). Numbers in parentheses represent *p*-value

and CUSUMSQ are portrayed in Fig. 4.1 (for Lebanon) and Fig. 4.2 (for Tunisia). The diagnostic tools of the long-run asymmetry test (expressed in Table 4.6) show sufficient specifications in the case of Tunisia, where the model elapses the misspecification test of Ramsey's RESET, alongside the model does not suffer from autocorrelation in the errors, and shows stability in terms of the CUSUM and CUSUMSQ tests. However, for Lebanon this is not the case, where the long-run asymmetry suffers from autocorrelation, plus Ramsey's RESET test shows the model is not well specified, in addition to the unstable long-run relationship evident by the CUSUM and CUSUMSQ tests.

4.5   Conclusions and Policy Implications

Kisswani et al. (2020b) give a brief review of the previous studies that reported negative outcome of oil prices-tourism nexus (see also: Yeoman et al. 2007; Becken and Lennox 2012). However, most of these studies assumed symmetric effect. For this reason, in this study we diverge from this path and we explore the asymmetric effect (nonlinear) instead of the symmetric effect. Consequently, we decompose the oil price (P_t) to partial sums of the positive and negative changes of the oil price (P_t^+ and P_t^-), and then employ the nonlinear autoregressive distributed lags (NARDL) model of Shin et al. (2014). Furthermore, in the analysis we consider the structural breaks of the series. Such breaks where first identified by the multiple structural breaks test of Bai and Perron (1998), and then integrated it in the NARDL model as dummy variables.

We dealt in this study with seven MENA countries (Egypt, Israel, Jordan, Lebanon, Morocco, Tunisia, and Turkey). The data is annual frequencies over the period 1995–2018. But, because the annual frequencies would generate small sample size issue, we transform the annual frequencies into quarterly series using the quadratic match-sum method. The findings of the NARDL analysis reveal a long-run association (cointegration) involving tourism receipts and the positive, as well as the negative changes in oil price (P_t^+ and P_t^-) for all seven countries. However, when testing for the long-run asymmetric impact, evidence was only found for Lebanon and Tunisia. What is more, when we examine the existence of the short-run asymmetry, the NARDL analysis gave support for it in the case of Jordan, Lebanon, and Tunisia only.

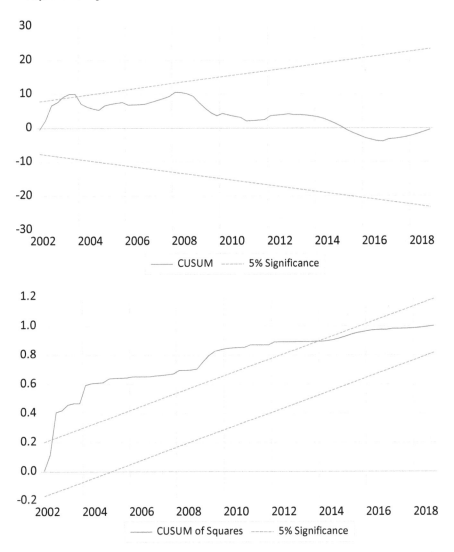

Fig. 4.1 CUSUM and CUSUMSQ graphs for Lebanon

The findings imply several important policy implications. When oil price increase is significantly affecting tourism in a negative way, then policymakers should design policies that can offset the decrease in number of international travelers, through encouraging domestic tourism. Additionally, MENA countries should start engaging tourism activities in different energy sources, or try to encourage tourism activities to be more labor intensive which can reduce the effect of oil price volatility, and create more jobs. Finally, decision makers should pay attention to the asymmetric impact of oil prices at tourism in the MENA countries, provided that tourism is an important

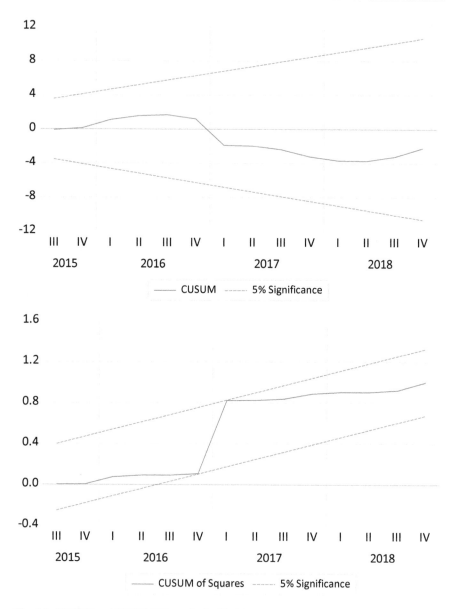

Fig. 4.2 CUSUM and CUSUMSQ graphs for Tunisia

injection to their GDP since tourism industries are good source of jobs that can be very helpful in designing policies for reducing unemployment whether in terms of number or gender of workers.

References

Acikgoz S, Ben Ali MS (2019) Where does economic growth in the Middle Eastern and North African countries come from? Q Rev Econ Finance 73:172–183

Acikgoz S, Ben Ali MS, Mert M (2016) Sources of economic growth in MENA countries: Technological Progress, Physical Or Human Capital Accumulations? Economic development in the Middle East and North Africa. Springer/Palgrave Macmillan, New York, pp 27–69

Arezki R, Nabli MK (2012) Natural resources, volatility, and inclusive growth: perspectives from the Middle East and North Africa. In: IMF working paper, No. 111–12. International Monetary Fund, Washington, DC

Albalate D, Bel G (2010) Tourism and urban public transport: holding demand pressure under supply constraints. Tour Manag 31(3):425–433

Álvarez LJ, Hurtado S, Sánchez I, Thomas C (2011) The impact of oil price changes on Spanish and euro area consumer price inflation. Econ Model 28(1–2):422–431

Bai J, Perron P (1998) Estimating and testing linear models with multiple structural changes. Econometrica 66(1):47–78

Becken S (2008) Developing indicators for managing tourism in the face of peak oil. Tour Manag 29(4):695–705

Becken S, Lennox J (2012) Implications of a long-term increase in oil prices for tourism. Tour Manag 33(1):133–142

Bernini C (2009) Convention industry and destination clusters: evidence from Italy. Tour Manag 30(6):878–889

Blackstock KL, White V, McCrum G, Scott A, Hunter C (2008) Measuring responsibility: an appraisal of a Scottish National Park's sustainable tourism indicators. J Sustain Tourism 16(3):276–297

Blake A, Cortes-jiménez I (2007) The drivers of tourism demand in the UK. A report prepared by Christel DeHaan Tourism and Travel Research Institute-University of Nottingham for the Department of Culture, Media and Sport. UK Parliament, London

Brown RL, Durbin J, Evans JM (1975) Techniques for testing the con-stancy of regression relationships over time. J Roy Stat Soc 37:149–192

Cheng M, Chung L, Tam C-S, Yuen R, Chan S, Yu I-W (2012) Tracking the Hong Kong Economy. Occasional Paper 03/2012. Hong Kong Monetary Authority. Hong Kong

Cheung C, Law R (2001) Determinants of tourism hotel expenditure in Hong Kong. Int J Contemp Hospitality Manag 13(3):151–158

Choi H-C, Sirakaya E (2006) Sustainability indicators for managing community tourism. Tour Manag 27(6):1274–1289

Donayre L, Wilmot NA (2016) The asymmetric effect of oil price shocks on the Canadian economy. Int J Energy Econ Policy 6(2):167–182

Dwyer L, Forsyth P (2008) Economic measures of tourism yield: what markets to target? Int J Tourism Res 10(2):155–168

Dwyer L, Forsyth P, Rao P (2000) The price competitiveness of travel and tourism: a comparison of 19 destinations. Tour Manag 21(1):9–22

Gregory AW, Nason JM, Watt DG (1996) Testing for structural breaks in cointegrated relationships. J Econometrics 71:321–341

Habibi F (2017) The determinants of inbound tourism to Malaysia: a panel data analysis. Curr Issues Tourism 20(9):909–930

Hamdi H, Sbia R, Shahbaz M (2014) The nexus between electricity consumption and economic growth in Bahrain. Econ Model 38:227–237

Hanafiah MHM, Harun MFM (2010) Application of gravity model in estimating tourism demand in Malaysia. In: Proceedings of 2010 international conference on business, economics and tourism management, (Cbetm), pp 293–297

Holzner M (2011) Tourism and economic growth: the beach disease? Tour Manag 32(4):922–933

Jalil A, Mahmood T, Idrees M (2013) Tourism–growth nexus in Pakistan: evidence from ARDL bounds tests. Econ Model 35:185–191

Katircioglu S (2009a) Revisiting the tourism-led-growth hypothesis for Turkey using the bounds test and Johansen approach for cointegration. Tour Manag 30(1):17–20

Katircioglu S (2009b) Tourism, trade and growth: the case of Cyprus. Appl Econ 41(21):2741–2750

Katircioglu ST, Sertoglu K, Candemir M, Mercan M (2015) Oil price movements and macroeconomic performance: evidence from twenty-six OECD countries. Renew Sustain Energy Rev 44(C):257–270

Kisswani K (2017) Evaluating the GDP—energy consumption Nexus for the ASEAN-5 countries using nonlinear ARDL model. OPEC Energy Rev 41(4):318–343

Kisswani K (2019a) Asymmetric gasoline-oil price nexus: recent evidence from non-linear cointegration investigation. Appl Econ Lett 26(21):1802–1806

Kisswani K (2019b) The dynamic links between oil prices and economic growth: recent evidence from non-linear cointegration analysis for the ASEAN-5 countries. Emerg Markets Finance Trade (Forthcoming). https://doi.org/10.1080/1540496x.2019.1677463

Kisswani A, Kisswani K (2019) Modelling the employment-oil price nexus: a non-linear cointegration analysis for the U.S. market. J Int Trade Econ Dev 28(7):902–918

Kisswani K, Harraf A, Kisswani A (2019) Revisiting the effects of oil prices on exchange rate: asymmetric evidence from the ASEAN-5 countries. Econ Change Restructuring 52(3):279–300

Kisswani K, Kisswani A, Harraf A (2020a) The impacts of oil price shocks on tourism receipts for selected MENA countries: do structural breaks matter? Tourism Anal (Forthcoming). https://doi.org/10.3727/108354220x15758301241891

Kisswani K, Zaitouni M, Moufakkir O (2020b) An examination of the asymmetric effect of oil prices on tourism receipts. Curr Issues Tourism 23(4):500–522

Lim C, McAleer M (2001) Modelling the determinants of International Tourism demand to Australia, ISER discussion paper 0532, Institute of Social and Economic Research, Osaka University. Japan

Meo M, Chowdhury M, Shaikh G, Ali M, Masood Sheikh S (2018) Asymmetric impact of oil prices, exchange rate, and inflation on tourism demand in Pakistan: new evidence from nonlinear ARDL. Asia Pacific J Tourism Res 23(4):408–422

Moshiri S (2015) Asymmetric effect of oil price shocks in oil-exporting countries: the role of institutions. OPEC Energy Rev 39(2):222–246

Naccache T (2010) Slow oil shocks and the weakening of the oil price-macroeconomy relationship. Energy Policy 38(5):2340–2345

Narayan PK (2004) Fiji's tourism demand: the ARDL approach to cointegration. Tourism Econ 10(2):193–206

Pesaran MH, Shin Y, Smith RJ (2001) Bounds testing approaches to the analysis of level relationships. J Appl Econometrics 16:289–326

Quayson J, Var T (1982) A tourism demand function for the Okanagan, BC. Tourism Manag 3(2):108–115

Romilly P, Song H, Liu H (2001) Car ownership and use in Britain: a comparison of the empirical results of alternative cointegration estimation methods and forecasts. Appl Econ 33(14):1803–1818

Salleh N, Othman R, Ramachandran S (2007) Malaysia's tourism demand from selected countries: the ARDL approach to cointegration. Int J Econ Manag 1(3):345–363

Shaeri K, Adaoglu C, Katircioglu ST (2016) Oil price risk exposure: a comparison of financial and non-financial subsectors. Energy 109:712–723

Shin Y, Yu BC, Greenwood-Nimmo M (2014) Modelling asymmetric cointegration and dynamic multipliers in a nonlinear ARDL framework. In: Sickels R, Horrace W (eds) Festschrift in Honor of Peter Schmidt: econometric methods and applications. Springer, New York, NY, pp 281–314

Song H, Witt SF (2000) Tourism demand modelling and forecasting: modern econometric approaches. Routledge, Oxford

Song H, Wong KF (2003) Tourism demand modeling: a time-varying parameter approach. J Travel Res 42(3):57–64

Tang CF, Abosedra S (2014) Small sample evidence on the tourism-led growth hypothesis in Lebanon. Curr Issues Tourism 17(3):234–246

World Tourism Organization (2019) International Tourism Highlights, 2019 Edition. UNWTO. Madrid. https://doi.org/10.18111/9789284421152

WTO (2006) http://www.e-unwto.org/doi/book/10.18111/9789284413 492

Yeoman I, Lennon J, Blake A, Galt M, Greenwood C, McMahon-Beattie U (2007) Oil depletion: what does this mean for Scottish tourism? Tour Manag 28:1354–1365

Chapter 5
Youth Unemployment and Quality of Education in the MENA: An Empirical Investigation

Mohammad Reza Farzanegan and Hassan F. Gholipour

Abstract The Middle East and North Africa (MENA) region has the highest rate of youth unemployment worldwide. High records of youth unemployment have increased the risk of political instability and other social concerns. Our study aims to investigate the role of quality of education in explaining the within country variation of youth unemployment in the MENA region. We use fixed effect regression methodology for a panel of 18 MENA countries from 2007 to 2017. Our results show a significant and robust negative (decreasing) effect of higher quality of education system on youth unemployment rate. This decreasing effect is robust to control of other drivers of youth unemployment, country and year fixed effects. Including full set of control variables, we show that a one unit increase in perceived quality of education systems from the Global Competitiveness Reports is associated with approximately 4 percentage points decline in youth unemployment. Our general specification explains approximately 70% of within-country variation of youth unemployment rate in the MENA region. Among control variables, only trade openness and foreign direct investment (FDI) share of GDP show statistically significant (negative) association with youth unemployment, meaning that trade and foreign investment openness contribute to employment of youth in the region. We suggest some recommendations for policy makers in the region.

Keywords Youth unemployment · Quality of education · MENA · Panel regression

M. R. Farzanegan (✉)
School of Business and Economics, Economics of the Middle East Research Group,
Philipps-Universität Marburg, Center for Near and Middle Eastern Studies (CNMS), Marburg,
Germany
e-mail: farzanegan@uni-marburg.de

H. F. Gholipour
School of Business, Western Sydney University, Sydney, Australia
e-mail: H.Fereidouni@westernsydney.edu.au

© The Author(s), under exclusive license to Springer Nature Switzerland AG 2021   65
M. S. Ben Ali (ed.), *Economic Development in the MENA Region*, Perspectives
on Development in the Middle East and North Africa (MENA) Region,
https://doi.org/10.1007/978-3-030-66380-3_5

5.1   Introduction

Economic growth and its determinants have been a continuous question not only for scholars but also for policy makers worldwide. An important input for long-term economic growth is the demographic structure of a country. Countries with larger share of working age population (15–64 years) in total population should in theory have more possibilities for production and thus economic growth. Discussing the case of economic growth in Asia, Bloom and Williamson (1998), and Bloom et al. (2000) have demonstrated that approximately one third of the fast economic growth in the "Asian Tigers" in the 1970s and 1980s can be related to demographic transition (i.e. reduction of fertility rate and increase of working ag population). The interest in understanding the determinants of economic growth is the Middle East and North Africa (MENA) is also important. The MENA region has experienced a rapid increase in its working age population between 1976 and 2006 which was comparable to the growth rate in East Asia (0.7% annual growth based on geometric end-point growth method). However, the economic growth impact of such a similar increase in demographic transition in these two regions was significantly different. Some authors like Bloom et al. (2007) suggest that the quality of institutions is responsible for different income effects of demographic structure. Bjorvatn and Farzanegan (2013) show in a theoretical and empirical study that the degree of dependency on natural resource rents is one of the main reasons for different income effects of age structure, explaining the paradox of economic development and demographic transition in the MENA region.

Other studies also engage in exploring the determinants of growth in the MENA region. For example, Acikgoz and Ben Ali (2019) argue that capital accumulation rather than productivity growth is the main driver of economic growth in a sample of MENA countries (also see Acikgoz et al. 2016; Ben Ali et al. 2016; Ben Ali and Krammer 2016, Apergis and Ben Ali 2020 for the role of corruption and natural resources in economic growth of the MENA).

As it is shown by Bjorvatn and Farzanegan (2013), the MENA countries were less able to benefit from their demographic transition and a significant share of young working age population have not been channelized into productive activities, leading to high numbers of unemployed young population. Therefore, a part of literature on the MENA economic development focuses on the topic of youth unemployment, aiming to explain its drivers besides the consequences. Youth unemployment is one of critical challenges in the MENA region, increasing the risk of political instability. In 2017, the youth unemployment rate in the MENA region reached almost 30%, which is considered as the highest level among all regions in the world. Figure 5.1 shows a trend of youth unemployment worldwide comparing the MENA region with other global regions from 2007 to 2017 (World Bank 2020).

Moreover, young people in the MENA region search for years to find a job and this stage is called "waithood" that delays the phase of adulthood. The high level of youth unemployment (which varies also across the MENA countries, see Fig. 5.2) has different reasons. For example, we can refer to slow economic growth, unclear job

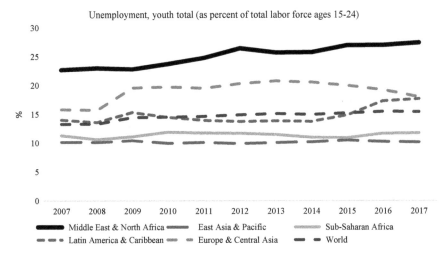

Fig. 5.1 Trend of youth unemployment rate in various global regions (2007–2017). *Source* World Bank (2020)

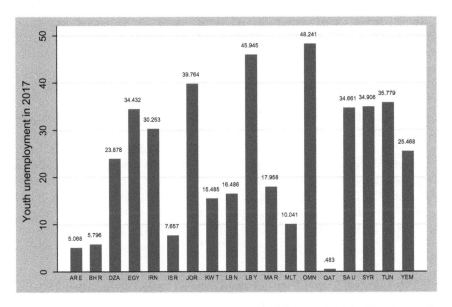

Fig. 5.2 Cross country variation of youth unemployment (percentage) in the MENA countries in 2017. *Source* World Bank (2020). *Note* ARE (United Arab Emirates); BHR (Bahrain); DZA (Algeria); EGY (Egypt); IRN (Iran); ISR (Israel); JOR (Jordan); KWT (Kuwait); LBN (Lebanon); LBY (Libya); MAR (Morocco); MLT (Malta); OMN (Oman); QAT (Qatar); SAU (Saudi Arabia); SYR (Syria); TUN (Tunisia); YEM (Yemen)

market information, career path and undefined required qualifications. Additionally, the poor education system that does not prepare youth with skills and knowledge needed for the candidates in the job market is another driver of high youth unemployment rates. Furthermore, the long queue of the young graduates over the public sector due to high wages, secured jobs, and other benefits may also explain part of the challenge of youth unemployment. Likewise, the private sector is excessively regulated and that can be seen as burden in the way of finding jobs for youth.

Oil rents may also both positively and negatively affect the jobs for youth. Depending on type of institutions, oil rents may boost investment and labor-intensive economic projects which then may open new opportunities for youth. It may also foster conflict (Farzanegan et al. 2018; Bjorvatn and Farzanegan 2015), corruption and rent-seeking and additionally due to the Dutch disease leads to lower employment opportunities for the youth. For example, Farzanegan (2014) shows a negative and significant link between oil rents dependency and small business formation (which are the main source of employment).

Demographic transition may also explain part of the youth unemployment problem in the MENA region. Increasing working age population in oil-based economies is not leading to higher income growth, adding pressure in job market for youth (Bjorvatn and Farzanegan 2013). Moreover, globalization and trade openness can provide new chances for the youth in job market by increasing investment and trade opportunities. Nevertheless, increasing trade openness may also boost competition and affects the local industries by lowering their profit margin and thus reducing the employment rates in less competitive and labor intensive industries of an economy.

Our focus in this study is on the impact of quality of education system in shaping the development of youth unemployment rate in the MENA countries. Youth unemployment in the MENA region is high partly due to mismatch between education system and skills that are required by the job market. The low quality of education system is mainly affected by reliance of these countries on natural resource rents (Farzanegan and Thum 2020). The key question is whether we can find a strong empirical support for the relevance of quality of education in youth employability in the MENA region, controlling for other important drivers of youth unemployment.

5.2 Review of Literature on the Link Between Education and Youth Unemployment

The link between education and unemployment (including youth unemployment) has been broadly analyzed in the literature over the past four decades. Most of existing studies find that educated workers experience less unemployment and shorter duration of unemployment (e.g. Ashenfelter and Ham 1979; Mincer 1991; Riddell and Song 2011; Farber 2004; Nickell 1979; Wolbers 2000; Kettunen 1997; Biagi and Lucifora 2008). This is mainly because additional education enhances individuals' ability to make more efficient decisions in the face of shifting economic environments and improve individual's adaptive capacity and adjustability to new technology (e.g. Fullan and Loubser 1972; Schultz 1975; Globerman 1986). In other words, education makes an individual more productive both in the production of goods and services and in the attainment of additional education which decreases the costs of training undertaken by companies (Magnussen 1979). Thus, workers with higher level of education are more attractive for employers.

Although most researchers have strongly emphasized on the positive effect of education on employment, there are some researchers who do not support this view. For example, Yang (2018), Li et al. (2014), Erdem and Tugcu (2012) show that the incidence of unemployment is significantly higher among young people with university degrees than those with lower level of education. They argue that the young graduates are unemployed mainly because they are either over-educated or their skills mismatch industries' expectations.

For the MENA countries, Kamyab (2013) notes that severe educational deficiencies within the higher education systems is one the main drivers of high youth unemployment. In the same strand, Ahmed (2012) concludes that education in the region is not a guarantee against unemployment because education systems in the MENA region fail to produce graduates with required skills by industries. Kabbani (2019) also suggests that policymaker in the MENA region should reform their education systems to advance cognitive, non-cognitive and technical skills. The similar suggestion is provided by Fakih et al. (2020) to tackle youth unemployment in a set of MENA countries. Msigwa and Kipesha (2013) also show that the youth unemployment problem is related to educational background and degrees possessed by the young people as compared to the qualification demanded in the job market. Yizengaw (2018) argues that quality of teaching staff, availability of learning facilities, quality and updated learning material are important factors in improving university graduates' employability. O'Reilly et al. (2015) review several studies on youth unemployment and conclude that the expansion of education in European Union is weakly aligned to the shifting structure of skills required by firms which lead to higher youth unemployment in the region. Based on their analyses, they suggest that government sponsored trainings have positive medium-run impacts on youth employment, if they are delivered in high quality and customized to the labor market needs. A recent study by PWC (2018) also shows that youth unemployment rate is lower in countries with higher level of educational attainment, high quality vocational training and a high level of support for young disadvantaged people. A study conducted by OECD (2015) argues that one of the main drivers of youth unemployment in the era of rapid technological change and globalization is that most young people lack access to quality education and their skills mismatch the industries' demand. Neuman and Ziderman (1999), Riphahn and Zibrowius (2016) and Ryan (2001) show that in countries with established vocational and apprenticeship education and training, youth participating in these programs experience a quicker entry into the job market than youth entering the labor market after taking part in general education. Tomic and Taylor (2018) provide evidence that the youth unemployment in Croatia is mainly caused by poor quality education (e.g. general lack of practical orientation in all stages of education which has led to the mismatch of main education and training programs with the knowledge and skill demanded by firms). The similar issue appears in Slovenia where educational policy is not completely aligned with the employers' requirements, which lead to high rate of unemployment among young people (Čepar et al. 2018).

While existing studies provide valuable insights on the link between education and youth unemployment, to the best of our knowledge, there is no empirical study that examines the relationship between quality of education system and youth unemployment in the MENA region with recent data. Our study addresses this research gap in the literature.

5.3 Research Design and Results

5.3.1 Data and Model

Our hypothesis is that a higher level of quality of education system reduces the youth unemployment rate, ceteris paribus. We use a panel of 18 MENA counties over the period 2007–2017. The list of sample countries are Algeria, Bahrain, Egypt, Iran, Israel, Jordan, Kuwait, Lebanon, Libya, Malta, Morocco, Oman, Qatar, Saudi Arabia, Syria, Tunisia, United Arab Emirates and Yemen. We estimate the following specification with fixed effects regression methodology.

$$\text{youth\_unemployment}_{it} = \text{cons} + \beta_1 \text{ quality\_education}_{it}$$
$$+ \beta_2 Z_{it} + \mu_i + \theta_t + \varepsilon_{it} \tag{5.1}$$

youth_unemployment is unemployment of youth (as percentage of total labor force ages 15–24), *cons* is a constant term, quality_education is perceived quality of education system, Z is a vector that captures control variables (economic development, oil rent, trade and investment openness, population growth, quality of governance and government expenditures on education); μ_i is country fixed-effect, θ_t is year fixed-effect and ε is an error term.

Our dependent variable is unemployment of youth (as percentage of total labor force ages 15–24) and it refers to "the share of the labor force ages 15–24 without work but available for and seeking employment" (World Bank 2020). The data are obtained from the World Bank (2020) and the main inputs for calculation of this variable is from ILOSTAT database of International Labour Organization. In our sample of MENA counties for period of 2007–2017, the youth unemployment rate varies from minimum of 0.45% (Qatar in 2016) to the maximum of 48.24% (Oman in 2017) and with the average of 22%.

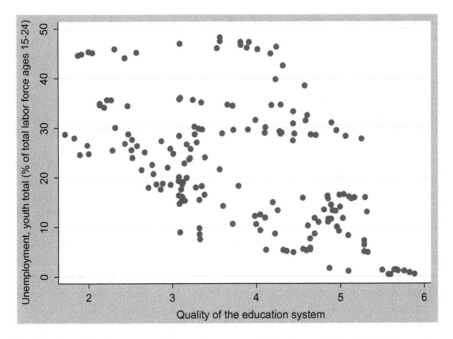

Fig. 5.3 Association between youth unemployment and education quality in the MENA countries
Source World Bank (2020) and WEF (2018)

In line with the literature, a set of independent variables are considered in our study. *Quality of education system*: To measure the quality of education system, we use perceived quality of education systems from the Global Competitiveness Reports of the World Economic Forum (WEF)[1]. There are different questions which aim to measure the quality aspects of education system in this survey. We utilize the following question in the survey: "How well does the educational system in your country meet the needs of a competitive economy?" The index varies from 1 (not well at all) to 7 (very well). The data for our analysis is available from 2007 to 2017. This measure reflects the opinion of executives on the effectiveness of the educational setting in responding to the demands in job market and is used in other studies such as Farzanegan and Thum (2020). The WEF quality of education system in our sample of the MENA countries varies from minimum of 1.71 (Yemen in 2011) to a maximum of 5.88 (Qatar in 2015) and with an average of 3.81. Figure 5.3 shows the association between youth unemployment rate and quality of education system in our sample of MENA countries.

Besides quality of education, which is our main variable of interest, we have controlled for other possible confounding variables that possibly affect the youth unemployment such as gross domestic product (GDP) per capita, oil rents, trade openness, share of foreign direct investment (FDI) in GDP, population growth

---

[1] http://reports.weforum.org/global-competitiveness-index-2017-2018/downloads/.

rate, government expenditures on education as a percentage of GDP and quality of governance.

GDP per capita: We use the logarithm (log) of GDP per capita in constant USD to control for the effect of economic development on job market in general and the situation of youth employment in particular. Countries are not only different due to their varying degree of quality of education, but they may also have a significant differences in terms of economic development. It is important to check the impact of quality of education on youth unemployment independent from differences in income per capita.

Oil rents (as % of GDP): "Oil rents are the difference between the value of crude oil production at world prices and total costs of production" (World Bank 2020). The MENA region is rich in oil resources and on average 16% of GDP of the region depends on oil rents. There is also a substantial cross-country variation within the MENA regarding the role of oil rents in economic development (Ben Ali et al. 2016). This share ranges from a minimum of 0 (Lebanon and Malta) to a maximum of 60% (Kuwait in 2011). Oil rents may have both positive and negative impacts on the employment opportunities for youth. On one side, higher rents through the channel of Dutch disease may reduce the competitiveness of local industries in global markets by appreciation of real effective exchange rate (e.g. Farzanegan and Markwardt 2009) and thus reduces their market share and job opportunities. On the other side, if the rents are managed efficiently and allocated for promotion of non-oil private sector through financial credits and investment in infrastructure and human capital, then we may also observe the blessing part of rents (for example, Farzanegan and Thum 2020 show that the final impact of oil rents on education spending, depends on quality of governance). This lack of clear effect of rents on youth unemployment is also visible in Fig. 5.4, which shows the association between these two variables in the sample of MENA region. We can observe that some countries with relatively high reliance on oil rents have very low levels of youth unemployment (e.g. Qatar) and there are also countries with negligible oil rents but high records of youth unemployment. Thus, the final effect will be an empirical question which we investigate in the next section.

Trade (% of GDP): "Trade is the sum of exports and imports of goods and services measured as a share of GDP" (World Bank 2020). A higher degree of trade may provide new opportunities for local producers, as the larger international market is available. It is discussed that higher trade through its positive impact on economic growth may also reduce the risk of political instability (Farzanegan and Witthuhn 2017). However, higher trade openness at the absence of strong institutions may increase illicit trade, smuggling and corruption (see Farzanegan 2009 for the case of Iran). In such a situation, youth may not benefit from increasing trade openness and we may even observe a higher degree of income inequality between the well-connect individuals and firms (to government) and those without such connections. The increasing inequality during trade liberalization may then increase risk of conflict (Barbieri and Schneider 1999) and negatively impact the job market conditions. Figure 5.5 shows the association between trade openness and youth unemployment in the MENA countries.

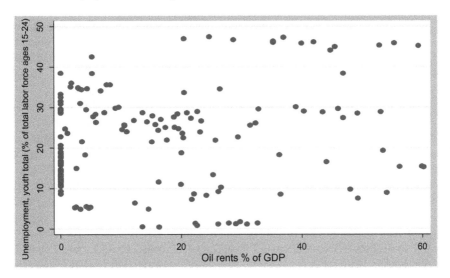

Fig. 5.4 Youth unemployment rates and oil rents dependency in the MENA region. *Source* World Bank (2020)

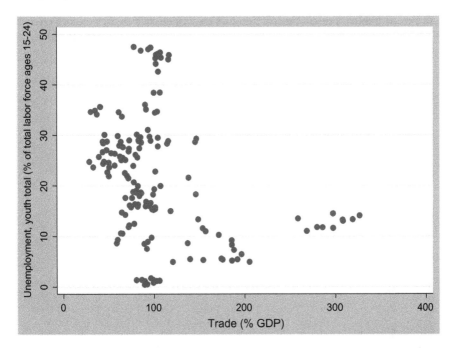

Fig. 5.5 Youth unemployment and trade openness in the MENA. *Source* World Bank (2020)

Overall, we can see that countries with higher share of trade in their economies have lower records of youth unemployment. However, we can find a significant variation in youth unemployment rate, keeping the level of trade openness fixed. In other words, there are also other important factors which may explain the reasons of within and cross-country differences of youth unemployment.

FDI (% of GDP): FDI, net inflows (% of GDP) is another control variable which may shape the youth unemployment rate. Based on definition of the World Bank (2020), "foreign direct investment are the net inflows of investment to acquire a lasting management interest (10 percent or more of voting stock) in an enterprise operating in an economy other than that of the investor. It is the sum of equity capital, reinvestment of earnings, other long-term capital, and short-term capital as shown in the balance of payments". As in the case of trade openness, the final effect of foreign investment on youth unemployment is ambiguous. On one side, higher investment may generate more new job opportunities and thus have a favorable effect on economic growth and political stability. The latter positive development may then invite more investors and thus benefit even more the youth part of population. On the other side, as Farzanegan and Witthuhn (2017) mention, growing investment and increasing economic activities may generate new opportunities for politicians to implement favoritism. The possible positive association between investment (especially at the public sector) and corruption is also mentioned by Tanzi and Davoodi (1998). As Fig. 5.6 shows, we may not see a clear association between FDI and youth

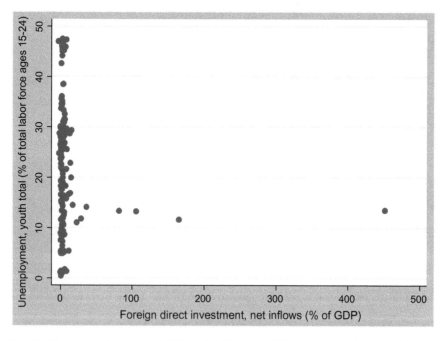

Fig. 5.6 Youth unemployment and FDI % of GDP in the MENA. *Source* World Bank (2020)

unemployment rate. We do see a significant variation in records of youth unemployment at the similar levels of FDI share in GDP, reminding us that other factors may be also relevant for explanation of youth unemployment.

Population growth rate: Demographic aspects may also matter in explanting the youth unemployment rate. Countries with higher population growth may experience an increasing pressure on scarce resources and impoverish individuals, which then may reduce the opportunity cost of civil disorder and lower investment and growth. Of course, higher population growth may not automatically lead to instability and conflict. This nexus depends on the capacity of countries in resources allocation and keeping safety and order. Our data show a significant variation in population growth rate in the MENA region. It ranges from −3% (Syria in 2014) to a maximum of 16% (Qatar in 2007). Figure 5.7 shows the association between population growth rate and youth unemployment rate in the MENA region. We observe that there are countries with two digits growth rate of population which have a low records of youth unemployment (e.g. Qatar and UAE). Their high records of population growth are partly explained by higher income levels of households and government transfers in a form of various subdues, reducing the economic costs of raising children and possibly high level of inflow of migrants.

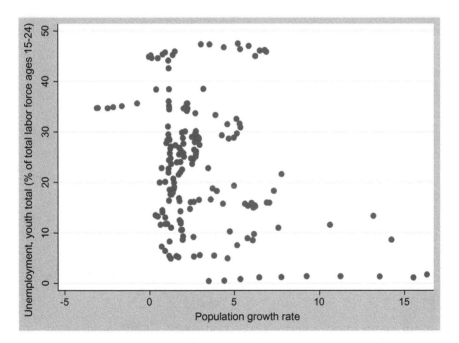

Fig. 5.7 Youth unemployment and population growth in the MENA. *Source* World Bank (2020)

Governance index: This is a mean of three dimensions of quality of governance namely political stability, rule of law and regulatory quality from the World Governance Indicators of the World Bank (WGI 2020). They are measuring the perception of country experts regarding some critical aspects of governance, which are relevant for economic performance, investment, doing business and thus employment opportunities for the youth. We expect countries with higher levels of quality of governance also show a lower records of youth unemployment. This measure varies from minimum of −2.19 (Syria in 2016) to the maximum of 1.36 (Malta in 2010). Figure 5.8 shows the negative correlation between governance and youth unemployment in the region.

Government spending on education % of GDP: Finally we are controlling for the share of government spending on education in GDP. According to the World Bank (2020), "general government expenditure on education (current, capital, and transfers) is expressed as a percentage of GDP and includes expenditure funded by transfers from international sources to government. General government usually refers to local, regional and central governments". The MENA region, on average, allocated 4% of its GDP to education, which is not less than of other regions. It varies from a minimum level of 1.6% (Lebanon in 2010) to a maximum of 7.8% (Malta in 2013). The effect of government spending on education on the youth unemployment depends on how such spending is effective in increasing relevant skills among youth. Such cognitive skills are important drivers of economic growth in long run and

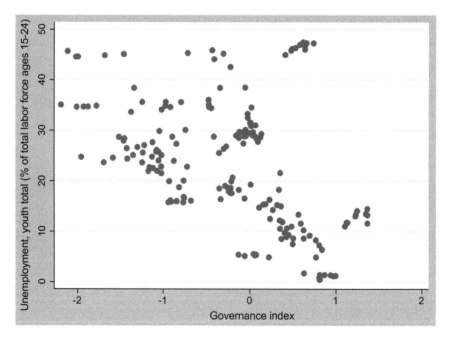

Fig. 5.8 Youth unemployment and governance in the MENA. *Source* WGI (2020) and World Bank (2020)

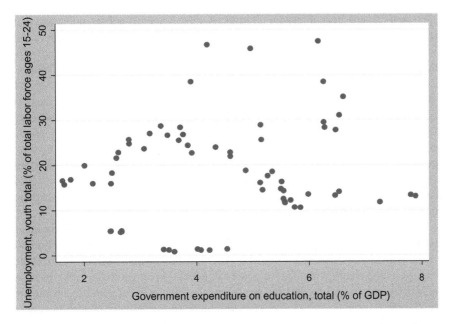

Fig. 5.9 Youth unemployment and government spending on education % of GDP in the MENA. *Source* World Bank (2020)

employment opportunities for youth (Hanushek 2013; Jamison et al. 2007). But, the role of government spending on education to improve education quality which is needed to reduce youth unemployment depends on quality of institutions and effectiveness of the state in allocating of such budgets (Hanushek 2005; Farzanegan and Thum 2020). Figure 5.9 shows the association between youth unemployment and government spending on education (as % of GDP) for the MENA region during period of analysis.

5.3.2 Results and Discussion

Our conceptual framework hypothesizes that the higher level of quality of education is reducing the youth unemployment rate in the MENA region, ceteris paribus. Dependent and independent variables are explained in earlier section. Adjusting for all factors that theoretically influence quality of education and youth unemployment in different countries is essentially impossible. An often-used alternative is to account for all factors that, at a given point in time, affect all countries by controlling time fixed effect. For example, international financial crisis in years 2008–09 or the Arab Spring in 2011 are the year specific shocks which are affecting countries in our sample. Likewise, there may be country-specific factors that influence a given country at all times that can be adjusted for by controlling a country fixed effect.

The country fixed effect allows for all invariant observed and unobserved factors that differentiate countries from each other (e.g. geography, history, culture, religion, and so on), and the quality of education effect is therefore estimated by comparing what happens within countries for youth unemployment when education quality changes.

Table 5.1 shows the results of country and year fixed effects regressions. Model 1 includes only quality of education (which is changing from 1.7 to 5.8) besides the country and year fixed effects which are included in all models. A one-unit increase in quality of education index is associated with approximately 3 percentage points decrease in youth unemployment. About 15% of within country variation in youth unemployment is explained by within country variation in quality of education and fixed effects. This finding lends empirical support to the descriptive arguments of Kamyab (2013), Ahmed (2012) and Kabbani (2019) who note that improving the quality of education can reduce youth unemployment in the MENA region.

Model specifications represented in columns 2 to 8 of Table 5.1 control for other discussed explanatory variables which may be correlated with both youth unemployment and quality of education. Controlling for these other variables does not affect the decreasing and significant effect of quality of education on youth unemployment in the MENA countries. Specification represented in column 8 that includes a complete set of control variables shows that a one unit increase in quality of education system is associated with about 4 percentage points decline in youth unemployment.

Among control variables, only trade openness and FDI share of GDP show statistically significant (negative) association with youth unemployment in some models, meaning that trade and foreign investment openness contribute to employment of youth in the region.

In Table 5.1, we assume that there is no bidirectional relationship between education and youth unemployment. However, earlier studies suggest that higher levels of youth unemployment may discourage young population to invest in cognitive skills and thus may negatively shape the quality of education (for further debates see Farzanegan and Thum 2020). To reduce the problem of reverse feedback and simultaneously bias, we use one-year lag of selected right hand side variables in Table 5.2. The results re-confirm earlier results on the decreasing effect of quality of education on youth unemployment. An increase in education quality by one score in the previous year decreases youth unemployment by 2.3 percentage points in current period. The effect is statistically significant at 5% level. In addition, we do find a significant decreasing effect of both FDI and trade on youth unemployment rate. Countries which promote trade and foreign investment are more able to reduce their levels of youth unemployment, controlling for oil dependency and income per capita as well country and year fixed effects.

5.3.3   Conclusion and Policy Implications

Youth unemployment is one of the main challenges for the MENA region. Due to high records of youth unemployment, the countries in the MENA region are highly

Table 5.1 Youth unemployment and education quality in the MENA: panel fixed effects findings

	(1)	(2)	(3)	(4)	(5)	(6)	(7)	(8)
	Dependent variable: youth unemployment rate %							
Quality of education	-3.134***	-3.276***	-3.314***	-2.932***	-2.923***	-2.742***	-2.448	-4.905***
	(-3.16)	(-3.06)	(-3.04)	(-3.36)	(-3.31)	(-3.38)	(-1.72)	(-3.13)
log of GDP per capita		-4.743	-4.589	-4.246	-4.767	-5.064	-4.021	-1.615
		(-0.76)	(-0.70)	(-0.55)	(-0.60)	(-0.63)	(-0.50)	(-0.12)
Oil rents % GDP			-0.033	-0.062	-0.067	-0.070	-0.067	-0.171
			(-0.41)	(-0.81)	(-0.83)	(-0.90)	(-0.79)	(-0.97)
Trade % of GDP				-0.067*	-0.072**	-0.062*	-0.060	-0.073
				(-2.09)	(-2.30)	(-1.89)	(-1.71)	(-1.09)
FDI % of GDP					-0.007	-0.005	-0.005	-0.025*
					(-1.32)	(-1.05)	(-0.74)	(-2.18)
Population growth rate						0.135	0.120	-0.181
						(0.86)	(0.68)	(-0.36)
Governance index							-1.734	3.398
							(-0.36)	(0.78)
Government spending on education % GDP								0.708
								(1.61)
Country fixed effect	Yes	Yes	Yes	Yes	Yes	Yes	Yes	Yes

(continued)

Table 5.1 (continued)

	(1)	(2)	(3)	(4)	(5)	(6)	(7)	(8)
Year fixed effect	Yes	Yes	Yes	Yes	Yes	Yes	Yes	Yes
Observations	176	150	150	143	143	143	143	53
R-sq	0.15	0.18	0.18	0.25	0.26	0.26	0.27	0.68

Notes Estimation method is ordinary least squares with Huber-robust standard errors (t statistics are reported in parentheses) clustered at the country level. Significantly different from zero at *90% confidence, **95% confidence, ***99% confidence

Table 5.2 Youth unemployment and education quality in the MENA: panel fixed effects results (with one-year lag of selected independent variables)

	Dependent variable: Youth unemployment %
L. Quality of education	−2.366**
	(−2.85)
L. Trade (% GDP)	−0.066**
	(−2.63)
L. FDI (% GDP)	−0.007**
	(−2.25)
L. Oil rents (% GDP)	−0.140
	(−1.46)
L. log GDP p.c.	−3.974
	(−0.58)
Country fixed effect	Yes
Year fixed effect	Yes
Obs.	143
R-sq	0.25

L. refers to one-year lag. Estimation method is ordinary least squares with Huber-robust standard errors (t statistics are reported in parentheses) clustered at the country level. Significantly different from zero at *90% confidence, **95% confidence, ***99% confidence

at risk of revolts and protests. Also, in the recent political and economic protests in countries such as Iran, Iraq, and Lebanon we can see a strong presence of youth population. Lack of economic perspective is reducing the economic opportunity costs for repressed youth population in the region in destabilizing the political system which is shown to be economically costly (see Farzanegan 2020 for the case study of Iran).

In this study, we discuss the impact of quality of education on youth unemployment. The quality of education system has recently attracted attention of organizations such as the World Bank and other researchers. It is shown that the MENA countries (especially those which are dependent on oil rents) are suffering from low quality of education system. Farzanegan and Thum (2020) provide a detailed analysis on the link between oil rents dependency and education quality and presents different explanatory arguments for possible channels through which oil rents may weaken quality of education.

In our panel regression study for 18 MENA countries over the period 2007-2017, we find a robust decreasing effect of quality of education system (based on subjective evaluation by experts in Global Competitiveness Reports of WEF) on the youth unemployment rate. This negative impact remains after controlling for other possible confounding variables such as GDP per capita, oil rents dependency, trade openness, foreign direct investment, quality of governance, government spending on education, country and year fixed effects. Moreover, using one-year lag of independent variables to decrease the risk of reverse feedback re-confirms our main findings.

International organizations and policymakers in the MENA region should invest more on quality of education system and increase the relevant academic and professional skills which are needed in job market. The quality of education is the key factor in dealing with youth unemployment in the MENA region. Moreover, we find empirical evidence on the constructive role of trade openness and FDI in dampening the youth unemployment rate in the region. This latter finding is consistent with study of Farzanegan et al. (2020) which finds the diminishing effect of economic liberalization on informal economy in case of Egypt.

References

Acikgoz S Ben, Ali MS (2019) Where does economic growth in the Middle Eastern and North African countries come from? Q Rev Econ Finance 73:172–183

Acikgoz S, Ben Ali MS, Mert M (2016) Sources of Economic growth in MENA countries: technological progress, physical or human capital accumulations? Economic development in the Middle East and North Africa. Springer/Palgrave Macmillan, New York, pp 27–69

Ahmed M (2012) Youth Unemployment in the MENA region: determinants and challenges. Published in the World Economic Forum's Addressing the 100 Million Youth Challenge—Perspectives on Youth Employment in the Arab World in 2012, June 2012. https://www.imf.org/en/News/Articles/2015/09/28/04/54/vc061312

Apergis N, Ben Ali MS (2020) Corruption, rentier states and economic growth: where do the GCC countries stand? In: Miniaoui H (eds) Economic development in the Gulf cooperation council countries: from rentier states to diversified economies. Springer, Berlin

Ashenfelter O, Ham J (1979) Education, unemployment and earnings. J Polit Econ 87:S99–S166

Barbieri K, Schneider G (1999) Globalization and peace: assessing new directions in the study of trade and conflict. JPeace Res 36:387–404

Ben Ali MS, Krammer S (2016) The role of institutions in economic development. Economic development in the Middle East and North Africa, pp 1–25. Springer/Palgrave Macmillan, New York

Ben Ali MS, Cockx L, Francken N (2016) The Middle East and North Africa: cursed by natural resources? Economic development in the Middle East and North Africa. Springer/Palgrave Macmillan, New York, pp 71–93

Biagi F, Lucifora C (2008) Demographic and education effects on unemployment in Europe. Labour Econ 15(5):1076–1101

Bjorvatn K, Farzanegan MR (2013) Demographic transition in resource rich countries: a bonus or a curse? World Dev 45:337–351

Bjorvatn K, Farzanegan MR (2015) Resource rents, balance of power, and political stability. J Peace Res 52:758–773

Bloom DE, Williamson JG (1998) Demographic transitions and economic miracles in emerging Asia. World Bank Econ Rev 12(3):419–455

Bloom DE, Canning D, Malaney PN (2000) Demographic change and economic growth in Asia. Population Dev Rev 26(Suppl.):257–290

Bloom DE, Canning D, Mansfield RK, Moore M (2007) Demographic change, social security systems, and savings. J Monetary Econ 54(1):92–114

Čepar Ž, Ojteršek M, Milost F (2018) Youth unemployment and higher education, the case of Slovenia. Sotsialno-ekonomichni problemy i derzhava [Socio-Econ Prob State] 18(1):4–16

Erdem E, Tugcu CT (2012) Higher education and unemployment: a cointegration and causality analysis of the case of Turkey. Eur J Educ 47:299–309

Fakih A, Haimoun N, Kassem M (2020) Youth unemployment, gender and institutions during transition: evidence from the Arab Spring. Soc Indic Res. https://doi.org/10.1007/s11205-020-02300-3

Farber HS (2004) Job loss in the United States, 1981 to 2001. Research in Labor Economics 23:69–117

Farzanegan MR (2009) Illegal trade in the Iranian economy: evidence from structural equation model. Eur J Polit Econ 25(4):489–507

Farzanegan MR (2014) Can oil-rich countries encourage entrepreneurship? Entrepreneurship Reg Dev 26:706–725

Farzanegan MR (2020) The economic cost of the Islamic Revolution and war for Iran: synthetic counterfactual evidence. Defence and Peace Economics. https://doi.org/10.1080/10242694.2020.1825314

Farzanegan MR, Markwardt G (2009) The effects of oil price shocks on the Iranian economy. Energy Econ 31(1):134–151

Farzanegan MR, Thum M (2020) Does oil rents dependency reduce the quality of education? Empirical Econ 58:1863–1911

Farzanegan MR, Witthuhn S (2017) Corruption and political stability: does the youth bulge matter? Eur J Polit Econ 49:47–70

Farzanegan MR, Lessmann C, Markwardt G (2018) Natural resource rents and internal conflicts: can decentralization lift the curse? Econ Syst 42:186–205

Farzanegan MR, Hassan M, Badreldin A (2020) Economic liberalization in Egypt: a way to reduce of the shadow economy? J Policy Model 42:307–327

Fullan Michael, Loubser Jan J (1972) Education and adaptive capacity. Sociol Educ 45:271–287

Globerman S (1986) Formal education and the adaptability of workers and managers to technological change. In: Craig Riddell W (ed) Adapting to change: labour market adjustment in Canada. University of Toronto Press, Toronto, pp 41–69

Hanushek EA (2005) The economics of school quality. German Econ Rev 6(269):286

Hanushek EA (2013) Economic growth in developing countries: the role of human capital. Econ Educ Rev 37:204–212

Hanushek EA, Woessmann L (2008) The role of cognitive skills in economic development. J Econ Lit 46:607–668

Jamison EA, Jamison DT, Hanushek EA (2007) The effects of education quality on income growth and mortality decline. Econ Educ Rev 26:771–788

Kabbani N (2019) Youth employment in the Middle East and North Africa: revisiting and reframing the challenge. Policy Briefing/February 2019. Brookings Doha Center. https://www.brookings.edu/research/youth-employment-in-the-middle-east-and-north-africa-revisiting-and-reframing-the-challenge/

Kamyab S (2013) Higher education and youth unemployment in the Middle East and North Africa. Comp Int Higher Educ 5:14–15

Kettunen J (1997) Education and unemployment duration. Econ Educ Rev 16:163–170

Li S, Whalley J, Xing C (2014) China's higher education expansion and unemployment of college graduates. China Econ Rev 30:567–582

Magnussen O (1979) Further aspects of the education-employment relationship: youth unemployment and education. Eur J Educ 14:285–288

Mincer J (1991). Education and Unemployment. NBER Working Paper No. w3838

Msigwa R, Kipesha EF (2013) Determinants of youth unemployment in developing countries: evidences from Tanzania. J Econ Sustain Dev 4:67–77

Neuman S, Ziderman A (1999) Vocational education in Israel: wage effects of the VocEd-occupation match. J Hum Res 34(2):407–420

Nickell S (1979) Estimating the probability of leaving unemployment. Econometrica 47:1249–1266

O'Reilly J, Eichhorst W, Gábos A, Hadjivassiliou K, Lain D, Leschke J, McGuinness S et al (2015) Five characteristics of youth unemployment in europe flexibility, education, migration, family legacies, and EU Policy. SAGE Open 5(1):1–19

OECD (2015) Setting objectives for achieving better youth employment outcomes. Prepared for the third G20 Employment Working Group Meeting, 23–24 July 2015, Turkey

PWC (2018). The long term impact of being "not in employment, education or training" on our young people https://www.pwc.com.au/government/government-matters/youth-unemployment.html

Riddell WC, Song X (2011) The impact of education on unemployment incidence and re-employment success: evidence from the U.S. labour market. Labour Economics 18:453–463

Riphahn RT, Zibrowius MJ (2016) Apprenticeship, vocational training and early labor market outcomes—evidence from East and West Germany. Educ Econ 24:33–57

Ryan P (2001) The school-to-work transition: a cross-national perspective. J Econ Lit 39(1):34–92

Schultz T (1975) The value of the ability to deal with disequilibria. J Econ Lit 13(3):827–846

Tanzi V, Davoodi H (1998) Corruption, Public Investment, and Growth. In: Shibata H., Ihori T (eds) The Welfare State, Public Investment, and Growth, pp 41–60, Springer, Tokyo. https://doi.org/10.1007/978-4-431-67939-4_4

Tomic CH, Taylor K (2018) Youth unemployment, the brain drain and education policy in Croatia: a call for joining forces and for new visions. Policy Futures Educ Special issue: Educ Policies Central and Eastern Eur 16(4):501–514

WGI (2020) World governance indicators. World Bank, Washington DC

Wolbers MHJ (2000) The effects of level of education on mobility between employment and unemployment in The Netherlands. Eur Sociol Rev 16:185–200

World Bank (2020) World Development Indicators, Washington DC

Yang L (2018) Higher education expansion and post-college unemployment: understanding the roles of fields of study in China. Int J Educational Dev 62:62–74

Yizengaw JY (2018) Skills gaps and mismatches: private sector expectations of engineering graduates in Ethiopia, vol 49, issue no. (5). Institute of Development Studies, Brighton, UK, IDS Bulletin, pp 55–70

Chapter 6
Military Spending and Economic Development: Evidence from the MENA Region

Cristian Ortiz, Rafael Alvarado, and Mohamed Sami Ben Ali

Abstract Military spending can have positive or negative impact on economies. In the empirical literature, there is evidence for both hypotheses. In practice, the effect of military spending on the economy will depend on the geographic context and the type of military spending. The Middle East and North Africa (MENA) region is composed of a group of countries with high military spending. This chapter examines the relationship between military expenditure in MENA countries with a set of economic, social, and institutional indicators. Our results show a growing military spending in the region. One possible explanation is the constant conflicts, ethnic, cultural, and religious tensions. Additionally, our findings highlight a possible link between military spending, natural resources, human capital, and economic development. Policymakers in the MENA region have to cope with the international drop in oil prices and the slowdown in several economies. The promotion of foreign investment aimed at improving the endowment of human capital through technology transfer and the improvement of the national productive capacity could promote the achievement of the region's sustainable development objectives.

Keywords Military spending · MENA · Economic growth · Economic development

C. Ortiz (✉)
Departamento de Economía, Universidad Católica del Norte, Antofagasta, Chile
e-mail: cristian.ortiz@unl.edu.ec

C. Ortiz · R. Alvarado
Carrera de Economía, Universidad Nacional de Loja, Loja, Ecuador

M. S. Ben Ali
College of Business and Economics, Qatar University, Doha, Qatar

© The Author(s), under exclusive license to Springer Nature Switzerland AG 2021
M. S. Ben Ali (ed.), *Economic Development in the MENA Region*, Perspectives on Development in the Middle East and North Africa (MENA) Region,
https://doi.org/10.1007/978-3-030-66380-3_6

6.1   Introduction

Military spending is one of the government budget items that generate a broad debate in society. The Stockholm International Peace Research Institute (SIPRI) is an institution that provides information on military spending, cooperation, and armed conflicts. SIPRI includes current military spending and investment expenditures of the armed forces for the preservation of peace, the defense of territorial integrity or for other specific purposes. These military expenditures are composed of civilian and military personnel working in activities related to the military sector. It also include pensions and social services for retired personnel, costs for operations and maintenance, expenses for imports of military equipment, expenditures for research and development for military purposes, and donations to other countries. Military spending leads to the hypothesis that increased military spending should promote countries' economic growth. However, the impact of military spending on economic, social, and institutional development largely depends on the export or import orientation of weapons (Dunne and Tian 2016; Ortiz et al. 2019). Understandably, the industries that produce military equipment for export are entities that could generate employment and income. However, there is a substantial outflow of foreign currency when military spending is spent on the import of military equipment.

Military spending raises several concerns in developing countries because of the scarcity of their resources. The social budgets dedicated to investment in education, health, and infrastructure are possible ways in which these countries can make a great leap to economic progress. Arrow (1994) suggests that there is no particular merit in military spending than any other form of government spending. Furthermore, it has been confirmed that higher military expenditures are associated with higher levels of corruption (Gupta et al. 2001). It have been documented that corruption can even displace the allocation of public investment from education and health (Mauro 1998; Swaleheen et al. 2019).

One of the regions with considerable military spending is the Middle East and North Africa (MENA) region, having a strategic geographical position and possess a vast reserves of natural resources, particularly oil (Acikgoz and Ben Ali 2019; Acikgoz et al. 2016). This chapter aims to analyze the relationship between military spending and a set of economic, social, and institutional indicators. Specifically, we evaluate the link between military spending and a selected economic development and social well-being indicators in the context of vast energy resources. First, we present a debate on the fundamentals of military spending on welfare and economic development, focusing on the theoretical and empirical literature. Second, we analyze military spending as a percentage of GDP in 19 selected countries in the MENA region comparatively with military spending in other regions of the world. Third, we analyze the link between ethnic and religious tensions, military in politics, and external conflicts with military spending. Besides, we incorporate a brief description of the relationship between military expenditure and natural resources. Fourth, we evaluate the link between military spending with a set of economic indicators: human development index, income inequality, human capital, life expectancy, production, unemployment, freedom of trade, R&D, and economic complexity. Fifth, the chapter ends with an analysis between military spending as a percentage of GDP with institutional aspects: law and order, democracy index, and corruption index (for a survey on institutional indicators see Ben Ali and Krammer 2016).

6.2 Military Spending and Economic Development: A Literature Overview

Various approaches have attempted to explain the causal mechanisms that relate military spending to economic development and social welfare (Beniot 1973; Hwang 2012; Arrow 1994). One of the most comprehensive approaches is the Keynesian theory of public spending and economic dynamics. In this approach, public spending is a policy instrument that allows increasing employment, income, and in general, the well-being of the population through multipliers (Chen et al. 2014). Several empirical investigations show inconclusive results on the spillover effects of military spending. However, there is sufficient evidence in favor of the externalities of military research and development in promoting the emergence of products for civilian use, in encouraging the formation of highly specialized human capital, and in generating productive linkages with other industries (Yildirim and Öcal 2016). For example, Qiong and Junhua (2015) point out that military spending increases the efficiency of physical and social capital, generating an increase in investment and employment. Likewise, Huang et al. (2017) points out that public spending in the military sector increases human development in the long term. In contrast, Ali (2012) found that increases in military expenditures produce a reduction in inequality through job creation and economic efficiency. Increased human development and reduced inequality occur, primarily through employment and income generated by the industry associated with military activities. The indirect impact of the spillover effect of military production and research and development can translate into improved quality of life.

There are numerous illustrative examples on how public spending on research and development for military purposes can improve the civilian society. A clear example is the Internet, which emerged as a military communication infrastructure called ARPANET, run by the United States Department of Defense and the Research Projects Agency (ARPA). The project was launched to exchange scientific and military information, saving costs by replicating computers' capabilities in multiple locations. Furthermore, the project attempted to waterproof nuclear attacks or natural disasters (Stiglitz 1999).

There is an empirical literature stating that some countries use military supremacy to gain access to natural resources, promote their economic interests with other countries through cooperation, trade, and investment agreements (Agnew and Crobridge 2002; Ortiz et al. 2019). However, there is also applied research that shows that military spending does not significantly affect countries' economic growth, particularly in the long term. In some cases, military spending may be associated with corruption, weak institutions, low levels of democracy, and high levels of shadow economy. Likewise, the literature shows that military spending can directly impact external debt in some developed countries (Zhang et al. 2016). This problem also occurs in developing countries with internal political issues, with social polarization, or governance conflicts (Bodea et al. 2016; d'Agostino et al. 2016). Other research has shown that the amount spent in the military sector produces essential changes on the economic, social, and institutional indicators. For example, Albalate et al. (2012) find that in governmental presidential systems', countries spend more resources on military items than countries with parliamentary systems.

The empirical evidence dealing with the military spending - economic development nexus has increased over time since the seminal research by Beniot (1973). d'Agostino et al. (2011) point out that the allocation of more funds to the United States military sector did not increase its well-being while the positive relationship between military spending and economic indicators occurred in most developed countries (Wang et al. 2012; Desli et al. 2017; Kollias and Paleologou 2019). This relationship can be explained by the military supremacy that allows net exporters of military equipment to generate net financial inflows into the country (Ortiz et al. 2019). Leontief et al. (1965) show that the military industry generates positive externalities with other industries and sectors that benefits the consolidation of existing companies or promote the emergence of new business opportunities.

On the other hand, there is empirical evidence showing that increases in military spending is associated with lower levels of economic growth (Abu-Bader and Abu-Qarn 2003; Manamperi 2016; d'Agostino et al. 2017), especially in the least developed countries (Dunne and Tian 2013, 2015, 2016). Similarly, Kollias et al. (2020) find that military spending effects do not decrease unemployment levels in the United States. Other research has associated military spending with higher levels of external debt (Caruso and Di Domizio 2015, 2016), with high levels of corruption (Gupta et al. 2001), and with dictatorial or autocratic governments (Desli et al. 2017). In this last line of thought, some recent studies has corroborated that higher military expenditures are slightly associated with democratic regimes and high levels of social inequality (Harrison and Wolf 2012; Töngür et al. 2015). Also, it have been argued that the impact of military spending on economic, social, and institutional indicators depends on whether the industry is located within the country and if any externalities are generated or not with other more productive sectors.

6.3 Military Spending in MENA Countries

The MENA region is a particular case to analyze military spending for at least three reasons. First, several countries in the region are rich in natural resources that have fueled investment and economic growth. Geopolitical literature has indicated that countries with abundant natural resources, new or in exploitation, are in permanent risk of armed conflict, which could explain the increase in military spending for defensive purposes (Ali and Abdellatif 2015). Second, some of the

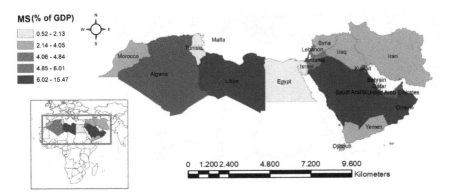

Fig. 6.1 Military spending as a percentage of GDP in MENA countries, 2017. *Source* Authors based on SIPRI data. *Note* The MS data for Libya, Qatar, United Emirates Arab (UAE), Yemen and Syria correspond to the years 2015, 2010, 2014, 2014 and 2010 respectively, because there is no data from those countries in 2017

region's countries belong to zones of armed conflict, with external threats and high levels of ethnic and religious tensions along with autocratic regimes. Third, one of the region's objectives is to strengthen military alliances with external powers to combat terrorism. These territorial characteristics have an essential impact on military spending, which directly affects the growth, development, and institutionalization of the region. Figure 6.1 shows military spending (MS) as a percentage of GDP for 19 MENA countries in 2017. The results indicate that Saudi Arabia, Libya and Oman have the highest military spending. In recent years, Saudi Arabia was involved in a military conflict in Yemen. In the case of Libya, there is a conflict between internal armed groups, although the conflict have external connections.

According to SIPRI (2018), the military spending has followed an increasing trend during the recent years, due to the geopolitical tensions in the world and in this region in particular. During 2019, world military spending experienced its highest increase since the 1960s. Five countries namely United States, China, India, Russia and Saudi Arabia concentrate 60% of the world military spending. Ortiz et al. (2019) point out that this increase is explained by the reactivation of several military conflicts in various parts of the world. In monetary terms, military spending in 2019 reached USD 1.9 billion, equivalent to a 3.6% increase in one year. This increase is the highest since the end of the Cold War, raising serious concerns about the future of the relations between countries with conflicting strategic interests. The MENA countries have also experienced an increase in military spending, where at least four simultaneous conflicts occur: the war in Syria, Libya, Yemen, and the Palestinian-Israeli conflict. Figure 6.2 shows the evolution of the per capita military spending for seven regions around the world during the last three decades. One of the evidenced results is that the MENA countries are the second region with the highest military spending. Moreover, the MENA region has higher military spending compared to other regions around the world.

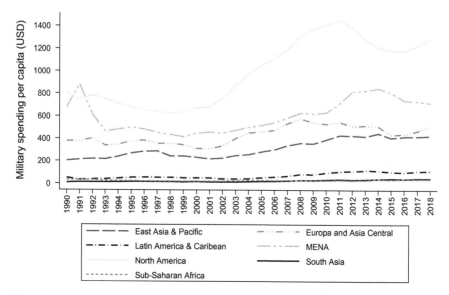

Fig. 6.2 Per capita military spending (USD) 1990–2018. *Source* Authors based on SIPRI data

Figures 6.1 and 6.2 show that MENA countries region have high military spending as a percentage of GDP and in terms of per capita military spending. The following sections show a detailed analysis of the implications of military spending on a set of variables.

6.3.1 Ethnic and Religious Tensions, Politics, External Conflicts and Military Spending

Since the end of World War I, the Middle East has been in recurring armed conflicts, both within and between countries. The prevailing geopolitical conditions in the region do not allow the creation of an institutional framework that promotes economic development as if it is being achieved by Qatar and the United Arab Emirates, among others (Ben Ali and Krammer, 2016; Ben Ali and Saha 2016, Shrabani and Ben Ali 2017). After the Arab Spring, which occurred in mid-2010, the MENA region entered a new phase of political confrontations. The possibility that the turmoil will continue in the following years before the region can reach the full long-term stability is high. Uncertainty about these changes can lead countries to increase their military capacity against external or internal threats. In practice, military accumulation in this region would persist for the years to come. Currently, the MENA region spends an average of 4.5% of the GDP on military spending, while the average for developed countries is around 1.5%. Factors that can influence the volume of military spending are diverse: ethnic and religious tensions, military's presence in politics and external

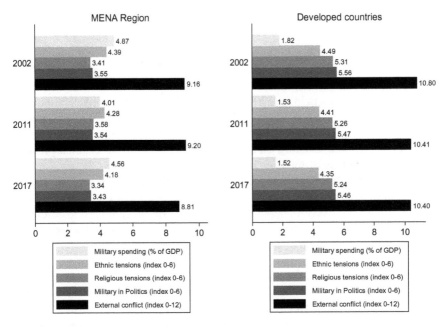

Fig. 6.3 Military spending (% of GDP) and conflict risk index. *Source* Authors based on SIPRI and ICRG data

conflicts. Figure 6.3 display some risk indices for the 19 countries analyzed. This information is compared with the same indicators from a sample of 69 developed countries. Statistical information is obtained from the International Country Risk Guide (ICRG). The theoretical and empirical literature has identified that ethnic, religious tensions, or the risk of foreign interference are some determinants that could increase military spending (Odehnal and Neubauer 2018). Figure 6.3 shows that the regional average of military spending during the last three years (2002, 2011 and 2017) has fluctuated between 4.01 and 4.87% of the GDP. The ethnic tension index (Scale from 0 to 6), assesses the degree of tension within a country attributable to ethnic differences, nationality, or linguistic divisions. The risk index has lower points in countries where race and nationality tensions are high because opposite groups are intolerant and unwilling to compromise. Higher ratings are displayed for countries where tensions are minimal. Israel, Iraq, and Syria are most at risk of conflict due to ethnic tensions. Likewise, the countries with the lowest risk of conflict due to ethnic tensions are Qatar, UAE, and Tunisia.

The religious tensions index that measures religious tensions denotes a significant difference between MENA countries and developed countries. The religious tensions index (Scale from 0 to 6) is a measure of the domination of society and the government by a single religious group trying to substitute civil law by religious law and exclude other religions from the political and social processes. A low index means a higher risk while a high index indicates a lower one. The Figure suggests that religious tensions rather than ethnic tensions are a critical factor in explaining military spending in the

MENA region. Likewise, the index capturing military persons participating in politics have a scale ranging from 0 to 6 (lower index, higher risk). In the MENA region, this index fluctuates between 3.43 and 3.55, compared to developed countries where extreme values ranges between 5.26 and 5.56. The data suggest that relatively high military expenditures (as a percentage of GDP) may be explained by the high risk of military regimes' participation in politics. We also evaluate an index of external conflict (on a scale from 0 to 12), capturing a measure of war by foreign inference. The risk can range from non-violent external pressure (diplomatic pressures, trade restrictions, territorial disputes, sanctions, and others) to violent external pressure (cross-border conflicts of total war). A lower index score means the existence of a high risk. In the MENA region, the external conflict index show a high risk of foreign interference than developed countries. This fact may explain why military expenditures are relatively higher in the MENA countries as compared to developed ones. In this sense, fear of external pressure at any level may motivate higher military spending than in a situation of a total absence of risk.

It is also obvious that there is a high degree of military participation in politics (index risk of 3.00). This last indicator could explain why for example the military category is so high in Libya. Using 2017 data, Saudi Arabia display a military spending of 10.25% of GDP, followed by Oman and Algeria, with 9.56% of GDP and 6.01% of GDP, respectively. Although Saudi Arabia does not have a high risk of ethnic conflicts (5.00), the risk of religious conflict is however high (3.50). Likewise, the risk of external conflict seems high since it reflects an index of around 8.0 (on a scale of 0 to 12). This context could explain the high military spending as a percentage of GDP. The three countries with the highest military spending in the region are classified as high and medium–high income countries (excluding Libya). Countries most at risk of external conflict are Syria, Lebanon, and Yemen. At the same time, the countries with the lowest risk of conflict are Malta, Oman, and Bahrain. The results suggest that internal and external conflict risk factors may explain the level of military spending in MENA countries. The existence of a risk of conflict can motivate the public spending to increase military spending and keeps the government in power. The countries with the lowest religious tension are Morocco, Malta, and Libya, while the countries with the most significant religious tension are Iraq, Iran, and Algeria.

6.3.2 Military Spending and Natural Resources in the MENA Region

As documented in numerous studies, many countries in the MENA region are undergoing a "natural resource curse" that has led to poor economic outcomes and a mismanagement of natural resource (Ben Mim and Ben Ali 2020; Apergis and Ben Ali 2020; Ben Ali et al. 2016). There is an evidence to suggest that the discovery of new natural resources greatly increases the risk of conflict, especially if the natural resource is oil (Bannon and Collier 2003). Erdoğan et al. (2020) found that, despite the volatility of oil prices, military spending in the Gulf Cooperation Council (GCC) countries has not been reduced. In many cases, rising oil revenues have been accompanied by a rapid increase in military spending, especially from imported arms. Importing manufactured weapons is a quick and direct process of getting weapons ready for use when in-house technology is not enough to make military equipment.

Several reasons drive the increase of military spending when there is a high dependence on income from natural resources. First, military spending acts as a protection against possible risks of foreign inference to seize resources (Ali 2012), which can be a constant concern for the stability of governments. The army plays a dominant role in several countries' economic affairs in the MENA region, as evidenced by the growing military-industrial complex (Ali 2012). Varisco (2010) documented the existence of a correlation between armed conflicts and the existence of abundant natural resources.

Figure 6.4. illustrates the nexus between military spending and income from natural resources. Although the pattern that follows the relationship between the two variables is not clear, several countries with greater dependence on income from natural resources have high levels of spending on weapons. The trend is not obvious as the budget of military spending might not be always and completely officially declared by some countries in the region. The countries most dependent on income from natural resources are Iraq, Kuwait, Libya, Oman, Qatar, and Saudi Arabia, are among the countries with the highest military spending. In these countries, the income from natural resources as a percentage of GDP exceeds 30%.

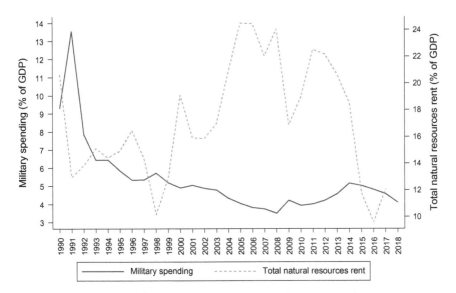

Fig. 6.4 Military spending (% of GDP) and natural resources rent (% of GDP) in MENA region. *Source* Authors based on SIPRI and World Development Indicators (WDI)

6.3.3 Military Spending and Economic Development Indicators in the MENA Region

In practice, military spending depends on fiscal capacity, strategic objectives, the need to defend territorial integrity, and a geopolitical component of each country. Abu-Bader and Abu-Qarn (2003) found that military spending have reduced economic growth in countries such as Egypt, Israel, and Syria, which have participated directly or indirectly in conflicts during the recent years. These results are consistent with the findings of Desli and Gkoulgkoutsika (2020), who find that military spending has a negative effect on economic growth. Likewise, Chang et al. (2011) point out that increased military spending leads to slower economic growth in low-income countries in Africa, Eastern Europe, the Middle East, South Asia, and the Pacific. Figure 6.5 display military spending, the human development index (HDI), income inequality (INQ), human capital (HCI), and life expectancy (LE) at birth. The upper left graph illustrates the relationship between military spending and the human development index, where it is possible to notice that the fall in military spending in the long term is related to a sustained growth of human development. We can also notice a negative relationship between military spending and income inequality, human capital index and life expectancy.

Figure 6.6 display the potential relationship between military spending and the behavior of the unemployment rate and the logarithm of the real per capita product

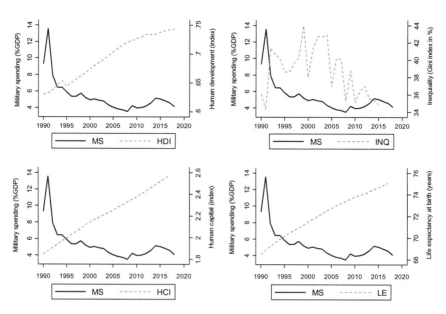

Fig. 6.5 Military spending, human development, inequality, human capital index, and life expectancy at birth in MENA region. *Source* Authors based on SIPRI, Pen World Tables (PWT), Human development reports, and WDI data

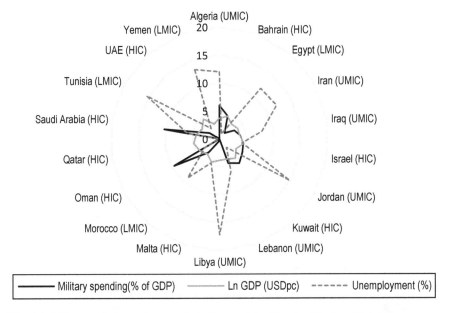

Fig. 6.6   Military spending and economic indicators. *Note* The classification: High-income countries (HIC), upper-middle-income countries (UMIC), lower-middle-income countries (LMIC) and low-income countries (LIC) were obtained from the World Bank Atlas method classification

compared to the military spending in the 19 selected MENA countries. The data shows that Jordan, Libya, Tunisia, Iran, and Egypt have high unemployment rates as compared to the other countries. High unemployment rates are associated with high levels of social discontent, which increases social protests and encourages the increase of military spending to maintain social order and internal peace.

6.3.4   Military Spending and Institutional Indicators in MENA

Figure 6.7 displays the potential link between military spending (as a % of GDP) and three institutional indicators extracted from the ICRG database. The three institutional indicators ranges from 0 to 6. Table 6.1 expands the information on the possible link between military spending with a set of institutional indicators. The data for Saudi Arabia, show a high risk of corruption (index of 3.04) and is one of the countries with the highest military expenditure in the region. Relatively similar results are observed for Oman. Overall, we can establish a negative relationship between institutional variables and military spending.

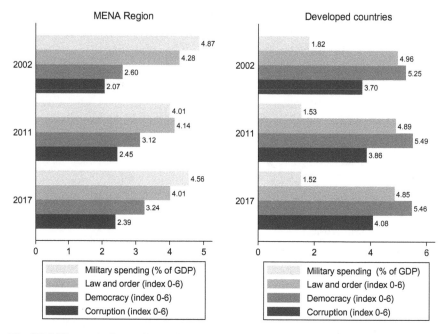

Fig. 6.7 Military spending and institutional factors in MENA region versus 69 developed countries. *Source* Authors based on SIPRI and ICRG data

6.4 Conclusions and Policy Implications

Military spending has several impacts on economic and social variables. MENA countries are natural resources rich, particularly oil. During the last decades, this region has increased military spending, generating a large number of investigations aimed at determining the impact that this spending could create on social, economic, and institutional indicators.

We examine in this chapter the military spending in MENA countries and their possible relationships with a broad set of indicators. Our results offer evidence that the military spending is correlated with the main economic, social, and institutional indicators. Data from 19 countries in the MENA region is compared to a sample of 69 developed countries. The findings show that the MENA countries have higher military spending as compared to developed ones. In general, our analysis shows that military spending aimed at purchasing of weapons does not necessarily favor economic development and the well-being of the population. Numerous policy recommendations can emerge from our study. Countries in the MENA region need to strengthen human capital so that foreign investments in the military or civilian sphere can have improving results on economic growth. In addition, these countries have some challenges, such as improving the quality of institutions, promoting FDI inflows associated with human capital and technology transfer, and improving human capital formation.

Table 6.1 Military spending and Institutional Indicators in 18 MENA countries in 2017

	Military spending	Corruption	Democracy	Law and order
Country	(% of GDP)	(index 0–6)	(index 0–6)	(index 0–6)
Algeria	6.01	2.00	3.50	3.00
Bahrain	4.39	2.50	3.50	4.50
Egypt	1.42	2.00	2.17	3.00
Iran	3.11	1.50	3.00	4.00
Iraq	3.84	1.00	4.00	1.50
Israel	4.43	3.50	6.00	5.00
Jordan	4.84	3.00	3.00	3.88
Kuwait	5.63	2.67	3.00	4.00
Lebanon	4.60	1.67	4.50	4.00
Libya	15.47[**]	1.00	2.00	4.00
Malta	0.51	3.50	6.00	5.00
Morocco	3.19	3.00	4.50	4.00
Oman	9.56	3.00	2.00	5.00
Qatar	1.49[+]	3.67	2.00	5.00
Saudi Arabia	10.25	3.04	2.00	5.00
Syria	4.05[c]	1.00	1.00	4.50
Tunisia	2.13	2.50	4.50	5.00
UAE HIC	5.64[a]	4.00	2.50	4.00
Yemen LIC	3.96[b]	1.00	2.50	2.00

Source Authors, using SIPRI and ICRG data

Note ** denotes the 2015 data; + corresponds to the 2010 data; "a" corresponds to the 2014 data, and "b" corresponds to the 2014 data, "c" corresponds to the 2010 data since data are missing for those countries in 2017. This data is closest to the year that we want to illustrate

References

Abu-Bader S, Abu-Qarn AS (2003) Government spending, military spending and economic growth: causality evidence from Egypt, Israel, and Syria. J Policy Model 25(6):567–583

Acikgoz S, Ben Ali MS (2019) Where does economic growth in the Middle Eastern and North African countries come from? Q Rev Econ Finance 73:172–183

Acikgoz S, Ben Ali MS, Mert M (2016) Sources of economic growth in MEN countries: technological progress, physical or human capital accumulations? Economic development in the Middle East and North Africa. Springer/Palgrave Macmillan, New York, pp 27–69

Agnew J, Crobridge S (2002) Mastering space: hegemony, territory and international political economy. Routledge

Albalate D, Bel G, Elias F (2012) Institutional determinants of military spending. J Comp Econ 40(2):279–290

Ali HE (2012) Military expenditures and inequality in the Middle East and North Africa: a panel analysis. Defence Peace Econ 23(6):575–589

Ali HE, Abdellatif OA (2015) Military expenditures and natural resources: evidence from rentier states in the Middle East and North Africa. Defence and Peace Economics 26(1):5–13

Apergis N, Ben Ali MS (2020) Corruption, rentier states and economic growth: where Do the GCC countries stand? In: Miniaoui H (ed) Economic development in the Gulf cooperation council countries: from rentier states to diversified economies. Springer, Berlin.

Arrow KJ (1994) International peace-keeping forces: economics and politics. The economics of international security. Palgrave Macmillan, London, pp 81–86

Bannon, I., Collier, P. (2003). Natural resources and violent conflict: options and actions. The World Bank.

Ben Ali MS, Krammer S (2016) The role of Institutions in economic development. Economic development in the Middle East and North Africa. Springer/Palgrave Macmillan, New York, pp 1–25

Ben Ali MS, Saha S (2016) Corruption and economic development. Economic development in the Middle East and North Africa. Springer/Palgrave Macmillan, New York, pp 133–154

Ben Mim S, Ben Ali MS (2020) Natural resources curse and economic diversification in GCC countries. In: Miniaoui H (ed) Economic development in the Gulf cooperation council countries: from rentier states to diversified economies. Springer, Berlin.

Ben Ali MS, Cockx L, Francken N (2016) The Middle East and North Africa: cursed by Natural resources? Economic development in the Middle East and North Africa. Springer/Palgrave Macmillan, New York, pp 71–93

Benoit E (1973) Defense and economic growth in developing countries. FAO. Working paper.

Bodea C, Higashijima M, Singh RJ (2016) Oil and civil conflict: Can public spending have a mitigation effect? World Dev 78:1–12

Caruso R, Di Domizio M (2015) The Impact of US military spending on Public Debt in Europe (1992–2013): a note. Peace Econ Peace Sci Pub Policy 21(4):459–466

Caruso R, Di Domizio M (2016) Interdependence between US and European military spending: a panel cointegration analysis (1988–2013). Appl Econ Lett 23(4):302–305

Chang HC, Huang BN, Yang CW (2011) Military spending and economic growth across different groups: a dynamic panel Granger-causality approach. Econ Model 28(6):2416–2423

Chen PF, Lee CC, Chiu YB (2014) The nexus between defense spending and economic growth: new global evidence. Econ Model 36:474–483

d'Agostino G, Dunne JP, Pieroni L (2011) Optimal military spending in the US: a time series analysis. Econ Model 28(3):1068–1077

d'Agostino G, Dunne JP, Pieroni L (2016) Government spending, corruption and economic growth. World Dev 84:190–205

d'Agostino G, Dunne JP, Pieroni L (2017) Does military spending matter for long-run growth? Defence Peace Econ 28(4):429–436

Desli E, Gkoulgkoutsika A (2020) Military spending and economic growth: a panel data investigation. Econ Change Restructuring 1–26

Desli E, Gkoulgkoutsika A, Katrakilidis C (2017) Investigating the dynamic interaction between military spending and economic growth. Rev Dev Econ 21(3):511–526

Dunne JP, Tian N (2013) Military expenditure and economic growth: a survey. Econ Peace Secur J 8(1):5–11

Dunne JP, Tian N (2015) Military expenditure, economic growth and heterogeneity. Defence Peace Econ 26(1):15–31

Dunne JP, Tian N (2016) Military expenditure and economic growth, 1960–2014. Econ Peace Secur J 11(2)

Erdoğan S, Çevik Eİ, Gedikli A (2020) Relationship between oil price volatility and military expenditures in GCC countries. Environ Sci Pollut Res 1–13

Gupta S, De Mello L, Sharan R (2001) Corruption and military spending. Eur J Polit Econ 17(4):749–777

Harrison M, Wolf N (2012) The frequency of wars 1. Econ Hist Rev 65(3):1055–1076

Huang TY, Wu PC, Liu SY (2017) Defense–growth causality: considerations of regime-switching and time-and country-varying effects. Defence Peace Econ 28(5):568–584

Hwang SH (2012) Technology of military conflict, military spending, and war. J Pub Econ 96(1–2):226–236

Kollias C, Paleologou SM (2019) Military spending, economic growth and investment: a disaggregated analysis by income group. Empirical Econ 56(3):935–958

Kollias C, Paleologou SM, Tzeremes P (2020) Defence spending and unemployment in the USA: disaggregated Analysis by gender and age groups. Peace Econ Peace Sci Publ Policy 1(ahead-of-print)

Leontief W, Morgan A, Polenske K, Simpson D, Tower E (1965) The economic impact--industrial and regional—of an arms cut. Rev Econ Stat 217–241

Manamperi N (2016) Does military expenditure hinder economic growth? Evidence from Greece and Turkey. J Policy Model 38(6):1171–1193

Mauro P (1998) Corruption and the composition of government expenditure. J Pub econ 69(2):263–279

Odehnal J, Neubauer J (2018) Economic, security, and political determinants of military spending in NATO countries. Defence Peace Econ 1–15

Ortiz C, Alvarado R, Salinas A (2019) The effect of military spending on output: new evidence at the global and country group levels using panel data cointegration techniques. Economic Anal Policy 62:402–414

Qiong L, Junhua H (2015) Military expenditure and unemployment in China. Procedia Econ Finance 30:498–504

Shrabani S, Ben Ali MS (2017) Corruption and economic development: new evidence from the Middle Eastern and North African Countries. Econ Anal Policy 54:83–95

SIPRI (2018) Military Expenditure: SIPRI Yearbook. Stockholm, International Peace Research Institute (SIPRI)

Stiglitz JE (1999) Knowledge as a global public good. In: Kaul I, Grunberg I, Stern MA (eds) Global public goods: International cooperation in the 21st century. Oxford university press, New York, pp 308–325

Swaleheen M, Ben Ali MS, Temimi A (2019) Corruption and public spending on education and health. Appl Econ Lett 1–5

Töngür Ü, Hsu S, Elveren AY (2015) Military expenditures and political regimes: evidence from global data, 1963–2000. Econ Model 44:68–79

Varisco AE (2010) A study on the inter-relation between armed conflict and natural resources and its implications for conflict resolution and peacebuilding. J Peace Conflict Dev 15(1):38–58

Wang TP, Shyu SHP, Chou HC (2012) The impact of defense spending on economic productivity in OECD countries. Econ Model 29(6):2104–2114

Yildirim J, Öcal N (2016) Military expenditures, economic growth and spatial spillovers. Defence Peace Econ 27(1):87–104

Zhang X, Chang T, Su CW, Wolde-Rufael Y (2016) Revisit causal nexus between military spending and debt: a panel causality test. Econ Model 52:939–944

Chapter 7
Foreign Aid, Development, and International Migration: An Exploration of the MENA Region

Jonas Gamso and Farhod Yuldashev

Abstract A large literature has emerged to explore the relationship between foreign aid and emigration from aid-recipient countries. Scholars suggest that aid affects international migration from these countries through its impacts on economic growth, civil conflict, and political institutions. This chapter builds on this literature with specific attention to the Middle East and North Africa (MENA). The authors review the relevant literatures on aid, development, and international migration, discuss key characteristics of the MENA region, describe the volume and composition of aid to MENA countries, and reflect on how aid is affecting migration patterns. They also offer some preliminary statistical analysis, finding a negative correlation between aid and emigration from the MENA region. After presenting preliminary results, a research agenda is offered for economic development specialists interested in further investigating aid and migration in the MENA context.

Keywords Foreign aid · International migration · MENA

7.1 Introduction

Foreign aid and international migration are of great importance to economic development. While the relationship between aid and development has been hotly debated for many years (Gulrajani 2011), compelling evidence suggests that aid can bolster economic growth (Headey 2008; Minoiu and Reddy 2010) and improve other facets of human development (Riddell and Niño-Zarazúa 2016). Likewise, international migration has important consequences for development, in light of its impacts on human capital in home and destination countries (Saxenian 2006), as well as the

J. Gamso (✉)
Thunderbird School of Global Management, Arizona State University, Phoenix, United States
e-mail: jonas.gamso@thunderbird.asu.edu

F. Yuldashev
Graduate School of Public and International Affairs, Pittsburgh, United States
e-mail: fyuldashev@pitt.edu

potential of remittances from emigrants to support economic growth in their home countries (Ben Mim and Ben Ali 2012; Maïga et al. 2016).

In recent years, a large literature has emerged around the relationship between foreign aid and international migration and, in particular, on the effects of aid on emigration from aid-recipient countries. Some scholars argue that aid will deter individuals in aid-recipient countries from emigrating (Böhning 1994), whereas others argue that aid may enable them (de Haas 2007). Foreign aid has a host of effects on developing countries, impacting economic growth (Lof et al. 2015), conflict mitigation (de Ree and Nillesen 2009), and political development (Jones and Tarp 2016). The impacts that aid has on these variables may, in turn, affect migration patterns and, indeed, scholars have identified relationships between aid and international migration (e.g., Gamso and Yuldashev 2018a, b; Lanati and Thiele 2018a, b, 2020).

While the scholarship on aid and migration has produced important insights, researchers must look more closely at the unique characteristics of individual regions and countries. In this chapter, we explore the Middle East and North Africa (MENA), as a starting point to understanding how aid may affect emigration from countries in the region. We do so over several sections. In Sect. 7.2, we review the relevant literature on aid, development, and international migration. In Sect. 7.3, we discuss key characteristics of the MENA region. Section 7.4 describes the volume and composition of aid to MENA countries, using data from the AidData project. In Sect. 7.5, we offer statistical analysis and then lay out a research agenda for economic development specialists interested in exploring aid and migration in the MENA context. Section 7.6 offers a brief conclusion and addresses some policy implications.

7.2 Literature Review: Aid, Development, and International Migration

Few topics in development studies have attracted as much attention as foreign aid.[1] Researchers have explored the effects of aid on economic growth (Chatterjee and Turnovsky 2007; Lof et al. 2015), inequality and poverty (Chong et al. 2009), civil conflict (de Ree and Nillesen 2009; Savun and Tirone 2012), political development and stability (Jones and Tarp 2016; Morrison 2009), and public health (Williamson 2008), among other things.

Recently, the literature has turned to the relationship between aid and migration (Clemens and Postel 2018). While this topic is not entirely new to the development literature (e.g. Morrison 1982; Böhning 1994), there has been a surge of recent interest. This likely reflects the political salience of immigration in the USA and Western Europe (Goodwin and Heath 2016; Scribner 2017), as well as the refugee crises stemming from conflicts in Syria and Libya (Baldwin-Edwards and Lutterbeck

---

[1] See Qian (2015) for a thorough review of the foreign aid literature.

Fig. 7.1 Aid as deterring migration

2019; Ostrand 2015). Western policymakers have expressed interest in the relationship between aid and migration, seeing aid as a development friendly approach to stemming immigration inflows (Baldwin-Edwards et al. 2019).

While there is considerable attention on foreign aid as a tool to manage immigration, the theoretical and empirical evidence is mixed.[2] Theoretically, foreign aid inflows may reduce emigration from aid-recipient countries by alleviating the push factors that lead individuals to seek better lives in foreign countries (Morrison 1982). These may include economic push factors, such as poverty and joblessness, or political push factors, such as state repression or corruption. Likewise, if aid reduces civil conflict, improves the state of public health, or otherwise enhances human development, then the residents of countries that receive aid will enjoy a better quality of life at home, which may in turn deter them from seeking better lives elsewhere. Figure 7.1 provides a conceptual model of the "aid as deterring migration" narrative.

On the other hand, and although it may seem counterintuitive, improving economies through aid may encourage emigration. In particular, higher incomes and economic growth may give individuals access to resources that they would not otherwise have, which they may in turn use to emigrate (de Haas 2007). Likewise, to the extent that aid fosters conflict resolution and greater political rights (Savun and Tirone 2012; Wright 2009), it may allow for freer movements for citizens, which will in turn facilitate emigration (Breunig et al. 2012).[3] Figure 7.2 provides a conceptual model for the "aid as facilitating migration" narrative.[4]

Empirical research can offer insights as to whether the aid as deterring or aid as facilitating narrative is more accurate, but results have been mixed. For example, Berthélemy et al. (2009) find that aid has a positive effect on migration, consistent with the aid as facilitating line of argument, whereas Lanati and Thiele (2018a, b) identify a negative relationship, suggesting that aid deters emigration. Gamso and

---

[2]See Clemens and Postel (2018) for a review of this literature.

[3]Likewise, although civil conflict is likely to force some individuals to leave their countries (Ibáñez and Vélez 2008), it may also lead to restrictions on freedom of movement or border closures (Vignal 2017). This suggests that reduced civil conflict may facilitate emigration as these restrictions are lifted.

[4]It should also be noted that the effectiveness of foreign aid is much debated (Thérien 2002) and some studies fail to find positive relationships between aid and economic growth (Mallik 2008), political development (Knack 2004), or conflict resolution (Mousseau 2020).

Fig. 7.2 Aid as facilitating migration

Yuldashev (2018a, b) find that the effect of aid on migration is contingent on the type of aid, with rural development aid and aid for political development being accompanied by reductions in migration outflows from aid-recipient countries. This indicates that some types of aid deter emigration.[5] It may also be that aid targeted toward alleviating environmental degradation (Arndt and Tarp 2017), promoting education (Riddell and Niño-Zarazúa 2016), and advancing health and medicine (Mishra and Newhouse 2009) impacts international migration trends, as each of these have been shown to affect the movement of people (Afifi 2011; Kalipeni and Oppong 1998; Williams 2009).

7.3 Key Characteristics of the MENA Region

Cross-national data analysis, of the sort done in most of the studies discussed above, has its weaknesses when applied to a given country or region. Each region has its own unique features and circumstances, and MENA is no different, as countries in this area have characteristics that affect the aid that they receive, as well as the impacts that this aid then has on population movements. Additionally, MENA countries have arrangements with donor countries that revolve around managing population movements in exchange for foreign aid (Tsourapas 2019), as we discuss below.

In general terms, the region is facing a host of changes, including population growth, urbanization, and environmental stresses (McKee et al. 2017). Many countries in the region have poor political institutions (Saha and Ben Ali 2017; Ben Ali and Saha 2016; Bhuiyan and Farazmand 2020; Khondker 2019). Most MENA nations are categorized as "mostly unfree" or "moderately free," according to the Heritage Foundation's Economic Freedom Index, and the average MENA score from the World Bank's World Governance Indicators shows poor governance (Ben Ali and Krammer 2016). Additionally, several MENA countries have high rates of poverty and inequality (Ncube et al. 2014), high youth unemployment (Ben Ali and Krammer 2016), and persistent conflict and terrorism (Fearon 2017; Honig and Yahel 2019).

---

[5]It should be noted that these studies suggest small effects, such that aid deters migration at a high dollar-per-migrant cost (Clist and Restelli 2020).

This has fostered significant grievances, aimed in particular at political elites (Ali 2020).

Poor institutions, poverty, inequality, and conflict are all potential push factors that could lead individuals to leave MENA countries. Indeed, the region has experienced a large amount of emigration: According to the International Organization for Migration (2016) approximately 24 million individuals from MENA lived outside of their birth country in 2015, constituting approximately 10% of international migrants. Approximately half of these emigrants live in other MENA countries, with Europe being the second leading destination.[6] Countries in the MENA region also generate more refugees than any other (over 6 million, in 2015, with approximately 4.9 million coming from Syria).[7] Fargues (2008) argues that four characteristics of MENA countries have driven emigration: (1) large youth populations, (2) poor employment conditions at home, partly reflecting poor economic policies, (3) population density, leading to pressures on water resources, and (4) various unresolved conflicts in the region. Other push factors highlighted in the literature include climate change (Wodon and Liverani 2014), weak political institutions (Dibeh et al. 2019), and cultural traits (Docquier et al. 2020).[8]

7.4 Foreign Aid to the MENA Region

In theory, push factors such as unemployment and weak political institutions could be alleviated by foreign aid. There is a body of scholarship on the effectiveness of aid in MENA countries, but before delving into this literature it is worthwhile to provide an overview of aid to the region. As a starting point, it should be noted that the MENA region is a significant recipient of aid, despite having relatively high levels of development (Root et al. 2016). Additionally, the purposes of this aid vary, both in terms of the interests of donors (Bicchi 2010; Pellicer and Wegner 2009; Wildeman and Tartir 2014) and in terms of the sectors that aid is allocated toward.

We begin by providing a snapshot of aid to the MENA region, using descriptive statistics from AidData (Tierney et al. 2011). Figure 7.3 shows aid flows to MENA countries, as a share of total aid, for the period from 1990 to 2013. Aid to MENA constituted over 20% of total aid in 1991, 1994, 2004, 2005, and 2007, and for all years combined the MENA region receives about 15 percent of foreign aid. This is especially notable when you consider that MENA countries accounted for less than six percent of the global population during each of these years, according to data from the World Bank.

---

[6]Mangin and Zenou (2016) estimate that approximately one million irregular migrants from the MENA region moved to Europe in 2015.

[7]MENA countries, such as Jordan and Lebanon, also host large refugee populations, and MENA countries attract many immigrants from abroad, with Saudi Arabia and the United Arab Emirates being the top destinations.

[8]It is likely that the decision to emigrate is attributable to a number of intersecting factors (Crawley and Hagen-Zanker 2019), suggesting that no single variable drives migrants.

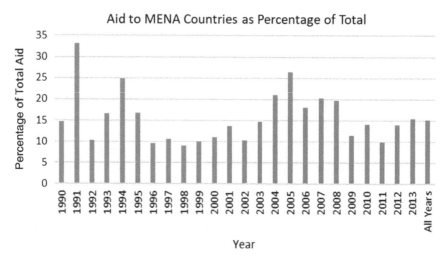

Fig. 7.3 Aid to MENA countries as percentage of total

Table 7.1 Top aid recipients in MENA region

Aid recipient	Aid commitment (in millions)	Percent of total aid to Mena region (%)
Iraq	$61,652.8	23.86
Egypt	$60,206.93	23.3
Morocco	$34,463.02	13.34
Palestinian adm. areas	$18,620.47	7.21
Tunisia	$18,034.25	6.98
Jordan	$14,951.09	5.79
Other Mena countries[a]	$207,928.6	19.53
Total	$258,388.4	100

[a]Other countries ordered from highest to lowest aid recipient: Algeria, Yemen, Lebanon, Syria, Iran, Israel, Saudi Arabia, Oman, Bahrain, Libya, Kuwait, Qatar, United Arab Emirates

Next, we identify the MENA countries that received the most aid during the 1990–2013 period, those being Egypt, Iraq, Jordan, Morocco, Palestine, and Tunisia (see Table 7.1). Iraq and Egypt have received particularly large amounts of aid, with nearly 50 percent of aid to the region flowing to those two countries. Aid to Iraq peaked in 2005, during the height of the US-led occupation, while aid to Egypt peaked in 1991 and then rose dramatically again during and in the aftermath of the Arab Spring.[9]

---

[9]Putting Egypt aside, the Arab Spring appears not to have dramatically affected aid to the region, as Heydermann (2014: 50) explains: "Western patterns of foreign assistance exhibit remarkable

Aid Commitments (In Millions)

Fig. 7.4 Aid commitments to MENA countries, by type

Foreign aid is not uniform in its intent or in its effectiveness, as the type of aid allocated has important implications for development outcomes (Jones and Tarp 2016) and for migration (Gamso and Yuldashev 2018a, b), among other things (Savun and Tirone 2018). As such, it is instructive to consider the type of aid that flows into MENA countries. To do so, we disaggregate aid by type. Figure 7.4 shows that most aid to the MENA region is for debt relief, while energy generation and supply, government and civil society, and water supply and sanitation also receive significant attention.

When these aid projects are put into the categorization utilized by Jones and Tarp (2016), we see that aid to improve governance makes up about 8.65% of aid to the MENA region. This is the only sort of aid that Gamso and Yuldashev (2018a) find to be negatively related to emigration, suggesting that most aid to MENA countries will not lead to reductions in migrant outflows.[10] That said, it may be that specific characteristics of aid-recipient MENA countries are such that other types of aid affect migration.

---

continuity, despite the scale of the uprisings and their effects, and despite the commitment of Western governments to expand assistance in support of the aspirations of Arab protestors."

[10]Governance aid has also been found to improve political institutions (Jones and Tarp 2016) and to reduce terrorism (Savun and Tirone 2018), suggesting that aid of this sort would reduce key push factors that generate emigration.

7.4.1 Donor Motives

It is worth briefly considering the motives of donors, as these may potentially affect the aid that they provide and the effectiveness of this aid. In general, aid provision may reflect recipient need or donor interests, with the latter being particularly important in explaining bilateral aid (Maizels and Nissanke 1984). Donors are likely to be compelled by foreign policy interests as well as domestic considerations.[11] On the foreign policy side, aid has been speculated to serve as a form of bribery to garner support in international organizations (Kuziemko and Werker 2006), to complement military interventions (Kisangani and Pickering 2015), and to secure access to foreign markets (Lancaster 2007). For example, receiving US aid is strongly related to votes in favor US-supported resolutions in the United Nations General Assembly (Dreher et al. 2008). Domestic political considerations also affect aid provision. For example, conservative governments tend to give aid that encourages trade, while left-leaning governments give more disaster relief (Green and Licht 2018).[12]

Research suggests that aid to the MENA region is similarly political in nature, such that strategic concerns are paramount for major donors' aid allocations (Pellicer and Wegner 2009). Reducing international migration appears to be one of these strategic concerns. This is particularly true of European donors, who have made financial support for migrant-sending countries a key component of their immigration management policy. Consistent with the "aid as deterring" strategy, EU member states intend to use aid as a tool to promote economic development in MENA countries, thereby reducing the economic push factors that lead to emigration (Arroyo 2019).

7.4.2 Aid Effectiveness

The next concern is about the effectiveness of foreign aid, a subject that has generated great debate (Engel 2014). Although some scholars are skeptical of aid (e.g., Easterly 2007), studies offer evidence that aid can reduce poverty, promote political development, and advance the resolution of conflict. For example, Mahembe et al. (2019) survey the literature and find that most studies reveal a negative relationship between aid and poverty. Likewise, Wright (2009) finds that aid promotes democratization, while Jones and Tarp (2016) find that aid targeted toward governance projects promotes better political institutions. Several studies likewise suggest that aid can prevent or help to halt civil wars.[13] For example, aid may reduce the grievances that lead to conflict (Collier and Hoeffler 2004), preventing wars from happening in the first place. Likewise, governments can use aid to pay rebels off or to win support

---

[11]This is not to discount the importance of humanitarian and moral concerns, which also drive foreign aid donors, particularly in the context of multilateral aid (Lumsdaine 1993).

[12]For additional work on domestic politics and foreign aid, see Fleck and Kilby (2001) and Thérien and Noel (2000).

[13]As with most aid-literatures, studies offer mixed findings on this topic (Findley 2018).

from citizens, thereby helping to weaken non-state combatants and bringing wars to a close more quickly (Azam and Delacroix 2006; Azam and Mesnard 2003).

It is also likely that the effectiveness of aid is conditional on factors such as quality of governance and existing levels of poverty and inequality in recipient countries (Burnside and Dollar 2000; Collier 2007), making its impacts on any one country or region contingent on these (and perhaps other) factors. The implication is that aid may fail to produce positive outcomes in countries such as those in the MENA region, many of which have high levels of inequality and poverty (Ncube et al. 2014), as well as poor governance quality (Bhuiyan and Farazmand 2020). Studies focused on the effectiveness of aid in the MENA region specifically show mixed effectiveness for aid. For example, Baliamoune-Lutz (2016) finds that aid is effective in terms of promoting women's political empowerment MENA countries, whereas Amin (2014) finds that aid did not generate development in Egypt during and after the Arab Spring.

7.5 Aid and Migration in the MENA Context: Current and Future Research

The aid-migration nexus has received some attention in the MENA context as well, both from policymakers and scholars. As noted above, European policymakers are especially keen to use foreign aid as a tool to deter immigration from neighbors to the South (Arroyo 2019). This reflects the hope that promoting development in MENA countries will reduce push factors in those countries, thereby deterring emigration (de Haas 2007).

The European Commission and leaders from individual EU member states have proposed making aid conditional on sending countries making efforts to halt irregular emigration. EU leaders have also provided foreign aid and other diplomatic favors to large transit countries in the region such as Morocco and Turkey in order to reduce the flow of migration into Europe (Kent et al. 2019; Norman 2020). Tsourapas (2019) argues that leaders in Jordan, Lebanon, and Turkey maintain refugee populations within their own borders in exchange for aid from Europe. This suggests that aid serves to prevent emigration from MENA countries, but that it does so through quid pro quo arrangements rather than via its impacts on development.

Gamso and Yuldashev (2018b) use survey data from the Arab Barometer to clarify their finding that rural development aid can reduce internal and international migration from rural areas. Findings from this survey suggest that agricultural workers in Arab countries are less eager to migrate, such that rural development aid that supports agricultural production and employment deters migration from rural areas. This suggests that development-focused aid can reduce emigration from countries in the region by lowering unemployment.

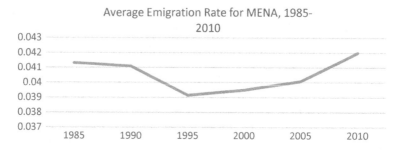

Fig. 7.5 Average emigration rates for MENA countries, 1985–2010

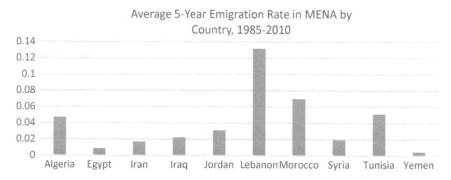

Fig. 7.6 Average emigration rates for individual MENA countries

7.5.1 Data Analysis

Having earlier provided descriptive data on foreign aid to MENA countries, it is now useful to similarly reflect on emigration rates. Using data from Brücker et al. (2013), which offers emigration rate data in five-year intervals (1985, 1990, 1995, 2000, 2005, and 2010),[14] we begin with emigration rates from all MENA countries for which data is available (see Fig. 7.5). As the figure shows, emigration rates have ranged from 0.039 to 0.042 across the time series, and they dipped to their lowest point in the mid-1990s before reaching their highest point in 2010.

Next, we offer data on individual MENA countries. In Fig. 7.6, we show the average emigration rates of countries for which data is available, over the 1985–2010 period. This data shows that Egypt and Iraq, the countries that received the highest amounts of foreign aid, had among the lowest emigration rates, while countries

---

[14]Emigration rate data measures the "proportion of migrants over the pre-migration population (defined as the sum of residents and migrants in each source country)," using Census data from 20 OECD countries that are destinations for international migrants: Australia, Austria, Canada, Chile, Denmark, Finland, France, Germany, Greece, Ireland, Luxembourg, Netherlands, New Zealand, Norway, Portugal, Spain, Sweden, Switzerland, UK, and USA. Additional details are available here: https://www.iab.de/en/daten/iab-brain-drain-data.aspx#Methodology.

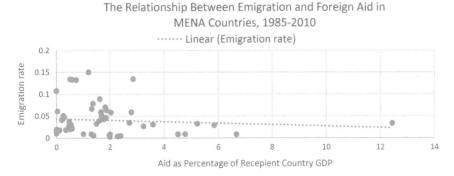

Fig. 7.7 The relationship between emigration and foreign aid for MENA countries, 1985–2010

like Lebanon and Algeria that received low levels of foreign aid have had high emigration rates. However, it should be noted that Iran and Syria, countries that received low levels of foreign aid, also had low emigration rates, suggesting that aid and international migration are not always linked.

In order to determine whether there is a negative or positive relationship between foreign aid and emigration from MENA countries, we offer a correlation analysis of these variables for the ten MENA countries for which both aid and emigration data is available. The Pearson correlation coefficient is -0.0589. Figure 7.7 offers visualization of this relationship, showing a negative trend line.

This offers some preliminary evidence in favor of the aid as deterring narrative, but clearly more thorough analysis is needed, given the small correlation coefficient and the importance of other variables. We have insufficient MENA-specific emigration data to carry out a multiple regression analysis, but we suggest future research take efforts to identify and analyze such data.

7.5.2 Future Research

We close this chapter by suggesting several research streams for development economists to move forward with. The first question for researchers to consider is whether aid is actually an effective deterrent to those who would otherwise emigrate from MENA countries. As discussed above, there have been a host of studies on the relationship between aid and migration, but results are mixed and few have focused on MENA countries in particular. Our preliminary analysis suggests that aid may deter emigration, but further analysis is necessary. Among other things, studies in this area can determine whether aid is more effective at deterring emigration from some countries than others (e.g., countries with higher or lower income levels) and whether some donors are more effective than others at targeting aid in a manner that deters emigration. Additionally, researchers may consider whether the state of bilateral relations, whether economic or political, between donor and recipient countries matter. This sort of research can also offer insights as to the mechanisms by which aid affects emigration from MENA countries.

A second question to consider is whether the composition and disbursement of aid affects emigration patterns from aid-recipient MENA countries. As discussed above, studies suggest that some types of aid are more effective at deterring emigration than others (e.g., Gamso and Yuldashev 2018a, b). While these studies are useful for understanding aid and migration across a large sample, MENA countries are unique in many ways and so the trends identified in the existing literature may not apply in the MENA context. A related matter is the disbursement of aid, which is often quite volatile (Hudson and Mosley 2008). This volatility may affect emigration from MENA countries (Gamso et al. 2020), either because it leads to economic or political hardships (Agénor and Aizenman 2010; Nielsen et al. 2011) that prompt migrant outflows, or because it undermines political deals between donors and recipient governments to stall migration (Tsourapas 2019).

A third area for researchers to explore is if and how aid moderates the effects of crises, such as political upheavals and civil wars, on migrant outflows. This is especially pertinent in the MENA context, considering the political upheavals of the Arab Spring and the civil conflicts that followed in Syria and elsewhere. Aid has been shown to help to ease democratic transitions (Savun and Tirone 2011) and to prevent civil war onset (Savun and Tirone 2012), suggesting a role for aid to relax the tensions in MENA countries that generate emigration. Likewise, given the growing number of natural disasters in the region (World Bank 2014), and the migrant outflows that typically accompany such disasters (Berlemann and Steinhardt 2017; Boustan et al. 2012), it is worthwhile to consider whether aid for disaster preparedness can help to ease emigration following natural disasters.[15]

Finally, scholars should explore the emergence of MENA countries as donors. In recent years, donations from Turkey and from the Gulf monarchies have grown (Altunişik 2014; Isaac 2014) and leaders in these countries increasingly see aid as a political tool (Farouk 2020). To what extent is migration control an objective for MENA donors? How have the aid flows from these countries affected emigration patterns from the countries receiving that aid? These are questions that future research should explore.

7.6 Conclusion and Policy Implications

Foreign aid is one of the most studied topics in development economics and its impacts on international migration have piqued the interests of policymakers and academics. While a literature has emerged to investigate the relationships between

---

[15] A related issue is climate change. Research suggests that climate change over the twenty-first century will lead to significant warming and reduced precipitation in the MENA region (Bucchignani et al. 2018), which are likely to spur large population movements if unaddressed (Scott et al. 2020). Researchers may wish to study whether aid for climate change mitigation and adaptation can offset some of the population displacements that would otherwise occur.

aid and migration, this research has tended to look at cross-national data spanning the entire developing world. From global perspective, there is some evidence that foreign aid can decrease emigration from aid-recipient countries (e.g., Lanati and Thiele 2018a)—particularly aid that focuses on developing governance and civil society institutions and that is more evenly distributed between urban and rural areas can have a substantive negative impact on emigration (Gamso and Yuldashev 2018a, b).

In this chapter, we have attempted to contextualize this research for MENA countries. The quantitative analysis we have shown offers evidence for a negative relationship between aid and emigration, but it does not provide a conclusive verdict. We have therefore recommended that scholars conduct further research in order to offer a more in-depth and comparative understanding of foreign aid, development, and international migration in MENA. Scholars should explore the research avenues that we suggest, as well as other related matters, in order to further refine our understanding of the aid-migration nexus.

References

Afifi T (2011) Economic or environmental migration? The push factors in Niger. Int Migration 49(s1):e95–e124

Agénor P, Aizenman J (2010) Aid volatility and poverty traps. J Dev Econ 91(1):1–7

Ali HA (2020) Public perception of rentier elites in the Middle East and North Africa. Int J Public Adm 43(5):392–403

Altunişik MB (2014) Turkey as an 'emerging donor' and the Arab uprisings. Mediterr Politics 19(3):333–350

Amin K (2014) International assistance to Egypt after the 2011 and 2013 uprisings: more politics and less development. Mediterr Politics 19(3):392–412

Arndt C, Tarp F (2017) Aid, environment and climate change. Rev DevEcon 21(2):285–303

Arroyo HT (2019) Using EU aid to address the root causes of migration and refugee flows. European University Institute, Migration Policy Centre, Florence

Azam J, Delacroix A (2006) Aid and the delegated fight against terrorism. Rev Dev Econ 10(2):330–344

Azam J, Mesnard A (2003) Civil war and the social contract. Public Choice 115(3–4):455–475

Baldwin-Edwards M, Lutterbeck D (2019) Coping with the Libyan migration crisis. J Ethnic Migr Stud 45(12):2241–2257

Baldwin-Edwards M, Blitz BK, Crawley H (2019) The politics of evidence-based policy in Europe's 'migration crisis'. J Ethnic Migr Stud 45(12):2139–2155

Baliamoune-Lutz M (2016) The effectiveness of foreign aid to women's equality organizations in the MENA. J Int Dev 28(3):320–341

Ben Ali, MS, Krammer, MS (2016) The Role of Institutions in Economic Development. Economic development in the Middle East and North Africa. Springer/Palgrave Macmillan, New York, pp 1–25

Ben Ali, MS, Saha, S (2016) Corruption and economic development. Economic development in the Middle East and North Africa. Springer/Palgrave Macmillan, New York, pp 133–154

Ben Mim S, Ben Ali M. S. (2012) Through which channels can remittances spur economic growth in MENA countries? Economics 6(33):1–27

Berlemann M, Steinhardt MF (2017) Climate change, natural disasters, and migration—a survey of the empirical evidence. CESinfo Economic Stud 63(4):353–385

Berthélemy J, Beuran M, Maurel M (2009) Aid and migration: substitutes or complements? World Dev 37(10):1589–1599

Bhuiyan S, Farazmand A (2020) Society and public policy in the Middle East and North Africa. Int J Public Adm 43(5):373–377

Bicchi F (2010) Dilemmas of implementation: EU democracy assistance in the Mediterranean. Democratization 17(5):976–996

Böhning WR (1994) Helping migrants to stay at home. Ann Am Acad Polit Soc Sci 534:165–177

Boustan LP, Kahn ME, Rhode PW (2012) Moving to higher ground: migration response to natural disasters in the early Twentieth Century. Am Econ Rev 102(3):238–244

Breunig C, Cao X, Luedtke A (2012) Global migration and political regime type: a democratic disadvantage. Br J Polit Sci 42(4):825–854

Brücker H, Capuano S, Marfouk, A (2013) Education, gender and international migration: insights from a panel-dataset 1980–2010, Mimeo

Bucchignani E, Mercogliano P, Panitz H, Montesarchio M (2018) Climate change projections for the Middle East-North Africa domain with COSMO-CLM at different spatial resolutions. Adv Clim Change Res 9(1):66–80

Burnside C, Dollar D (2000) Aid, policies, and growth. Am Econ Rev 90(4):847–868

Chatterjee S, Turnovsky SJ (2007) Foreign aid and economic growth: the role of flexible labor supply. J Dev Econ 84(1):507–533

Chong A, Gradstein M, Calderon C (2009) Can foreign aid reduce income inequality? Public Choice 140(1–2):59–84

Clemens MA, Postel HM (2018) Deterring emigration with foreign aid: an overview of evidence from low-income countries. Popul Dev Rev 44(4):667–693

Clist P, Restelli G (2020) Development aid and international migration to Italy: Does aid reduce irregular flows? The World Economy. Doi.org/10.1111/twec.13017

Collier P (2007) The bottom billion: why the poorest countries are failing and what can be done about it. Oxford University Press, New York

Collier P, Hoeffler A (2004) Greed and grievance in civil war. Oxford Econ Pap 56(4):563–595

Crawley H, Hagen-Zanker J (2019) Deciding where to go: policies, people and perceptions shaping destination preferences. Int Migr 57(1):20–35

de Haas H (2007) Turning the tide? Why development will not stop migration. Dev Change 38(5):819–841

de Ree J, Nillesen E (2009) Aiding violence or peace? The impact of foreign aid on the risk of civil conflict in Sub-Saharan Africa. J Dev Econ 88(2):301–313

Dibeh G, Fakih A, Marrouch W (2019) Labor market and institutional drivers of youth irregular migration in the Middle East and North Africa region. J Ind Relat 61(2):225–251

Docquier F, Tansel A, Turati R (2020) Do emigrants self-select along cultural traits? Evidence from the MENA countries. Int Migrat Rev 54(2):388–422

Dreher A, Nunnenkamp P, Thiele R (2008) Does US aid buy UN general assembly votes? A disaggregated analysis. Public Choice 136(1–2):139–164

Easterly W (2007) Was development assistance a mistake? Am Econ Rev 97(2):328–332

Engel S (2014) The not-so-great debate. Third World Q 35(8):1374–1389

Fargues P (2008) Emerging demographic patterns across the Mediterranean and their implications for migration through 2030. Migration Policy Institute, Washington DC

Farouk Y (2020) Saudi Arabia: aid as a primary foreign policy tool. In: Carnegie endowment for international peace. https://carnegieendowment.org/2020/06/09/saudi-arabia-aid-as-primary-for eign-policy-tool-pub-82003. Accessed 29 July 2020

Fearon JD (2017) Civil war & the current international system. Daedalus 146(4):18–32

Findley MG (2018) Does foreign aid build peace? Annu Rev Polit Sci 21:359–384

Fleck RK, Kilby C (2001) Foreign aid and domestic politics: voting in Congress and the allocation of USAID contracts across congressional districts. South Econ J 67(3):598–617

Gamso J, Yuldashev F (2018a) Targeted foreign aid and international migration: is development-promotion an effective immigration policy? Int Stud Quart 62(4):809–820

Gamso J, Yuldashev F (2018b) Does rural development aid reduce international migration? World Dev 110:268–282

Gamso J, Lu J, Yuldashev F (2020) Does foreign aid volatility increase international migration? Rev Int Organ. https://doi.org/10.1007/s11558-020-09400-2

Goodwin MJ, Heath O (2016) The 2016 referendum, Brexit and the left behind: an aggregate-level analysis of the result. Polit Q 87(3):323–332

Green ZD, Licht AA (2018) Domestic politics and changes in foreign aid allocation: the role of party preferences. Polit Res Q 71(2):284–301

Gulrajani N (2011) Transcending the great foreign aid debate: managerialism, radicalism and the search for aid effectiveness. Third World Q 32(2):199–216

Headey D (2008) Geopolitics and the effect of foreign aid on economic growth: 1970–2001. J Int Dev 20(2):161–180

Heydermann S (2014) Continuities and discontinuities in foreign assistance. Mediterr Politics 19(3):450–455

Honig O, Yahel I (2019) A fifth wave of terrorism? The emergence of terrorist semi-states. Terrorism Polit Violence 31(6):1210–1228

Hudson J, Mosley P (2008) Aid volatility, policy and development. World Dev 36(10):2082–2102

Ibáñez AM, Vélez CE (2008) Civil conflict and forced migration: the micro determinants and welfare losses of displacement in Colombia. World Dev 36(4):659–676

International Organization for Migration (2016) Migration to, from and in the Middle East and North Africa. https://www.iom.int/sites/default/files/country/mena/Migration-in-the-Middle-East-and-North-Africa_Data%20Sheet_August2016.pdf. Accessed 29 July 2020

Isaac SK (2014) Explaining the patterns of the Gulf monarchies' assistance after the Arab uprisings. Mediterr Politics 19(3):413–430

Jones S, Tarp F (2016) Does foreign aid harm political institutions? J Dev Econ 118:266–281

Kalipeni E, Oppong J (1998) The refugee crisis in Africa and implications for health and disease: aa political ecology approach. Soc Sci Med 46(12):1637–1653

Kent J, Norman KP, Tennis KH (2019) Changing motivations or capabilities? Migration deterrence in the global context. Int Stud Rev. https://doi.org/10.1093/isr/viz050

Khondker HH (2019) The impact of the Arab Spring on democracy and development in the MENA region. Soc Compass 13(9):e12726

Kisangani E, Pickering J (2015) Soldiers and development aid: military intervention and foreign aid flows. J Peace Res 52(2):215–227

Knack S (2004) Does foreign aid promote democracy? Int Stud Quart 48(1):251–266

Lanati M, Thiele R (2018a) The impact of foreign aid on migration revisited. World Dev 111:59–74

Lanati M, Thiele R (2018b) Foreign assistance and migration choices: disentangling the channels. Econ Lett 172:148–151

Lanati M, Thiele R (2020) Foreign assistance and emigration: accounting for the role of non-transferred aid. World Econ 43(7):1951–1976

Lancaster C (2007) Foreign aid: diplomacy, development, domestic politics. University of Chicago Press, Chicago

Lof M, Mekesha T, Tarp F (2015) Aid and income: another time-series perspective. World Dev 69:19–30

Lumsdaine D (1993) Moral vision in international politics: the foreign aid regime, 1949–1989. Princeton University Press, Princeton

Mahembe E, Odhiambo NM, Read R (2019) Foreign aid and poverty reduction: a review of international literature. Cogent Social Sci 5(1):1625741

Maïga EWM, Baliamoune-Lutz M, Ben Ali MS (2016). Workers remittances and economic development: which role for education? In: Economic development in the Middle East and North Africa, Springer/Palgrave Macmillan, New York, pp 95–114

Maizels A, Nissanke MK (1984) Motivations for aid to developing countries. World Dev 12(9):879–900

Mallik G (2008) Foreign aid and economic growth: a cointegration analysis of the six poorest African countries. Econ Anal Policy 38(2):251–260

Mangin S, Zenou Y (2016) Illegal migration and policy enforcement. Econ Lett 148:83–86

McKee M, Keulertz M, Habibi N, Mulligan M, Woertz E (2017) Demographic and economic material factors in the MENA region. Middle East and North Africa regional architecture: mapping geopolitical shifts, regional order and domestic transformations, Working Paper No. 3

Minoiu C, Reddy SG (2010) Development aid and economic growth: a positive long-run relation. Q Rev Econ Finance 50(1):27–39

Mishra P, Newhouse D (2009) Does health aid matter? J Health Econ 28(4):855–872

Morrison KM (2009) Oil, nontax revenue, and the redistributional foundations of regime stability. Int Org 63(1):107–138

Morrison TK (1982) The relationship of US aid, trade, and investment to migration pressures in major sending countries. Int Migrat Rev 16(1):4–26

Mousseau DY (2020) Does foreign development aid trigger ethnic war in developing states? Armed Forces Soc. https://doi.org/10.1177/0095327x20902180

Ncube M, Anyanwu JC, Hausken K (2014) Inequality, economic growth and poverty in the Middle East and North Africa (MENA). Afr Dev Rev 26(3):435–453

Nielsen RA, Findley MG, Davis ZS, Candland T, Nielson D (2011) Foreign aid shocks as a cause of violent armed conflict. Am J Polit Sci 55(2):219–232

Norman KP (2020) Migration diplomacy and policy liberalization in Morocco and Turkey. Int Migr Rev. https://doi.org/10.1177/0197918319895271

Ostrand N (2015) The Syrian refugee crisis: a comparison of responses by Germany, Sweden, the United Kingdom, and the United States. J Migr Human Secur 3(3):255–279

Pellicer M, Wegner E (2009) Altruism and its limits: the role of civil and political rights for American and French aid towards the Middle East and North Africa. J N Afr Stud 14(1):109–121

Qian N (2015) Making progress on foreign aid. Annu Rev Econ 7:277–308

Riddell A, Niño-Zarazúa (2016) The effectiveness of foreign aid to education: what can be learned? Int J Educ Dev 48:23–36

Root HL, Li Y, Balasuriya K (2016) The US foreign aid policy to the Middle East: the political economy of US assistance to the MENA region. Available at SSRN: https://ssrn.com/abstract=2716757 or http://dx.doi.org/10.2139/ssrn.2716757

Saha S, Ben Ali MS (2017) Corruption and economic development: new evidence from the Middle Eastern and North African countries. Econ Anal Policy 54:83–95

Savun B, Tirone DC (2011) Foreign aid, democratization, and civil conflict: how does democracy aid affect civil conflict? Am J Polit Sci 55(2):233–246

Savun B, Tirone DC (2012) Exogenous shocks, foreign aid, and civil war. Int Org 66(3):363–393

Savun B, Tirone DC (2018) Foreign aid as a counterterrorism tool: more liberty, less terror? J Conflict Resolut 62(8):1607–1635

Saxenian A (2006) The new argonauts: regional advantage in a global economy. Harvard University Press, Cambridge

Scribner T (2017) You are not welcome here anymore: restoring support for refugee resettlement in the age of trump. J Migr Human Secur 5(2):263–284

Scott M, Lennon M, Tubridy D, Marchman P, Siders AR, Main KL, Herrmann V, Butler D, Frank K, Bosomworth K, Blanchi R, Johnson C (2020) Climate disruption and planning: resistance or retreat? Plan Theory Pract 21(1):125–154

Thérien J (2002) Debating foreign aid: right versus left. Third World Q 23(3):449–466

Thérien J, Noel A (2000) Political parties and foreign aid. Am Polit Sci Rev 94(1):151–162

Tierney MJ, Nielson DL, Hawkins DG, Roberts JT, Findley MG, Powers RM, Parks B, Wilson SE, Hicks RL (2011) More dollars than sense: refining our knowledge of development finance using AidData. World Dev 39(11):1891–1906

Tsourapas G (2019) The Syrian refugee crisis and foreign policy decision-making in Jordan, Lebanon, and Turkey. J Global Secur Stud 4(4):464–481

Vignal L (2017) The changing borders and borderlands of Syria in a time of conflict. Int Aff 93(4):809–827

Wildeman J, Tartir A (2014) Unwilling to change, determined to fail: donor aid in occupied palestine in the aftermath of the Arab Uprisings. Mediterr Polit 19(3):431–449

Williamson CR (2008) Foreign aid and human development: the impact of foreign aid to the health sector. South Econ J 75(1):188–207

Williams N (2009) Education, gender, and migration in the context of social change. Soc Sci Res 38(4):883–896

Wodon Q, Liverani A (2014) Climate change and migration in the MENA region. MENA knowledge and learning quick notes series, no. 129. World Bank, Washington, DC

World Bank (2014) Natural disasters in the Middle East and North Africa: a regional overview. World Bank, Washington DC

Wright J (2009) How foreign aid can foster democratization in authoritarian regimes. Am J Polit Sci 53(3):552–571

Chapter 8
The Resource Curse: How Can Oil Shape MENA Countries' Economic Development?

Nicolas Clootens and Mohamed Sami Ben Ali

Abstract This chapter discusses whether the Middle East and North African (MENA) countries are prone to be cursed or blessed by their natural resources endowments. It thus reviews the literature on the resource curse theory. The existence of a resource curse is discussed and arguments against advocates of the resource curse are presented. Then, the resource curse transmission channels are presented. Finally, we present to what extent MENA countries are affected by the curse, drawing on existing literature as well as empirical data. The (scarce) literature shows that a resource curse may be underway in MENA economies. Broadly speaking, this literature often argues that the curse could be turned into a blessing through institutional improvements. The empirical data presented in this chapter tend to confirm this view. They show that the economic development of resource-rich MENAs has not been translated into human progress and has been largely non-inclusive. These results are stronger when the resource rent per capita is larger. Finally, the average institutional quality in resources-rich MENA countries appears to be lower than the average institutional quality in resources-poor MENA economies, suggesting some room for an institutional resource curse.

Keywords Natural resources curse · MENA · Economic development · Institutions

8.1 Introduction

The general audience often thinks that natural resources boost economic development as basic intuition would suggest that a country that owns some natural resources has an advantage compared to other countries that cannot benefit from them. This is indeed confirmed by history: the economic development of numerous OECD countries has

N. Clootens (✉)
Centrale Marseille, Aix-Marseille University, CNRS, AMSE, Marseille, France
e-mail: nicolas.clootens@centrale-marseille.fr

M. S. Ben Ali
College of Business and Economics, Qatar University, Doha, Qatar
e-mail: msbenali@qu.edu.qa

M. S. Ben Ali (ed.), *Economic Development in the MENA Region*, Perspectives on Development in the Middle East and North Africa (MENA) Region, https://doi.org/10.1007/978-3-030-66380-3_8

been fueled by the use of coal during the first industrial revolution and oil during the second one. However, several empirical studies suggest that this relationship between natural resources and economic performances goes in the other way since the late 1960s, giving rise to the idea of a resource curse. Table 8.1 represents wealth components in total wealth by income group. It shows that the share of natural capital in total wealth tends to decrease with the level of development, suggesting a resource curse. Conversely, the human capital share and the level of development seem positively associated.

In their seminal work, Sachs and Warner (1995) suggest that resource-rich countries have been characterized by a lower long-run economic growth than resource-poor countries. Indeed, the authors find a significant negative relationship between the GDP share of natural exports in 1970 and economic growth over the period 1970–1990. Figure 8.1 displays the negative relationship between the share of natural resource exports in GDP and the growth rate of per capita GDP over the period 1970–2017.

The work by Sachs and Warner (1995) has been replicated, and extended in several ways (see, e.g., Sachs and Warner 1999a, b, 2001; Kronenberg 2004; Davis 2013). Since the 2000s, a branch of the literature has followed the work of Gylfason (2001) trying to explain how natural resources dependence could affect economic growth through poor investment (Gylfason and Zoega 2006), insufficient human capital accumulation (Gylfason 2001; Stijns 2006), or loss of competitiveness through Dutch disease effects (Corden 1984; Krugman 1987; Torvik 2001; Matsen and Torvik 2005). This marks the beginning of a literature which tries to disentangle the curse's transmission channels. In more recent years, numerous scholars have studied the *institutional* explanations of the resource curse. They argue, for example, that natural resources fuel rent seeking and corruption (Leite and Weidmann 1999; Isham et al.

Table 8.1 Sub-components of total wealth by income group in 2014

Income group	Natural capital share (subsoil asset)	Produced capital share	Human capital share (%)
High income (OECD)	2.76% (1.13%)	27.66	70.36
High income (Non-OCDE)	30.23% (27.20%)	22.30	42.19
Upper middle income	16.81% (5.87%)	25.29	58.28
Lower middle income	26.78% (7.49%)	25.17	50.55
Low middle income	47.11% (4.17%)	14.43	40.82
World	9.40% (4.31%)	26.55	64.45

Source Own calculations based on Lange et al. (2018)

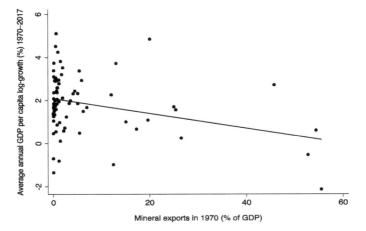

Fig. 8.1   The negative relationship between mineral exports and per capita GDP growth

2005), encourage conflicts (Collier and Hoeffler 2005; Berman et al. 2017), or reduce accountability of governments (Jensen and Wantchekon 2004).

Still, the existence of a resource curse is widely debated in the literature. Some criticisms are based on the proxy used to capture resource abundance (see, e.g., Lederman and Maloney 2006 or Brunnschweiler and Bulte 2008). Other authors suggest that the resource curse might be a statistical mirage, which merely depends on the studied period (James 2015). Finally, some authors suggest that a curse may exist, but that it is conditional to countries' specificities (Mehlum et al. 2006; van der Ploeg and Poelhekke 2009; Konte 2013; Clootens and Kirat 2017, 2020). According to these authors, the fact that natural resources depress growth cannot be taken as a law-like statement, but merely depends on countries' characteristics, either institutional, economical, or both.

The present chapter suggests to discuss the literature on the natural resource curse in order to see whether Middle East and North African (MENA) countries are likely to be affected by a resource curse. In addition, some empirical data are also proposed. The scarce literature on natural resource wealth and economic development in the MENAs tends to answer positively, largely emphasizing the importance of institutions in turning the curse into a blessing (Ben Ali et al. 2016). We confirm this view using empirical data. More specifically, we show that economic development of MENAs has not translated into human development and has been largely non-inclusive. The level of inequality indeed increases with the resource rent per capita. In addition, we suggest that the quality of governance, which is particularly low in resource-rich MENA countries, may explain these results.

The rest of the paper is organized as follows. The first section presents the debate among academics on the existence of a curse. The second section is devoted to the presentation of the possible transmission channel—both political and econom-ical—which could explain how the abundance of natural resources can generate poor economic outcomes. The third section deals with the specific case of MENAs by examining the existing literature and using empirical data. Finally, the last section concludes.

8.2   Curse or Blessing: What Does the Literature Tell Us About Natural Resources?

Since the seminal work of Sachs and Warner (1995), there exists a great debate in the literature on the existence of a resource curse itself. This debate is notably driven by the following straightforward empirical observation: resource-rich countries have exhibited different development patterns. The success story of the USA since independence is one of the best examples that natural resources (principally oil and coal) may be the engine of growth. However, there exist numerous elements suggesting that the relationship linking resource endowments and economic development goes in the other way since the 1960s. Perhaps one of the most striking examples is Nigeria, whose real GDP per capita measured in purchasing power parity (PPP) only increased by 2.2 times between 1966 and 2010, despite large oil revenues. Yet there are still countries whose economic performance seems to be fueled by natural resources. Between its independence in 1966 and 2010, Botswana's per capita GDP has been multiplied by a factor of 14.76 and the country has left the least-developed economies group. Other resource-rich countries with good economic performances over the period include Indonesia, Malaysia, and Thailand. These countries seem to have escaped the curse. However, some point out that they have performed less well than Hong Kong, Singapore, and South Korea, their resource-poor neighbors (van der Ploeg 2011). These various experiences have fueled the scientific controversy over the existence of a resource curse. Even recently, countries like Algeria, Russia, or Venezuela have experienced economic (and political for some) difficulties due to plummeting resource prices.

From a theoretical perspective, the very first economists such as Smith and Ricardo asserted that natural resources constituted a blessing for economic development. This vision was justified by the industrial revolution then underway in Western Europe and remained dominant until the 1980s with the emergence of the Dutch disease theory with Corden and Neary (1982) and Corden (1984). At that time, the Dutch economy was experiencing a decline in its manufacturing sector following a great gas discovery. The Dutch disease theory was the forerunner of the resource curse theory and is now widely seen as one of the many channels of transmission for the curse. The term *resource curse* has then been largely popularized by Auty (1993). The first cross-country study demonstrating a negative correlation between natural resource abundance and economic development—i.e. a resource curse—is the one by Sachs and Warner (1995). Then a very large literature trying to replicate or explain Sachs and Warner's results has developed. Notably, after Gylfason (2001), numerous papers interested in the curse's transmission channels were published. The main results of this literature are presented in the next section. Still, the fact that natural resources hamper economic development is far from being a consensual view.

Lederman and Maloney (2006, 2008) claim that talking about a curse in far from being evident. Reviewing the literature on the resource curse, they conclude that when some explanations of a curse are plausible, they are not specific to natural resources, and the underlying explanations could also apply to non-resource goods. For some other transmission channels, they conclude that they are not convincingly demonstrated because the authors proxy natural resource abundance with the GDP share of resource exports and the results are not robust to the introduction of different resource abundance indicators and alternative econometric methodologies. The question of resource abundance measurement is perhaps the most controversial issue in this literature. Indeed, the share of resource exports in GDP is more a proxy for resource dependence than abundance. This argument is present in Brunnschweiler and Bulte (2008) who introduce proxies for both dependence and abundance in growth regressions. They also argue that an endogeneity bias may exist because resource dependence is determined by economic decisions that can affect growth concomitantly. They find no negative effects of resource dependence after correcting for a potential endogeneity bias. More importantly, they find that natural resources abundance is growth-enhancing, suggesting that natural resources are a blessing. The same kind of exercise, however, leads to more moderate results in Van der Ploeg and Poelhekke (2010) and Clootens and Kirat (2017, 2020).

Another criticism which is addressed to the curse theory supporters is that the observation of a curse is highly dependent on the period of observation. During periods of rising (falling) resources prices, data are more likely to exhibit a positive (negative) relationship between resources endowments and economic growth. This argument is present in James (2015) who demonstrates the important role played by the industry composition. The mechanisms are very simple. In a country which is very resource-dependent, overall growth is strongly represented by the growth in the resource sector. If the resources prices decrease, it will strongly affect the overall growth rate of such a country. The author illustrates this statement with the case of Gabon in the 1980s, a period characterized by a sharp drop in resource prices. During the period, Gabon experienced both resource and non-resource sectors' growth above the world average. However, due to its strong resource dependence, its overall growth was about half of the world average. Nevertheless, the results found in James (2015) are themselves subject to criticism. The observation periods are somewhat short, which could explain the association between resource prices and economic performances by a price effect. On a longer horizon, such a price effect could be (over)compensated by some negative quantity effects due to curse mechanisms (which will be presented in the next section). In addition, the fact that resource-rich countries have, on average, not managed to diversify their economy in favor of growth-enhancing sectors might also be a manifestation of the resource curse.

Perhaps more reasonably, many articles suggest that it is not possible to infer law-like statements on natural resources as a curse or as a blessing. This branch of the literature argues for a *conditional* resource curse. The effects of natural resources on economic development can be conditioned by the type of resources considered. Indeed, point-source resources are more likely to generate curse mechanisms because the rents arising from their exploitation are easily appropriable. The likelihood that resource revenues from point-source deposits will benefit the entire population is therefore low. In addition, rent seeking behaviors, conflicts, and corruption to access the rent are more likely to appear. Conversely, diffuse resources are more likely to benefit the population in a broader way (Isham et al. 2005). Van der Ploeg and Poelhekke (2009) also confirm this insight for the resource price volatility transmission channel (which will be presented in the next section). Finite natural resources are also more likely to generate resource curse than reproducible resources because they are characterized by a scarcity rent that can amplify rent seeking behaviors.

The existence of a resource curse might also be conditional on institutional and constitutional variables. Andersen and Aslaksen (2008) argue that presidential regimes are more likely to be affected by a resource curse than parliamentary ones. The intuition is simple: corruption and rent seeking are easier in presidential regimes. In addition, this article also shows a (less robust) effect of the electoral system: a resource curse is more likely to appear with proportional electoral rules than with majoritarian ones. The level of institutional quality (broadly speaking, the policy outcomes determined by constitutional variables) also explains the differences in the relationship between natural resources and economic development. For example, Mehlum et al. (2006) show that resource-rich economies with good institutions benefit from their resources, while resource-rich economies with poor institutions experience a curse. Likewise, the existence (or the intensity) of a resource curse may be conditional to ethnic fractionalization, which increases the probability of conflict or rent seeking (Hodler 2006), human capital (Bravo-Ortega and De Gregorio 2005; Kurtz and Brooks 2011), trade openness (Arezki and van der Ploeg 2007), or financial development. More generally, Konte (2013) shows that the relationship between natural resources and economic development in an economy depends on the regime of growth to which it belongs, itself determined by the level of democracy. Along the same lines, Clootens and Kirat (2020) use threshold regressions to highlight the conditionality of the resource curse to the level of economic development. They show that natural resources significantly affect the growth of low-income countries and have no effect on the development of high-income economies. Resource abundance appears as a blessing while resource dependence appears as a curse in low-income countries. These suggest that low-income economies share common characteristics (low level of human capital, underdeveloped financial markets, poor institutional quality...) that explain how natural resources affect growth. The fact that resource abundance is a blessing and resource dependence a curse also calls for diversification policies in resource-rich low-income economies. They confirm previous findings given in Clootens and Kirat (2017) and Ben Mim and Ben Ali (2020).

The existence of a resource curse in itself is very debated in the literature. While it is not possible to infer a law-like statement that natural resources are a curse or a blessing, it is likely that the effects that natural resources have on economic development are conditional. Still, it is important to understand precisely how a wealth—natural resources—may hamper growth. This is the aim of the next section.

8.3 The Resource Curse Transmission Channels

As discussed in the previous section, the resource curse should not be seen as an universal law. Rather, it is a phenomenon that may appear when certain conditions are met. It is therefore important to understand how natural resources may restrain economic development. The literature has identified several transmissions channels which can be classified as political or economical.

8.3.1 Economic Transmission Channels

Talking about the resource curse, one often thinks of the *Dutch disease*, which actually refers to one of the many curse's transmission channels. This is a phenomenon that harmed the Dutch economy in the 1960s, when large gas fields were discovered. Following the discovery and exploitation of the deposits, the Netherlands experienced a significant currency inflow which in turn provoked an overvaluation of the local currency. This appreciation of the local currency then caused a fall in the non-resource sectors' competitiveness. Since positive externalities and increasing returns to scale are more likely to appear in the secondary and tertiary sectors than in the primary one, the currency appreciation has finally harmed the engine of growth, dampening the Dutch economy. This channel of transmission has been largely studied in the literature (see, e.g., Corden 1984; Krugman 1987; Bruno and Sachs 1982; Torvik 2001; Matsen and Torvik 2005).

Natural resources are also suspected to crowd out human capital investment, because they increase the agents' opportunity to invest in education (Sachs and Warner 1999b). As Gylfason (2001) stated: *"nations that are confident that their natural resources are their most important asset may inadvertently – and perhaps even deliberately! – neglect the development of their human resources, by devoting inadequate attention and expenditure to education. Their natural wealth may blind them to the need for educating their children."* This author indeed documents a negative association between the dependence to natural resources and several educational variables (public expenditures on education, expected years of schooling for women, gross secondary school enrollment). The existence of this channel is highly debated. For example, Stijns (2006) finds opposite results using resource abundance indicators.

Natural resources are also prone to shift investment from the engines of growth, *i.e.,* the secondary and tertiary sectors, to the primary industry which is less prone to yield gains of productivity (Sachs and Warner 1995).

Alongside with the previous mechanisms, it can be noted that (point-source) natural resources extraction industries are largely enclave industries with little positive spillover to the overall economy (Davis and Tilton 2005; Humphreys et al. 2007). Certainly, some countries grant extraction rights conditional on important investment in the local economy by the extraction company, but this is far from being the rule for all countries.

The last important economic channel relates to prices volatility. Government revenues in resource-rich economies often come from the extractive industry. Unfortunately, resource prices are very volatile, making the rent management very difficult. This tends also to generate macroeconomic volatility and hence discourages investment (van der Ploeg and Poelhekke 2009, 2010; Daniel 1992).

8.3.2 Political Transmission Channels

Besides the economic transmissions channels, the literature has also identified several political channels of transmission. Firstly, natural resources generate rents, which are often misused. Providing revenues to government, resources rents can allow policy makers to postpone, or even avoid, necessary (but unpopular!) structural reforms (tax collection for example). In the same spirit, they could be spent on unproductive social spending (Bomsel 1992). One famous example is the Pacific island of Nauru, which has known economic prosperity during few decades thanks to phosphate exploitation but failed to perpetuate this prosperity once phosphate exploitation ended. In that spirit, Ross (1999) argues that resources revenues of the government can ease resource-exporting economies' budget constraint, *"producing fiscal laxity and a tendency to over-borrow."* This is confirmed by Manzano and Rigobon (2001) who note that mineral abundance, which could be used as a collateral, is often associated with debt overhang.

Secondly, mineral resources are associated with weak institutions. Resource revenues may indeed be used to appease dissents, punish opposition, and avoid accountability pressure (Jensen and Wantchekon 2004; Karl 1999; Ross 2001). Corruption and rent seeking are phenomena that appear and develop with poor institutions (Ben Ali and Krammer 2016). The rent seeking, also called the *"political Dutch disease"* by Lam and Wantchekon (2003), is often present in resource-rich economies, where political interest groups ask for transfers that are not equated with economic or social contribution. Thus, a large share of the resource revenues is devoted to unproductive welfare expenditures that benefit a few individuals close to power and is not invested in pro-development projects, such as infrastructure, health, or education (Apergis and Ben Ali 2020). In addition, some entrepreneurs or workers that engage in rent seeking are less engaged in wealth creation (Deacon and Rode 2015). Another different (but very similar) major issue in resource-rich economies is corruption. In these countries, politicians are often suspected of accepting kickbacks from third persons or groups who attempt to gain or retain access to the rents. Using a panel of 31 oil-exporting countries, Arezki and Brückner (2011) demonstrate that an increase in the oil rent is associated with more corruption. This effect is reinforced when state participation in the oil sector is high.

Last, natural resources can generate conflicts (Collier and Hoeffler 2005). Of course, conflicts are multidimensional phenomena and natural resources can be one of the many sources of conflicts that can arise for greed or grievance motives (Collier and Hoeffler 2004). The greed theory asserts that rebels enter into armed conflict in order to gain or secure access to the resource rents. The value of the state (as a prize) increases with the presence of minerals, which is likely to induce conflicts. Soysa (2002) supports that view. On the contrary, the grievance theory asserts that social justice is the main source of conflicts (Cederman et al. 2011; Wimmer et al. 2009). According to this theory, rebels are motivated by rising inequalities caused by rent seeking and mismanagement of resource revenues. The probability of conflict is reinforced by ethnic fractionalization (Hodler 2006). In addition, natural resources provide revenues to belligerent and thus cause longer conflicts (Buhaug et al. 2009; Lujala 2010; Conrad et al. 2019).

8.4 Natural Resources and Economic Development in MENAs

The resource curse is a complex phenomenon, caused by various mechanisms. The present section discusses specifically the case of MENA countries. Are they prone to be cursed by their natural resources endowments? On the contrary, are natural resources a blessing for MENAs? These questions are of major importance given the importance of resource endowments in the MENA region which possesses, *e.g.*, approximately half of the world's oil reserves. This section first reviews the literature on natural resources in MENAs and then proposes an analysis based on comparative statistics.

8.4.1 Natural Resources in MENAs: The Existing Literature

The MENA countries are countries whose economic growth is mainly driven from physical capital rather from technology or productivity (Acikgoz and Ben Ali 2019; Acikgoz et al. 2016) deriving from the natural resources they own. Despite the obvious importance of these natural resources in many MENA countries and the vast literature linking natural resources and development, few articles have investigated the effects that natural resources have on economic development in MENAs. Ross et al. (2011) studies the linkages between natural resources rents and political economy trajectories in MENAs. They point out that natural resources have, on average, provided stability and limited the occurrence of violent conflicts, in accordance with the *rentier state* hypothesis. However, they also argues that policy choices that have emerged from those development models are becoming increasingly fragile, giving rise to a risk of instability in the region.

Nabli and Arezki (2012) study the economic performances of MENAs over the 1970–2008 period. They note that the region has achieved a high level of per capita income, but relatively slow and especially non-inclusive growth, which seems to generate social instability. The region has also been marked by high macroeconomic volatility, largely explained by its dependence on natural resources whose prices are very volatile. They note that the provision of goods and services such as health and education has increased but is still not sufficient. Finally, consistently with Ross et al. (2011), they argue that the economic success of MENA countries will largely depend on their ability to build strong and effective institutions. Apergis and Payne (2014) also confirm that view highlighting that better institutional quality allows to reduce the detrimental effect that oil reserves may have on economic performances. As documented in the literature, corruption is obviously linked to bad economic development indicators (Swaleheen et al. 2019; Saha and Ben Ali 2017; Ben Ali and Saha 2016). In this spirit, Al-Rawashdeh et al. (2013) argue that oil and gas exports dependence is negatively associated with economic development and explain this outcome by lack of democracy, corruption, military spending, and foreign funds outflows. Their main findings have been recently documented by Apergis and Ben Ali (2020) and Ben Mim and Ben Ali (2020) for the GCC countries as MENA region countries. In a similar setting, Bjorvatn et al. (2012) argue that the impact of resource wealth on growth is dependent on political fragmentation. Resource wealth is growth generating in the presence of a strong government, and it is growth depressing when the government is weak. Their results appear quite independent of the level of institutional quality.

Nabli and Arezki (2012) also point out that while the level of per capita income in the MENAs is relatively high and (slowly) increasing, the MENA region has experienced a decline in wealth between 1975 and 2005, due to a resource depletion that is not compensated by savings. It means that the MENA region does not meet the Hartwick's rule, which casts doubt on the sustainability of the development model. Majbouri (2015) estimates that, over a 40-year period, the oil producers in the MENA could have achieved a 17% higher income if they had used their natural resource revenues efficiently.

Bjorvatn et al. (2012) investigate the links between demographic transition, resource wealth, and growth. The question is of major interest for numerous MENA economies that have known a strong increase in their working-age populations. They show that resources rents determine the growth effects of demographic transitions, whatever the quality of institutions. Ben Ali et al. (2016) document the existence of a human capital curse in MENA countries. They show that health and primary educations spending are far below international level because resource rents generate bad incentives for policy makers. This could reveal problematic due to the demographic transition underway.

Matallah (2020) documents, on the contrary, that oil rents are very beneficial for the growth of oil exporters in the MENA region. However, he also points out that oil rents hamper economic diversification, which will be an important determinant of future growth. His results also tend to show that improving the quality of governance in the MENAs can change the association between oil rents and economic diversification. Again, the importance of institutions is also underlined, as economic diversification is highly influenced by several governance indicators.[1] He concludes that *"the enhancement of MENA oil-exporters' good governance capabilities is the way out of the resource curse because it is the only mediator that can reconcile the twin goals of diversifying economic activity and yielding benefits from oil endowment, hence turning oil wealth into a boon."*

8.4.2   Are MENAs Cursed by Their Natural Resources? Non-inclusiveness of Growth and Institutional Weaknesses

The MENA region is known for its large deposits of oil and gas. As previously stated, half of the worldwide oil reserves and one-third of the worldwide gas reserves are located in the MENAs. However, such an observation masks major disparities across MENA countries. Table 8.2 lists the MENA countries, their GDP per capita, and several measures of resource abundance and dependence. The list of MENAs was established according to the World Bank list. From this table, it appears that resources are unequally distributed among the countries in the region. We can classify MENA countries as resource-rich or resource-poor. We define that a country is resource-rich if its total wealth is made up of at least 25% of subsoil assets. For countries for which we have missing data, we rely on the classification done in Ross (2011).[2]

In the present section, we propose some descriptive statistics to analyze if MENA countries are affected or not by a resource curse. More specifically, we here focus on the link between resource wealth and the inclusiveness of growth in MENAs. We also propose to compare MENAs' institutional quality, conditionally to their resource wealth.

Table 8.3 shows the income per capita of MENA countries, their HDI, and their ranking in both criteria. It appears that resource-rich countries seem characterized by larger income per capita. However, their HDI is lowest than expected. Indeed, numerous resource-rich countries have a HDI ranking worse than their ranking on income per capita.

Figure 8.2a shows the relationship between the rent per capita and the difference between income per capita and HDI ranks for the MENAs. It documents a strong negative (and significant) correlation. This evidence suggests that the additional income provided by natural resources does not translate into improvements in human development. It also suggests that the growth may be largely non-inclusive.

---

[1]The governance indicators are namely control of corruption, rule of law, political stability and voice and accountability (Worldwide Governance Indicators database). Ben Ali and Sassi (2016) discuss more details about corruption indicators.

[2]We could also check the value of other indicators, such as the rents or exports when available. In any case, our classification meets Ross (2011)'s one, excepted for Bahrain. Given small known reserves in 2014, Bahrain appears not resource-abundant in our study despite an economic development fueled by oil, and a high level of fuel exports. A great field discovery done in 2018 may impose to reconsider our ranking.

Table 8.2 Resource dependence and abundance indicators in MENAs

Country	Resource Rich	GDP/capita (US$)	Population (millions)	Resource rents/capita (US$)	Fuel Net exports/capita (US$)	Fuel exports (% of GDP)	Subsoil asset (% of total wealth)
Algeria	Yes	3946	40.6	486	656	17.6	–
Bahrain	No	22,619	1.4	730	2550	17.8	5
Djibouti	No	2802	0.9	19	–	–	0
Egypt	No	3525	94.4	108	−48	1.2	11.4
Iran	Yes	5253	79.6	708	615	11.8	–
Iraq	Yes	4777	36.6	1497	–	27.2	67.3
Israel	No	37,322	8.5	62	−586	0.3	–
Jordan	No	4104	9.6	49	−293	0	4.7
Kuwait	Yes	27,653	4	8890	10,806	39.2	52.4
Lebanon	No	7630	6.7	0	−598	0	0
Libya	Yes	4035	6.5	907	–	–	–
Malta	No	25,133	0.5	0	−1951	6.8	0
Morocco	No	2941	35.1	65	−153	0.2	5.8
Oman	Yes	14,619	4.5	2875	4586	34.4	32.1
Qatar	Yes	57,163	2.7	8776	19,705	34.7	41.3
Saudi Arabia	Yes	19,879	32.4	3982	4324	22	48.6
Syria	Yes	–	17.5	–	–	–	–
Tunisia	No	3698	11.3	85	−123	1.8	7.8
UAE	Yes	38,142	9.4	4328	10,741	29.1	34.7
West Bank and Gaza	No	3074	4.4	0	–	–	0
Yemen	Yes	1034	27.2	7	–	–	29.2
MENA	–	7265	433.6	927	1192	18	40.6

Sources GDP/Capita, Population, Resource Rents/Capita, Fuel Net Exports/Capita and Fuel Exports are computed for 2016 thanks to the World Development Indicator database. Subsoil Assets/Total Wealth comes from World Bank Wealth Accounts and is computed for 2014

To confirm that view, Fig. 8.2b–d represents the relationship between the rent per capita and the pre-tax national income shares (top 1%, top 10%, and bottom 50%).[3] They show a strong positive relationship between the rent per capita and the top 1 and 10 percent shares of pre-tax national income, and a strong negative association with the bottom 50% share of pre-tax national income. Indeed, a 100 US$ increase in resource rent per capita is associated with a 0.11 (0.25) percentage point increase

---

[3] Source: World Inequality Database.

Table 8.3 GNI and HDI ranks

Country	Resource rich	HDI (Rank)	GNI/Capita PPP$ (rank)	GNI Rank-HDI Rank	Rersource rents/capita
Algeria	Yes	0.759 (82)	13,639 (82)	0	486
Bahrain	No	0.838 (45)	40,399 (27)	−18	730
Djibouti	No	0.495 (171)	3601 (147)	−24	19
Egypt	No	0.700 (116)	10,744 (100)	−16	108
Iran	Yes	0.797 (65)	18,166 (63)	−2	708
Iraq	Yes	0.689 (120)	15,365 (76)	−44	1497
Israel	No	0.906 (22)	33,650 (35)	13	62
Jordan	No	0.723 (102)	8268 (112)	10	49
Kuwait	Yes	0.808 (57)	71,164 (5)	−52	8890
Lebanon	No	0.730 (93)	11,136 (98)	5	0
Libya	Yes	0.708 (110)	11,685 (94)	−16	907
Malta	No	0.885 (28)	34,795 (34)	6	0
Morocco	No	0.676 (121)	7480 (118)	−3	65
Oman	Yes	0.834 (47)	37,039 (29)	−18	2875
Qatar	Yes	0.848 (41)	110,489 (1)	−40	8776
Saudi Arabia	Yes	0.857 (36)	49,338 (14)	−22	3982
Syria	Yes	0.549 (154)	2725 (161)	7	.
Tunisia	No	0.739 (91)	10,677 (101)	10	85
UAE	Yes	0.866 (35)	66,912 (7)	−28	4328
West Bank and Gaza	No	0.690 (119)	5314 (134)	15	0
Yemen	Yes	0.463 (177)	1433 (180)	3	7

Sources Resource Rents/Capita is computed for 2016 thanks to the World Development Indicator database. GNI/Capita and HDI are 2018 values taken from UN statistics

in the share of income held by the top 1% (top 10%) and with a decrease of 0.11 percentage point in the share of income held by the bottom 50%. These results seem to confirm the non-inclusiveness of resource-led economic development in MENAs, a source of instability according to Nabli and Arezki (2012).[4]

These bad performances of resource-rich countries may be explained by institutional quality as bad institutions could negatively impact all economic development dimensions (Ben Ali and Krammer 2016). Table 8.4 presents the governance quality index from the Worldwide Governance Indicators database (Kaufmann et al. 2009). It appears that on average, resource-poor MENA countries always perform better

---

[4]It makes no doubts that the consideration of several additional explanatory variables will affect the value of estimated coefficients. More empirical research is needed on this point.

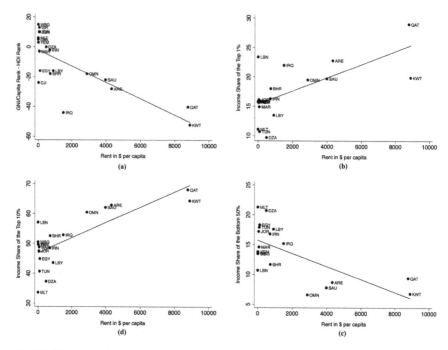

Fig. 8.2 The non-inclusiveness of economic development in MENAs

than resource-rich MENA economies. This may suggest that natural resource abundance generates bad institutional quality: more corruption, less accountability, more political instability, and so on. However, we find no evidence on a significant relationship between the size of the rent per capita and the governance indicators scores.[5] This last result may be explained, for example, by non-linearities in the relationship between wealth in natural resource and institutional quality. In any case, our results suggest a link and call for further studies on this point.

8.5   Conclusion and Policy Implications

In this chapter, we have discussed the resource curse hypothesis and its consistency for MENA countries. There exists a wide literature on the links between economic development and natural resources. As highlighted in the chapter, the literature is largely inconclusive since the results are affected by the choice of the proxy to measure resource wealth, the period of observation, or are conditional on

---

[5]We have only found a positive but low association between the size of the rent and the political stability indicator, consistently with Ross (2011).

Table 8.4 Governance indicators in MENAs

Country	Resource rich	Control of corruption	Regulatory quality	Rule of law	Government effectiveness	Political stability	Voice and accountability
Algeria	Yes	−0.678	−1.172	−0.857	−0.531	−1.098	−0.863
Bahrain	No	−0.016	0.608	0.456	0.328	−0.793	−1.372
Djibouti	No	−0.653	−0.7	−0.976	−0.974	−0.626	−1.373
Egypt	No	−0.645	−0.923	−0.517	−0.66	−1.438	−1.207
Iran	Yes	−1.387	−1.125	−1.626	−1.268	−2.314	−1.017
Iraq	Yes	−0.711	−1.229	−0.679	−0.191	−0.813	−1.343
Israel	No	1.187	1.313	1.072	1.345	−0.795	0.787
Jordan	No	0.265	0.052	0.304	0.134	−0.492	−0.713
Kuwait	Yes	−0.268	−0.074	0.028	−0.164	−0.05	−0.629
Lebanon	No	−0.965	−0.343	−0.83	−0.539	−1.619	−0.52
Libya	Yes	−1.627	−2.274	−1.817	−1.892	−2.283	−1.43
Malta	No	0.721	1.157	0.998	0.956	1.08	1.196
Morocco	No	−0.13	−0.235	−0.158	−0.106	−0.313	−0.626
Oman	Yes	0.339	0.61	0.408	0.192	0.76	−1.054
Qatar	Yes	0.901	0.696	0.794	0.736	0.9	−1.152
Saudi Arabia	Yes	0.231	0.079	0.338	0.261	−0.465	−1.729
Syria	Yes	−1.572	−1.666	−1.991	−1.819	−2.916	−1.987
Tunisia	No	−0.135	−0.47	−0.003	−0.229	−1.141	0.303
UAE	Yes	1.172	0.973	0.849	1.416	0.565	−1.05
West Bank and Gaza	No	−0.149	0.065	−0.344	−0.635	−1.976	−1.095
Yemen, rep.	Yes	−1.664	−1.48	−1.645	−1.825	−2.795	−1.692
MENA resource-rich	–	−0.866	−0.959	−0.987	−0.764	−1.55	−1.27
MENA resource-poor	–	−0.357	−0.523	−0.285	−0.36	−1.11	−0.831

Sources Worldwide Governance Indicators, 2016. Resource-rich and resource-poor averages are weighted by the size of the population. We obtain nearly the same outcome with unweighted averages, in the sense that MENA resource-poor countries always perform better than MENA resource-rich economies

other explanatory variables. Several potential transmissions channels are nevertheless identified in the literature and have been presented. Although the literature on the resource curse is very abundant, there are few articles dealing with the relationship between abundance of resources and economic performance for the specific case of MENAs. This is somewhat surprising since these countries own very large oil and gas deposits. As a whole, the literature tends to indicate the possibility of a resource curse in MENAs, and generally suggests that the existence, or intensity, of the resource curse can be conditional on the institutional quality.

We here provide evidence that economic development in the resource-rich MENAs has not translated into human progress, and has been largely non-inclusive. In addition, the data suggest that this failure of human and inclusive development can be explained by governance weaknesses. Of course, our results need to be confirmed by more detailed studies and call for further research. The evidence given in this chapter is nevertheless consistent with the conclusion in Ross (2011) that the development models followed by MENA resource-rich economies are becoming fragile. In addition, the descriptive statistics given in this chapter confirms findings in the literature (Ross 2011; Nabli and Arezki 2012) that economic success of MENA countries will depend on their ability to build strong and efficient institutions. Indeed, such institutions diminish the likelihood of rent seeking, corruption, and instability. On the contrary, they increase the likelihood that resource rents will be used more equitably, giving, *e.g.*, more opportunities to poor households to invest in their human capital. These results echo the one given in Ben Ali et al. (2016) who document a human capital curse in MENA countries.

References

Acikgoz S, Ben Ali MS (2019) Where does economic growth in the Middle Eastern and North African countries come from? Q Rev Econ Financ 73:172–183

Acikgoz S, Ben Ali MS, Mert M (2016) Sources of economic growth in MENA countries: technological progress, physical or human capital accumulations? In: Ben Ali MS (ed) Economic development in the Middle East and North Africa, Palgrave Macmillan, New York

Al-Rawashdeh R, Al-Nawafleh H, Al-Shboul M (2013) Understanding oil and mineral resources in a political economy context: the case of the middle east and north Africa (MENA). Mineral Econ 26(1–2):13–28

Andersen JJ, Aslaksen S (2008) Constitutions and the resource curse. J Dev Econ 87(2):227–246

Apergis N, Ben Ali MS (2020) Corruption, rentier states and economic growth: where do the GCC countries stand? In: Miniaoui H (ed) Economic development in the gulf cooperation council countries: from rentier states to diversified economies. Springer Nature, Singapore

Apergis N, Payne JE (2014) The oil curse, institutional quality, and growth in MENA countries: evidence from time-varying cointegration. Energy Econ 46:1–9

Arezki R, Brückner M (2011) Oil rents, corruption, and state stability: evidence from panel data regressions. Eur Econ Rev 55(7):955–963

Arezki R, van der Ploeg F (2007) Can the natural resource curse be turned into a blessing? the role of trade policies and institutions. IMF Working Paper WP/07/55

Auty R (1993) Sustaining development in mineral economies: the resource curse thesis. Routledge

Ben Ali MS, Cockx L, Francken N (2016) The Middle East and North Africa: cursed by natural resources? In: Ben Ali MS (ed) Economic development in the Middle East and North Africa, Palgrave Macmillan, New York

Ben Ali MS, Krammer MS (2016) The role of institutions in economic development. In: Ben Ali MS (ed) Economic development in the Middle East and North Africa, Palgrave Macmillan, New York

Ben Ali MS, Saha S (2016) Corruption and economic development. In: Ben Ali MS (ed) Economic development in the Middle East and North Africa, Palgrave Macmillan, New York

Ben Ali MS, Sassi S (2016) The corruption-inflation nexus: evidence from developed and developing countries. BE J Macroecon 16(1):125–144

Ben Mim S, Ben Ali MS (2020) Natural resources curse and economic diversification in GCC countries. In: Miniaoui H (ed) Economic development in the Gulf Cooperation Council Countries: from rentier states to diversified economies. Springer Nature, Singapore

Berman N, Couttenier M, Rohner D, Thoenig M (2017) This mine is mine! how minerals fuel conflicts in Africa. Am Econ Rev 107(6):1564–1610

Bjorvatn K, Farzanegan MR, Schneider F (2012) Resource curse and power balance: evidence from oil-rich countries. World Dev 40(7):1308–1316

Bomsel O (1992) The political economy of rent in mining countries. In: Tilton JE (ed) Mineral wealth and economic development. Resources For the Future, Washington, D.C., pp 59–79

Bravo-Ortega C, De Gregorio J (2005) The relative richness of the poor? natural resources, human capital, and economic growth. World Bank Policy research working paper 3483

Brunnschweiler CN, Bulte EH (2008) The resource curse revisited and revised: a tale of paradoxes and red herrings. J Environ Econ Manag 55(3):248–264

Bruno M, Sachs J (1982) Energy and resource allocation: a dynamic model of the "Dutch disease". Rev Econ Stud 49(5):845–859

Buhaug H, Gates S, Lujala P (2009) Geography, rebel capability, and the duration of civil conflict. J Conflict Resolut 53(4):544–569

Cederman L-E, Weidmann NB, Gleditsch KS (2011) Horizontal inequalities and ethnonationalist civil war: a global comparison. Am Polit Sci Rev 105(3):478–495

Clootens N, Kirat D (2017) A reappraisal of the resource curse. Econ Bull 37(1):12–18

Clootens N, Kirat D (2020) Threshold regressions for the resource curse. Environ Dev Econ. https:// doi.org/10.1017/S1355770X20000297

Collier P, Hoeffler A (2004) Greed and grievance in civil war. Oxford Econ Pap 56(4):563–595

Collier P, Hoeffler A (2005) Resource rents, governance, and conflict. J Conflict Resolut 49(4):625–633

Conrad JM, Greene KT, Walsh JI, Whitaker BE (2019) Rebel natural resource exploitation and conflict duration. J Conflict Resolut 63(3):591–616

Corden WM (1984) Booming sector and Dutch disease economics: survey and consolidation. Oxford Econ Pap 36(3):359–380

Corden WM, Neary JP (1982) Booming sector and de-industrialization in a small open economy. Econ J 92(368):825–848

Daniel P (1992) Economic policy in mineral-exporting countries: what have we learned? In: Tilton JE (ed) Mineral wealth and economic development. Resources For the Future, Washington, D.C., pp 81–121

Davis GA (2013) Replicating Sachs and Warner's working papers on the resource curse. J Dev Stud 49(12):1615–1630

Davis GA, Tilton JE (2005) The resource curse. Natural Res Forum 29(3):233–242

Deacon RT, Rode A (2015) Rent seeking and the resource curse. In: Congleton RD, Hillman AL (eds) Companion to the political economy of rent seeking. Edward Elgar Publishing, Cheltenham, UK, pp 227–247

Gylfason T (2001) Natural resources, education, and economic development. Eur Econ Rev 45(4):847–859

Gylfason T, Zoega G (2006) Natural resources and economic growth: the role of investment. World Econ 29(8):1091–1115

Hodler R (2006) The curse of natural resources in fractionalized countries. Eur Econ Rev 50(6):1367–1386

Humphreys M, Sachs J, Stiglitz JE (2007) Escaping the resource curse. Columbia University Press, New York

Isham J, Woolcock M, Pritchett L, Busby G (2005) The varieties of resource experience: natural resource export structures and the political economy of economic growth. World Bank Econ Rev 19(2):141–174

James A (2015) The resource curse: a statistical mirage? J Dev Econ 114:55–63

Jensen N, Wantchekon L (2004) Resource wealth and political regimes in Africa. Comp Polit Stud 37(7):816–841

Karl TL (1999) The perils of the petro-state: reflections on the paradox of plenty. J Int Aff 53(1):31–48

Kaufmann D, Kraay A, Mastruzzi M (2009) Governance matters VIII: aggregate and individual governance indicators, 1996–2008. World Bank Policy research working paper 4978

Konte M (2013) A curse or a blessing? natural resources in a multiple growth regimes analysis. Appl Econ 45(26):3760–3769

Kronenberg T (2004) The curse of natural resources in the transition economies. Econ Transit 12(3):399–426

Krugman P (1987) The narrow moving band, the Dutch disease, and the competitive consequences of Mrs. Thatcher: notes on trade in the presence of dynamic scale economies. J Dev Econ 27(1):41–55

Kurtz MJ, Brooks SM (2011) Conditioning the "resource curse": globalization, human capital, and growth in oil-rich nations. Comp Polit Stud 44(6):747–770

Lam R, Wantchekon L, (2003) Political Dutch disease. Department of Politics, New York University Working Paper

Lange G-M, Wodon Q, Carey K (2018) The changing wealth of nations 2018: building a sustainable future. The World Bank, Washington, DC

Lederman D, Maloney WF (2006) Natural resources, neither curse nor destiny. The World Bank, Washington, D.C

Lederman D, Maloney WF (2008) In search of the missing resource curse. World Bank Policy Research Working Paper 4766

Leite MC, Weidmann J (1999) Does mother nature corrupt: natural resources, corruption, and economic growth. IMF working paper WP/99/85

Lujala P (2010) The spoils of nature: armed civil conflict and rebel access to natural resources. J Peace Res 47(1):15–28

Majbouri M (2015) Calculating the income counterfactual for oil producing countries of the MENA region. Res Policy 44:47–56

Manzano O, Rigobon R (2001) Resource curse or debt overhang? NBER working paper no. 8390

Matallah S (2020) Economic diversification in mena oil exporters: understanding the role of governance. Res Policy 66:101602

Matsen E, Torvik R (2005) Optimal Dutch disease. J Dev Econ 78(2):494–515

Mehlum H, Moene K, Torvik R (2006) Institutions and the resource curse. Econ J 116(508):1–20

Nabli MMK, Arezki MR (2012) Natural resources, volatility, and inclusive growth: perspectives from the Middle East and North Africa. IMF working paper WP/12/111

Ross ML, Kaiser K, Mazaheri N (2011) The "resource curse" in MENA? Political transitions, resource wealth, economic shocks, and conflict risk. World Bank Policy Research working paper 5742

Ross ML (1999) The political economy of the resource curse. World Polit 51(02):297–322

Ross ML (2001) Does oil hinder democracy? World politics, pps 325–361

Sachs JD, Warner AM (1995). Natural resource abundance and economic growth. NBER working paper No. 5398

Sachs JD, Warner A (1999a) Natural resource intensity and economic growth. In: Mayer J, Chambers B, Farooq A (eds) Development policies in natural resource economies. Edward Elgar Publishing, Cheltenham, UK, pp 13–38

Sachs JD, Warner AM (1999b) The big push, natural resource booms and growth. J Dev Econ 59(1):43–76

Sachs JD, Warner AM (2001) The curse of natural resources. Eur Econ Rev 45(4):827–838

Saha S, Ben Ali MS (2017) Corruption and economic development: new evidence from the Middle Eastern and North African countries. Econ Anal Policy 54:83–95

Soysa ID (2002) Paradise is a bazaar? greed, creed, and governance in civil war, 1989-99. J Peace Res 39(4):395–416

Stijns J-P (2006) Natural resource abundance and human capital accumulation. World Dev 34(6):1060–1083

Swaleheen M, Ben Ali MS, Temimi A (2019) Corruption and public spending on education and Health. Appl Econ Lett 26(4):321–325

Torvik R (2001) Learning by doing and the Dutch disease. Eur Econ Rev 45(2):285–306

van der Ploeg F (2011) Natural resources: curse or blessing?. J Econ Lit 49(2):366–420

van der Ploeg F, Poelhekke S (2009) Volatility and the natural resource curse. Oxford Econ Pap 61(4):727–760

van der Ploeg F, Poelhekke S (2010) The pungent smell of "red herrings": subsoil assets, rents, volatility and the resource curse. J Environ Econ Manag 60(1):44–55

Wimmer A, Cederman L-E, Min B (2009) Ethnic politics and armed conflict: a configurational analysis of a new global data set. Am Sociol Rev 74(2):316–337

Chapter 9
Toward a Circular Economy in the MENA Region: Insights from the Water-Food Nexus

Mohammad Al-Saidi and Sudeh Dehnavi

Abstract The water-food nexus in the Middle East and Northern African (MENA) region is characterized by resource depletion, import dependence and environmental degradation. This contribution proposes that consumption awareness and resource circularity can be seen as a pathway to alleviate environmental problems and achieve long-term supply security in the water and food sectors. The chapter introduces wastewater recycling as a salient and highly relevant development in the MENA region. Current directions in using treated wastewater are analyzed. Furthermore, forerunner countries from different MENA sub-regions are briefly introduced with the focus on the particular characteristics and policy challenges in each of presented cases of wastewater reuse. Furthermore, crosscutting issues are presented. These include the need for addressing the large consumption footprints in MENA countries, the existence of distorting subsidies for agricultural water, the lack of communities' participation, the inadequacy of existing strategies and the suboptimal coordination mechanisms between water and food sectors. We suggest at the end of the paper some recommendations to policy makers in the region.

Keywords Water-food nexus · Circular economy · Wastewater reuse · Water recycling · Jordan · Gulf council countries (GCC) · Tunisia

9.1 Introduction

The Middle East and Northern African (MENA) region is mostly arid with limited availability of resources such as water and arable land. Water scarcity is constraining local food production in almost all countries, thus leading to an overuse of vulnerable

M. Al-Saidi (✉)
Center for Sustainable Development, College of Arts and Sciences, Qatar University, Doha, Qatar
e-mail: malsaidi@qu.edu.qa

S. Dehnavi
Institute for Technology and Resources Management the Tropics and Subtropics,
TH-Köln—University of Applied Sciences, Cologne, Germany
e-mail: sudeh.dehnavi@th-koeln.de

© The Author(s), under exclusive license to Springer Nature Switzerland AG 2021   139
M. S. Ben Ali (ed.), *Economic Development in the MENA Region*, Perspectives
on Development in the Middle East and North Africa (MENA) Region,
https://doi.org/10.1007/978-3-030-66380-3_9

water resources. MENA countries, particularly Arab countries in the Gulf, have been blessed with abundant carbon resources, that are being used to compensate for water scarcity (e.g., through desalination) and to import food (Al-Saidi et al. 2016; Woertz 2013). However, fossil fuels haven not always been positive for economic growth as they can be associated with lavish subsidies (e.g., energy subsidies in different forms), lack of economic diversifications, inefficiencies in resource use and economic underperformance in general (resource curse) (Ben Ali et al. 2016; Apergis and Ben Ali 2020; Ben Mim and Ben Ali 2020; Tsai 2018). Even in countries where water availability is relatively high, pressures on water and land resources are increasing due to the rapid growth of economies and populations, but also due to other combined factors such as mismanagement, resource overuse and conflicts (Al-Saidi 2020a).

Supplying the growing, and increasingly urban, populations of sufficient amounts of food in a decent quality and without causing a deterioration of water resources availability and quality is an important challenge. The issue is of particular importance given the nature of the economic growth trend in the region which has been intensive on physical capital (and less based on technology or human capital), thus leading to environmental exhaustion and resource depletion (Acikgoz and Ben Ali 2019; Acikgoz et al. 2016). In order to meet the challenge of basic supply security, alternative water resources are needed. The ideas of recycling water (e.g., reuse of wastewater or gray water) and using water of marginal quality (e.g., brackish water in lagoons) are promising ones. Water recycling or reuse can alleviate the pressures on freshwater resources (e.g., the depleted groundwater resources or the polluted rivers) or provide additional water for local food production. However, these ideas of closing loops in the use of vital resources can be expanded into broader strategies that center on restructuring both consumption and production patterns toward a low-metabolism and low-carbon development. Circular economy is such a sustainability strategy that seeks to enhance the circulation of products and consumers' awareness. The basic idea is to "close the loops" through business models fostering reuse and recycling. It can be quite relevant for arid regions and is generally heralded as a way to save resources and create growth (Geissdoerfer et al. 2018; Kalmykova et al. 2018; Korhonen et al. 2018; Stahel 2016).

The circular economy idea has been promoted through ambitious national and sectoral policies around the world, most prominently in China and the EU (McDowall et al. 2017). There are few applications of this idea for basic supply sectors although these sectors are arguably highly relevant in developing countries (Al-Saidi et al. 2020; Voulvoulis 2018). In fact, the broad agenda of the circular economy allows for various applications in basic supply sectors such as the water and food sectors. Al-Saidi et al. (2020) conceptualized the viable industrial applications of the circular economy in the water and food sectors though defining several circular strategies for basic supply, e.g., extraction/manufacturing/distribution efficiency and recovery, responsible/circular consumption or waste management and utilization. There is an extensive list of examples for circular economy applications in the water and food sectors depending on the value chain step and the circular economy loop. For example, the circular economy implies the use of more sustainable inputs for water and food productions such as renewable energies, bio-fertilizers, water of lesser quality or alternative feed for fish and livestock. Furthermore, it entails better ways of production including more energy- and water-saving technologies. Awareness-raising, retrieval of materials from waste and arrangements for donation and co-consumption (e.g., food sharing) are equally important. In fact, as to be explained in the following section, the circular economy idea is highly relevant for the water and food sectors due to the importance of these sectors, the increasing integration among them and the expected supply shortages in arid and rapidly growing regions.

This chapter aims at analyzing the circular economy idea in the practice of the water and food sectors in the MENA region. In particular, it focuses on water recycling for agricultural use as a prominent circular economy direction/loop in the MENA region. In this sense, the chapter analyzes how the circular economy can contribute to decouple local food production from the unsustainable water use in the Arab region. Such an analysis is timely considering the need to alleviate pressures on the increasingly vulnerable water and land resources in the MENA region. The chapter maps the wastewater reuse option in the region by embedding it within the circular economy concept, highlighting implementation models, challenges and pioneering countries as well as discussing missing links. It introduces the concept of circular economy as a practical sustainability paradigm in alignment with other sustainability ideas of low-metabolism or de-growth. Furthermore, the chapter discusses challenges and compares trends of treated wastewater reuse in some forerunner countries in the MENA region, namely Jordan, Tunisia and the Gulf states.

9.2 Resource Circularity and Waste Utilization in the Circular Economy-Economic Development Nexus

The circular economy concept is often embedded within broader strategies for sustainable economic growth or sustainable development. Rapid economic growth is associated with considerably wasteful practices, while it should not be an ulti-mate goal by itself (D'Alisa et al. 2015). It is important to consider the overall metabolism or physical throughput in an economy. At its core, the circular economy is geared toward industrial growth in way that incorporate resource circularity and waste utilization. It focuses on the transformation of businesses and industries by combining the economic and environmental pillars of sustainable development, e.g., redesigning processes, products and the handling of materials (Murray et al. 2017). In this sense, it is less focused on social aspects of sustainability and more geared toward business models and industrial applications. However, the framings of circular economy have varied depending on the country and the author's perspective. For example, China's circular economy strategies incorporate broader issues of environ-mental protection (e.g., pollution) or land-use planning (McDowall et al. 2017). One of the broader understandings of the circular economy is provided by Kirchherr et al. (2017) who reviewed several definitions of the concept. Accordingly, a comprehen-sive understanding of the circular economy needs to have a multi-systems perspective, i.e., a macro-perspective of the national level, a meso-perspective of the industry and a micro-perspective of the firm or consumer. It should also refer to sustainable development and its goals, e.g., environment protection, economic improvements, social equity and the rights of future generations. Furthermore, it also needs to include at least four of the famous R principles (i.e., reduce, reuse, recycle and recover) and prioritize them (i.e., first reduce, then reuse, then recycle and ultimately recover) (Kirchherr et al. 2017). In this sense, the circular economy can be seen as a means for sustainable (economic) development in general. This is similar to other concepts such as green economy, while the focus of the circular economy is on the contribution of waste utilization and recycling, in comparison with the green economy's focus on eco-innovations and green jobs (e.g., in renewable energies, or environmental technologies) (Engelmann and Al-Saidi 2019).

The circular economy idea has been around for a while now (since the early 1990s) and has found much attention in industrial ecology and economics literature. It is one of several concepts such as sustainable production or de-growth that represent popular banners for ideas stressing the need to change current unsustainable consumption and production patterns. In this context, concepts such as de-growth propose re-conceptualizing desirable growth through restructuring industries, reducing waste, recycling products and re-localizing consumption (Latouche 2009). In this sense, de-growth have lots in common with the idea of the circular economy as they both stress the circulation and the optimization of material flows (Schröder et al. 2019). In fact, there are many principles in the circular economy literature that seek to reduce waste and inefficiencies across the value chain steps (i.e., design, manufacturing, distribution, consumption and disposal) and to "close the loops" among these steps (Kalmykova et al. 2018; Pishchulov et al. 2018). Ultimately, the circular economy is characterized by low-metabolism, extensive systems for the reuse of (scarce) resources and sustainable business models (Geissdoerfer et al. 2018; Korhonen et al. 2018). It builds on other concepts of industrial ecology such as the steady-state economy (an economy with relatively stable size and consumption rates per capita) or the cradle-to-cradle product design (entirely recyclable or biodegradable products) (Kalmykova et al. 2018). The circular economy also implies considering the different economic functions of the environment and internalizing unpriced or underpriced commodities (Andersen 2007). Circular economy policies have been widely popular for designing industrial policies in China and some European countries through the provision of incentives and support to the manufacturing industry in order to enhance environmental considerations in product design and production as well as in waste utilization (McDowall et al. 2017). The assumption from these circular economy policies is that they can lead to decoupling economic growth from resource consumption (Kjaer et al. 2019). In fact, by introducing the aspect of recycling, the circular economy model can contribute to the improvement of environmental quality during growth, something that has been difficult to achieve through economic growth alone as put forward by the Environmental Kuznets Curve (EKC) (George et al. 2015).

9.3   Scarcity and Integration in the MENA Region's Water-Food Nexus

The water and food supply sectors represent bottlenecks for achieving long-term growth and sustainable development in the MENA region. While this region is characterized by aridity and thus high scarcity of water and land resources, a large portion of populations still work in the agricultural sector. Growing economies and populations have meant that water consumption increased and scarcity conditions worsened. Nowadays, most Arab countries exhibit high to very high water stress conditions (freshwater withdrawals as a percentage of available renewable water resources) while the inter-annual variability of available water is quite high in international comparison (Borgomeo et al. 2020). This means that water scarcity and water-related risks such as droughts or floods are increasingly affecting livelihoods and economic outcomes in the region. Alongside physical water scarcity, the MENA region is suffering from scarcities of organizational capacity and accountability for managing water resources in a sustainable manner (World Bank 2007). Furthermore, the failure to reform the water and food sectors in the last decades has led to disastrous outcomes in many countries. For example, the lavish subsidies for agricultural development (e.g., cheap loans or diesel subsidies) together with the lack of adequate water pricing have caused water depletion and hindered any measures to encourage sustainable use (Al-Saidi and Dehnavi 2020). The lack of sustainability policies has resulted in the decline of productive ecosystems, livelihood losses, the increase of land and water problems as well as political and economic disintegration across the Arab region (Al-Saidi 2020a).

There is a wide range of solutions to the ongoing water crisis in the MENA region. Alongside broad remedy packages such as the introduction of context-specific and integrated water management policies (Al-Saidi 2017) or holistically tackling water (and land) issues (e.g., both quality and quantity aspects, demand and supply, as well as regional and international issues) (Borgomeo et al. 2020), there are some concrete measures. A classical measure with increasing utilization has been the reliance on virtual water imported through food products to compensate local water deficits and vulnerabilities (Al-Saidi et al. 2016; Antonelli and Sartori 2015). Virtual water imports have been essential for meeting the requirements of food supply for the large populations in the region, particularly for hyper-arid countries such as the Arab Gulf states. Figure 9.1 shows how water stress in many MENA countries goes along with a high rate for food import dependency. Food import dependency is particularly high (between 90 and 100%) in most of the Gulf countries, and in Yemen, where water stress is quite high. In some big agricultural countries in the region such as Egypt, Sudan or Syria, food imports are still relatively low despite growing scarcities. Despite virtual water imports acting as a compensation for water scarcity, it did not lead to conservation or economic use since many MENA countries still have important annual water use deficits, while the Gulf countries, for example, have already depleted a good portion of their groundwater resources for local food production (Zubari et al. 2017). Therefore, it is important to seek other measures

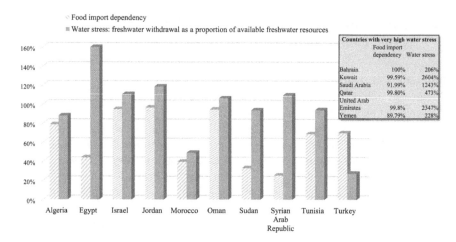

Fig. 9.1 Water scarcity and the need for food imports in some MENA countries. *Data sources* Food import dependency data for 2019 retried from (The Economist 2019). Water stress data for 2014 from (World Bank 2020)

such as the provision of additional (although more expensive) supplies (e.g., the use of desalinated water or water of marginal quality for food production), or the improvement of the use of current freshwater supplies through earlier-mentioned circular economy ideas.

Incorporating key strategies of the circular economy in the practice of the water and food sectors implies more integration and coordination between the two sectors, e.g., aligning water reuse strategies and infrastructure to the needs of the food sector or considering different water types for local food production. In fact, the basic supply sectors are already becoming highly integrated and interlinked. Water and food sectors have been an obvious tandem, while the requirements of better water use efficiency and productivity are even more important for food production in the case of aridity and water scarcity. So far, the water-food (and trade) nexus has been dominated by discourses such as virtual water calculations or the limits of local agricultural intensification, e.g. (Allan 2003; Ibarrola-Rivas et al. 2017). However, with the advancement of technologies of water treatment and reuse, the circulation of water in quasi-closed loops across the food supply chains (e.g., reuse of drainage water) and the diversion of domestic water for consequent uses in the agriculture sector (treated wastewater use for agriculture) have become more available and economic. In the next section, the directions and challenges of treated wastewater reuse in the MENA region are introduced and framed as a salient model for the implementation of the circular economy idea.

9.4 An Example of a Salient Model: Wastewater Recycling for Agricultural Use

9.4.1 Current Directions of Wastewater Reuse for Enhanced Food Security

The water use question in agriculture is highly relevant for achieving sustainability in both the water and food sectors. Naturally, water is needed for food production and it is the food sector that consumes most of water worldwide (a global average of around 70% of total annual freshwater withdrawals and up to 95% in some developing countries) (Seibert et al. 2013). In most dry countries in the MENA region, water use for agriculture is even higher than the global average, e.g., 85% of total water use in Arab countries (Al-Zubari 2017), or 88% Saudi Arabia although the added value of agriculture to the Saudi GDP is only around 2% (Al-Saidi and Saliba 2019). As mentioned earlier, MENA countries still largely depend on food imports for meeting local food demands and achieving food security. Here, the Gulf countries rank particularly high in the MENA region with regard to food security. This is due to their ability to provide accessible, good quality and affordable food thanks to the Gulf's large energy wealth. In fact, energy-abundant countries in the region (particularly the Gulf countries) seem to perform better with regard to food security (Fig. 9.2). However, this is not always the case, e.g., the relatively bad scoring for the energy exporting countries of Yemen and Sudan (both politically fragile) as well as Algeria. Israel also does not fit into this hypothesis since it is the second-highest food security score despite lacking energy-based wealth. However, Israel has invested

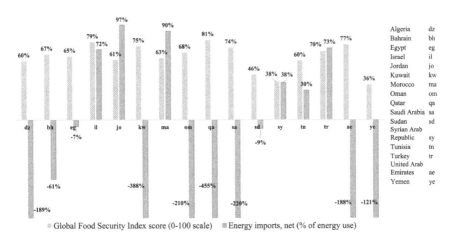

Fig. 9.2 Food security and energy abundancy in the MENA region. *Data sources* For the global food security index, 2019 data retrieved (The Economist 2019). Energy imports 2013 data from (World Bank 2020)

greatly in efficient water use in agriculture (e.g., drip irrigation) and also water reuse (Tal 2016).

While food security needs to be addressed through different measures (e.g., import policy, value chain optimization, nutrition aspects or quality and affordability strategies), circular economy can help enhancing food security in the MENA region through sustainably substituting some agricultural imports. For implementing the circular economy idea, there are several options for a better water circulation in agriculture. Some options include the treatment and use of water of marginal quality that is largely underutilized as brackish water, produced water from the hydrocarbon industry, or the combination of saline and freshwater agricultural systems (Brown et al. 2018). However, the most relevant options relate to enhancing the reuse of two types of water, namely agricultural drainage and wastewater. The recycling and reuse of agricultural drainage have been steadily increasing with Syria and Egypt leading in the Arab region in terms of drainage water volumes, e.g., around 9.3 billion cubic meters of agricultural drainage being reused in Egypt annually (AbuZeid 2020). Regarding wastewater reuse, this happens in different forms across the region. In many cases, wastewater is used without treatment, e.g., in highly arid regions or rural areas with no adequate water supply. For the treated wastewater, it is used either directly from the treatment plant (direct reuse) or indirectly through the discharge of treated water into surface water or groundwater (indirect reuse). Regarding the use purposes of treated/untreated wastewater, the water can be reused for landscaping, recreation, groundwater recharge or agriculture, the latter represents the focus of this chapter.

The use of treated wastewater is increasingly practiced across the MENA region although it is currently a small option, e.g., treated wastewater volumes accounting for only around 1% of the total water volumes used in Arab countries with the treatment rate of produced wastewater varying from very low in low-income MENA countries to almost 100% in the Arab Gulf countries (Al-Zubari 2017). At the same time, many countries are exploring the utilization of wastewater as a resource beyond the reuse of water. Wastewater has an economic value due to its by-products such as salt, nitrogen and phosphorus, and it can thus be used in the production of several goods such as fertilizers. In Arab countries, in 2013, 71% of wastewater was collected and 21% used (UNESCO WWAP 2017). The most common form of wastewater reuse is the indirect use through injection to surface water and groundwater as it is commonly practiced in the North Africa and the Mediterranean region (Ait-Mouheb et al. 2020). Jeuland (2015) examined the constraints to the expansion of wastewater reuse in the MENA region. The main constraints relate to the financial viability of treated wastewater and the low demand for this kind of water. In fact, a key challenge in the region is that the treated wastewater produced does not cover the treatment cost. If supplied to farmers at production costs, the price would be higher than freshwater (e.g., pumping surface water or groundwater) due to the lack of adequate pricing for agricultural water and the existence of significant energy subsidies across the MENA region (Ait-Mouheb et al. 2020; Al-Saidi and Dehnavi 2019, 2020; Jeuland 2015). There are many other challenges, which we discuss later in this chapter, e.g., the lack of systematic approaches and strategies, concerns about human health and pathogens and the lack of farmers' acceptance for using treated wastewater for edible agriculture.

9.4.2 State-of-Play and Challenges in Forerunner Countries

9.4.2.1 The Gulf Region

The water and food sectors, together with the energy sector, have been highly important for achieving a low-carbon and sustainable future in the countries of the Gulf Cooperation Council region (hereafter refers to as the Gulf region) (Al-Saidi and Elagib 2018; Al-Saidi and Saliba 2019). Since the Gulf countries are extremely arid, water is limited to groundwater aquifers in addition to wadis and streams mainly in Saudi Arabia and Oman. These limited freshwater resources have been the main source for agricultural water, while domestic water is almost entirely provided through desalination. Considering the mounting water scarcity problems due to groundwater depletion and large consumption rates per capita (Saif et al. 2014), the economic value of wastewater treatment and reuse is arguably quite high. Table 9.1 summarizes the Gulf experience in the use of treated wastewater, which is still an emerging water supply option. In 2010/12, only around 3% of water requirements of GCC countries were met by treated municipal wastewater (Al-Zubari 2017), with this number increasing steadily. However, much of treated wastewater is stored in lakes due to the lack of demand (Al-Saidi and Dehnavi 2020). Some of this water is also siphoned to the sea since only 39% of treated wastewater is used for purposes such as landscaping, forestry ornamental plants and grasses (Qureshi 2020). In fact, the combination of "hard" factors such as lack of transport infrastructure and "soft" factors in terms of unwillingness to adopt treated wastewater for agriculture or to reform the cheap water prices (see Table 9.1) has hindered this reuse option to reach its full economic potential. The utilization of wastewater as a resource is still "a lost opportunity" in the Gulf (Aleisa and Al-Zubari 2017), although some ambitious projects are underway to expand this option, e.g., for groundwater recharge or forage production. This is in addition to efforts focusing on the promotion of (combinations of) other types of marginal water, e.g., integrated seawater agriculture (saline groundwater or seawater with treated wastewater), produced water or saline water for terrestrial agriculture (Brown et al. 2018). These ideas hold the promise of a more sustainable water use through a greater circulation of water within the food production chains (Al-Saidi et al. 2020; Al-Saidi and Dehnavi 2020).

9.4.2.2 The Levant Region: Jordan

Jordan is one of the world's most water scarce countries. Long-term average annual precipitation in depth is about 111 mm/year, while the total annual water withdrawals in Jordan are about 1.044×10^9 m^3 (2016), 86% provided from freshwater resources;

Table 9.1 The wastewater reuse profile in the Gulf

Key characteristic	Description
Collection rate of wastewater	Around 50% of total domestic wastewater in the GCC in 2010[a]
Treatment rate (of collected wastewater)	In 2016, between 44% in Bahrain and 99% in Oman[b]
Reuse rate (of treated wastewater)	Less than 40% in 2010[a]
Future targets	Collection of 60% of municipal water by 2030, and reuse of 90% by 2035[a]
Main uses of treated wastewater	Landscaping, forestry, recreation, recharge of groundwater aquifers (emerging use), irrigation of livestock feed (emerging use)
Strengths of wastewater reuse experience	Use of advanced treatment technologies; strong engagement of national water suppliers; large-scale promotion by the state[c]
Uses in agriculture	Limited; occasional use for forage production; agricultural use still emerging
Specific constraints and challenges	Lack of infrastructure for water transport from wastewater plants; unwillingness to accept wastewater use for agriculture; heavy subsidization of water prices; lack of comprehensive strategies[d]
Information sources	[a](Zubari et al. 2017); [b](GCC-STAT 2016); [c](Al-Saidi and Dehnavi 2020); [d](Aleisa and Al-Zubari 2017; Al-Saidi and Dehnavi 2020; Brown et al. 2018; Qureshi 2020; Zubari et al. 2017)

13% from desalinated; 1% from direct use of treated municipal wastewater (AQUA-STAT 2019). Freshwater withdrawals are approximately 25 to 30% more than the internal resources can provide (Government of Jordan 2014). The figure for the total renewable water resources per capita in 2017 was about 96.58 m^3/capita/year, which is far below the global threshold of severe water scarcity (500 m^3/capita) and places Jordan in the category of water poverty (Al-Karablieh and Salman 2016). One reason is the continuous increase in population. Between 1992 and 2017, the total available renewable water resources per capita were more than halved (AQUASTAT 2019). Moreover, the gap between demand and available supply has widened due to climate change (Government of Jordan 2014).

Currently, the priority of using good quality water sources in Jordan is for domestic uses (over the agriculture sector). Still, the agriculture sector exhibits the highest demand for water. Therefore, the government has decided to invest into reuse of treated wastewater for agricultural purposes in order to decrease the pressure on freshwater and to shift water supply from agricultural to domestic and industrial uses. Only 1% of total annual water withdrawal in Jordan is from direct use of treated municipal wastewater (AQUASTAT 2019), still 93% of it is reused for agriculture (Government of Jordan 2015). However, the agriculture sector is only responsible for the production of about 5% of consumable items, with Jordan importing much of its needs for sugar, rice, powdered milk, tea, coffee, corn and vegetable oil (excluding olive oil) (Khraishy 2015). The agricultural sector is the largest consumer of water, while Jordan is a net food importing country (AQUASTAT 2019). The reuse of treated wastewater has been accelerated lately (Table 9.2) and treated wastewater is either used directly by farmers near the treatment plants or blended with freshwater. Famers need to obtain licenses to use treated wastewater and to declare the irrigated crops from the allowed ones, which include crops such as industrial crops, field crops, forages, fiber, oil, sugar and vegetables (only the ones eaten cooked). Fruits and

Table 9.2 The wastewater reuse profile in Jordan

Key characteristic	Description
Collection rate of wastewater	No recent data on collection rate; collected municipal wastewater volumes in 2012 of 0.115 (10^9 m^3/year) in comparison with 0.18 produced municipal wastewater in 2002[a]
Treatment rate (of collected wastewater)	About 98% in 2012
Reuse rate (of treated wastewater)	No recent data on reuse rate; direct use of treated municipal wastewater for irrigation purposes in 2010 was 0.103 (10^9 m^3/year)[a]; approximately 93% of treated wastewater used for agriculture[b]; 27 wastewater treatment plants produce 0.121 10^9 m^3/year, out of which 0.08 is produced by Al-Samra plant for indirect use in the Jordan Valley for irrigation[c]
Future targets	13% of water used in agriculture accounting stemming from treated wastewater by 2022[d]
Main uses of treated wastewater	Indirect irrigation in the Jordan Valley
Strengths of wastewater reuse experience	High treatment rate; relatively high volumes of treated wastewater used in irrigation (in regional comparison)
Uses in agriculture	Direct reuse occurs near treatment plants for fodder crops such as alfalfa, barley and maize, while indirect (blended freshwater and treated wastewater) reuse in the Jordan Valley for vegetable crops[e]
Specific constraints and challenges	Only a fraction of water reused is formalized (using permits and adhering to guidelines)[f]; little research/knowledge on the impact of treated wastewater on soil physiochemical conditions and fertility; high salinity and organic loads due to low average water consumption[g]; farmers' perception of water not reflecting actual quality[e]; low and ineffective water tariffs for agriculture[h]
Information sources	[a](AQUASTAT 2019); [b](Government of Jordan 2015); [c](Ait-Mouheb et al. 2020); [d](Ministry of Water and Irrigation 2009); [e](Carr et al. 2011); [f](Khreisat and Abu-Sharar 2018); [g](Ammary 2007); [h](Al-Saidi and Dehnavi 2019)

vegetables are irrigated indirectly by treated wastewater in the Jordan Valley (Carr et al. 2011).

9.4.2.3 The North Africa Region: Tunisia

With a long-term average annual precipitation of 207 mm per year, Tunisia is relatively less endowed with water resources in comparison with other Mediterranean countries (AQUASTAT 2019). Freshwater withdrawals have increased lately due economic and population growths. In total, 97% of the total water withdrawals stem from freshwater resources; 1.1% from desalinated water; 0.86% from direct use of treated municipal wastewater; and 0.2% from direct use of agricultural drainage water, while around 77% of these total withdrawals are used for agriculture (AQUASTAT 2019). The total water withdrawal per capita in Tunisia is 422.7 m^3/capita/year, which is more than four times higher than Jordan (AQUASTAT 2019). Tunisia has experienced a big shift in water allocation from municipal sector to the industry and agriculture sectors. Water withdrawal in the agriculture sector has increased from 2.644 10^9 m^3/year in 2011 to 3.773 in 2017; for industry from 0.165 to 0.965 for the same period (AQUASTAT 2019).

Due to the high amounts of water used in the agriculture sector and the high potential of drainage water reuse, Tunisia has been promoting of the reuse of drainage water as well as treated wastewater as new water sources (Table 9.3) that can transform the agriculture sector. The water reuse policies date back to the 1960s and they were relaunched at the beginning of the 1980s (Ait-Mouheb et al. 2020). The main applications of water reuse are agricultural irrigation and landscape irrigation. Some pilot projects have been launched or are under study for groundwater recharge, irrigation of forests and highways, and wetland development. Currently, most of reused wastewater is directed toward irrigation of industrial, fodder and tree crops as well as cereals while some water is reused for landscaping or recreation (Ait-Mouheb et al. 2020). There are strict criteria for the use of treated wastewater including types of crops, irrigation schemes, handling of treated wastewater, timing of usage and water quality monitoring (Dare et al. 2017).

9.5 Discussion of Crosscutting Issues

9.5.1 Some Missing Vital Rs: Rethink, Refuse and Reduce

The circular economy agenda goes beyond the enhanced circulation of materials and the establishment of more closed loops production systems. In fact, it is often linked to other sustainability concepts and sustainable development in general (Geissdoerfer et al. 2017; Korhonen et al. 2018) while the earlier mentioned broad definition relates it to contextual issues of development policies, lifestyles and the four R principles of

Table 9.3 The wastewater reuse profile in Tunisia

Key characteristic	Description
Collection rate of wastewater	Collected municipal wastewater in 2009 was 0.241 10^9 m^3/year, 84% of the total produced municipal wastewater[a]
Treatment rate (of collected wastewater)	In 2010, municipal wastewater was treated in 109 wastewater treatment facilities with about 94% treatment rate[a]
Reuse rate (of treated wastewater)	Around 30% in 2016[b]
Future targets	N/A
Main uses of treated wastewater	Overwhelmingly for irrigation, while a very small portion used for groundwater recharge and wetland conservation
Strengths of wastewater reuse experience	Good monitoring systems; old experience in reuse policies; clear formal regulations
Uses in agriculture	Fodder crops, trees and industrial crops, while irrigation of vegetables (consumed raw) prohibited[c]
Specific constraints and challenges	Water quality concerns regarding long-term effect of using treated wastewater due to high organic load and salt contents; farmers preferring using groundwater; need for updating policies and strategies[c]
Information sources	[a](AQUASTAT 2019); [b](Ait-Mouheb et al. 2020); [c](Dare et al. 2017)

reducing, reusing, recycling and recovering (Kirchherr et al. 2017). While encouraging wastewater utilization as a resource satisfies the principles of reducing freshwater demands in agriculture, recycling domestic wastewater volumes and recovering valuable by-products, the first principle is to encourage more environmental awareness, conservation and efficiency in consumption. Alongside the principle of reducing consumption, it is important rethink consumption and production patterns by questioning current designs of infrastructure systems and the nature of water and food demands. For example, wastewater reuse needs to be accompanied by water efficiency measures in the agriculture, while domestic water use should be characterized by awareness and responsible use. Furthermore, consumers should refuse waste of water and food, particularly in the Gulf region which exhibits some of the world's largest footprints in terms of food waste and water consumption—alongside equally large energy and carbon footprints (Al-Saidi and Elagib 2018; Al-Saidi and Saliba 2019). Wasteful patterns can be encountered in a lesser extent in lower-income countries of the region. At the same time, the poor state of infrastructure and the lack of modernization can encourage waste and inefficient use of resources. In this sense, it is highly needed to advance more comprehensive circular economy strategies in the MENA region beyond the current narrow focus on technologies for better resource circulation.

9.5.2 Socioeconomics of Incentives and Participation

In relation to the earlier mentioned missing principles, there are two socioeconomic issues required for a more conducive environment regarding the circular economy agenda. First, the relatively high level of water and energy subsidizations in the MENA region has caused disincentives to explore alternative resources such as treated wastewater. Although the level of subsidization has been steadily reduced, the region still holds a significant level of subsidization of fuel, agricultural water and domestic tariffs in order to promote affordability (Al-Saidi 2020b; Al-Saidi and Dehnavi 2019). Subsidies have meant that farmers prefer freshwater abstractions and consumers are less aware of the true or total economic cost of desalinated water or pumped water from the rivers, streams, lakes and aquifers. Second, the acceptance of certain new uses such as treated wastewater for edible agriculture, or even for closer-to-person uses such as drinking or bathing, remain low in the MENA region despite national-level differences. Although the water reuse acceptance is a quite complex social phenomenon, one can expect acceptance to increase with trust and participation. For example, encouraging farmers' participation in drafting reuse priorities and piloting wastewater reuse projects can increase the adoption of this option. Water consumers might be more willing to reduce water consumption or buy wastewater-based agricultural products if they are engaged in initiatives showcasing benefits and safety. For this, environmental education and role models (e.g., public figures promoting conservation and embracing the use of alternative, recycled products) can help in encouraging more circularity and responsibility in consumption.

9.5.3 Relevance of Strategies and Integration

The availability of integrated and holistic policies is quite relevant for advancing circular economy options. In the wastewater reuse planning, such policies should link food production to different sources of wastewater and to infrastructure planning. Traditionally, food policies in the MENA region have had little interlinkages to wastewater management, which is regarded as a concern for the municipal water subsector. Water policies from the 1990s and early twenty-first century on integrated water resources management (IWRM) have been formally successful in bundling water use concerns, including water in agriculture, into joint national water strategies and investments plans. However, IWRM policies were not effectively implemented (partly due the lack of support from the agriculture sector) (Al-Saidi 2017), while wastewater utilization did not figure highly as a priority. Recent food policies (e.g., national food strategies in the Gulf) have had more consideration of the water reuse issue, but they lack consistency in terms of implementation and linking different water types and systems in agriculture (Brown et al. 2018). It is also important to consider emerging integration issues in the MENA region. A closer integration and more coordination between the water, energy and food sectors are needed in the region in light of the advancement of renewable energies in agriculture and the mounting supply chain risks from climate change, rapid growth or internal vulnerabilities of the supply systems (Abulibdeh et al. 2019; Al-Saidi and Lahham 2019; Al-Saidi and Saliba 2019). Finally, Table 9.4 summarizes the mentioned crosscutting issues and compares them for the cases analyzed in this chapter.

Table 9.4 Comparative summary of crosscutting circular economy challenges for wastewater-food nexus

Comparison criteria	Comprehensiveness of circular economy principles in the wastewater-food nexus	Conduciveness of socioeconomic contexts	Availability of integrated, holistic wastewater reuse planning
The Gulf	Need for addressing awareness and responsible consumption; large footprints, e.g., water consumption of up to 700 liter per day in comparison with the average of 200 in the region (Al-Zubari 2017) and food waste of up to 650 kg per capita per year (El Bilali and Ben Hassen 2020)	Existence of high subsidization such as no fees for groundwater abstraction, discounts/no tariffs for domestic water for nationals; top-down policies; low acceptance for treated wastewater usage for close-to-person purposes	Lack of integration of wastewater plants to delivery infrastructure; need for more integrated and explicit national policies with better interlinkages between different (waste) water types, food production and clean energies
Jordan	Need to reduce water waste through food waste; high potential to reuse water through waste reuse (e.g., compost); very low irrigation efficiency with high potential to save water and produce more food; need for addressing awareness and responsible consumption (e.g., less meat); need for enhancing experience with promoting decentralized wastewater treatment and reuse	Low-performing water tariffs systems (Al-Saidi and Dehnavi 2019); subsidies for irrigation systems, and allocating state lands to peasants (Ministry of Environment 2015); low acceptance for treated wastewater usage for close-to-person purposes	Relatively clear strategies on wastewater reuse and integration strategies of wastewater plants to delivery infrastructure (Ministry of Water and Irrigation 2016); need for more integration to energy sector concerns (Al-Saidi and Lahham 2019)

(continued)

Table 9.4 (continued)

Comparison criteria	Comprehensiveness of circular economy principles in the wastewater-food nexus	Conduciveness of socioeconomic contexts	Availability of integrated, holistic wastewater reuse planning
Tunisia	Need for addressing the low irrigation efficiency and enhancing current policies to encourage investments in water-saving technologies (Frija et al. 2013); need to increase the reuse rate of wastewater for more productive uses (alongside the valuable experience with the reuse for landscaping and groundwater recharge) (UNU-FLORES 2017); lack of infrastructures to treat the amount of wastewater produced, especially in rural areas (GIZ 2016)	A lack of awareness of the health risk related to wastewater handling; big economic loss in agriculture sector due to poor water management practices and the loss of dam capacity; low acceptance for treated wastewater usage for close-to-person purposes; concerns of farmers about the marketability of agricultural products irrigated with wastewater	Some strategies existing (e.g., Water 2050) with wastewater as a priority; well-established national policies explicitly addressing the links between (waste)water and food; need for more coherent legislations regulating the environmental aspects of the reuse of reclaimed water and the requirements for its use (GIZ 2016)

9.6 Conclusions and Policy Implications

The water and food sectors in the MENA region are vital for ensuring basic supply despite the increasing demands, and for achieving key sustainability requirements such as conservation, ecosystems' protection and low-metabolism growth. In order to encourage the sustainable use of resources in these sectors, there is a need for more integration of issues and for holistic strategies. The circular economy thinking offers interesting insights for the water and food sectors in terms of improving the circulation of materials, closing the loops within and across the sectors and promoting low-intensity and more efficient production patterns. In addition to reusing, recovering and recycling resources, the circular economy emphasizes the need to rethink current practices, share resources and eliminate wasteful behavior. In this broad sense of the circular economy, there are several possible applications to the water-food nexus in the MENA region. These applications include awareness-raising, arrangements for responsible consumption, water- and food-saving technologies, alternative inputs and materials recovery. We highlighted in this chapter a very relevant option for enhancing the circular economy in the region, namely water recycling and reuse. This option can alleviate some of the pressures on the vulnerable water resources in the MENA region, which have been mismanaged and depleted for several decades.

With the advancement of water treatment technologies, it is now possible to clean and make available several types of water including drainage water, wastewater or produced water.

The use of treated wastewater has become a serious option (although not yet widely utilized) for augmenting water supplies in forerunner countries such as the Gulf states, Jordan and Tunisia. Much of the treated wastewater is now being reused for several purposes, e.g., mainly for landscaping in the Gulf, and for irrigation in both Tunisia and Jordan. There are several common challenges such as the acceptance of water quality provided by treatment plants, the provision of knowledge on long-term impacts of different recycled water quality on soil, the distorting effects of water and energy subsidies and the need for effective monitoring mechanisms. For wastewater reuse to become a viable option in a wider circular economy, there is a need for a comprehensive approach for the promotion of water reuse. Alongside reusing and recycling, addressing demand side issues of waste and inefficient use is necessary. Furthermore, engaging with the public (and especially user groups such as farmers) to embrace water reuse is important. It requires trust, role models and participation in water reuse initiatives. The right economic signals such as economic pricing for agricultural water can persuade water users of the need for water reuse as an integral option of water supply in contexts characterized by aridity and mounting scarcity. Finally, the recycling of wastewater should be linked to the recipient sectors (mainly agriculture) through clear national strategies that consider important factors such as infrastructure, the overall supply chains (including possible loops to close) and priorities in terms of uses and potential users.

References

Abulibdeh A, Zaidan E, Al-Saidi M (2019) Development drivers of the water-energy-food nexus in the Gulf Cooperation Council region. Dev. Pract. 29:582–593. https://doi.org/10.1080/09614524. 2019.1602109

AbuZeid KM (2020) Existing and recommended water policies in Egypt. In: Zekri S (ed) Water Policies in MENA Countries. Springer International Publishing, Cham, pp 47–62

Acikgoz S, Ben Ali MS, Mert M (2016) Sources of economic growth in MENA countries: technological progress, physical or human capital accumulations? Economic development in the middle east and North Africa. Springer/Palgrave Macmillan, New York, pp 27–69

Ait-Mouheb N, Mayaux P-L, Mateo-Sagasta J, Hartani T, Molle B (2020) Chapter 5—Water reuse: a resource for mediterranean agriculture. In: Zribi M, Brocca L, Tramblay Y, Molle F (eds) Water resources in the mediterranean region. Elsevier, pp 107–136

Aleisa E, Al-Zubari W (2017) Wastewater reuse in the countries of the Gulf cooperation council (GCC): the lost opportunity. Environ Monit Assess 189:553. https://doi.org/10.1007/s10661-017-6269-8

Allan JA (2003) Virtual water—the water, food, and trade nexus. Useful concept or misleading metaphor? Water Int 28:106–113. https://doi.org/10.1080/02508060.2003.9724812

Al-Karablieh E, Salman A (2016) Water resources, use and management in Jordan - A focus on groundwater. https://gw-mena.iwmi.org/wp-content/uploads/sites/3/2017/04/Rep.11-Water-resources-use-and-management-in-Jordan-a-focus-on-groundwater.pdf. Accessed 17 August 2020

Al-Saidi M (2017) Conflicts and security in integrated water resources management. Environ Sci Policy 73:38–44. https://doi.org/10.1016/j.envsci.2017.03.015

Al-Saidi M (2020a) Contribution of water scarcity and sustainability failures to disintegration and conflict in the arab region—the case of Syria and Yemen. In: Amour PO (ed) The regional order in the Gulf region and the middle east: regional rivalries and security alliances. Springer International Publishing, Cham, pp 375–405

Al-Saidi M (2020b) Instruments of energy subsidy reforms in Arab countries—the case of the Gulf Cooperation Council (GCC) countries. Energy Reports 6:68–73. https://doi.org/10.1016/j.egyr.2019.08.020

Al-Saidi M, Dehnavi S (2019) Comparative scorecard assessment of Urban water pricing policies—the case of Jordan and Iran. Water 11:704. https://doi.org/10.3390/w11040704

Al-Saidi M, Dehnavi S (2020) Marginal water resources for food production—challenges for enhancing de-growth and circular economy in the Gulf Cooperation Council (GCC) countries and Iran. In: UNESCO i-WSSM (ed) Water reuse within a circular economy context. UNESCO, Paris, France, under publication

Al-Saidi M, Elagib NA (2018) Ecological modernization and responses for a low-carbon future in the Gulf Cooperation Council countries. WIREs Clim Change 9:e528. https://doi.org/10.1002/wcc.528

Al-Saidi M, Lahham N (2019) Solar energy farming as a development innovation for vulnerable water basins. Dev Pract 29:619–634. https://doi.org/10.1080/09614524.2019.1600659

Al-Saidi M, Saliba S (2019) Water, energy and food supply security in the Gulf Cooperation Council (GCC) countries—a risk perspective. Water 11:455. https://doi.org/10.3390/w11030455

Al-Saidi M, Birnbaum D, Buriti R, Diek E, Hasselbring C, Jimenez A, Woinowski D (2016) Water resources vulnerability assessment of MENA countries considering energy and virtual water interactions. Procedia Eng 145:900–907. https://doi.org/10.1016/j.proeng.2016.04.117

Al-Saidi M, Das P, Saadaoui I (2020) Circular economy in basic supply: framing the approach for the water and food sectors of the Gulf Cooperation Council (GCC) Countries. Under publications

Al-Zubari WK (2017) Status of water in the arab region. In: Amer K, Adeel Z, Böer B, Saleh W (eds) The Water, energy, and food security nexus in the arab region. Springer International Publishing, Cham, pp 1–24

Ammary BY (2007) Wastewater reuse in Jordan: present status and future plans. Desalination 211:164–176. https://doi.org/10.1016/j.desal.2006.02.091

Andersen MS (2007) An introductory note on the environmental economics of the circular economy. Sustain Sci 2:133–140. https://doi.org/10.1007/s11625-006-0013-6

Antonelli M, Sartori M (2015) Unfolding potential of the virtual water concept. What is still under debate? Environ Sci Policy 50:240–251. https://doi.org/10.1016/j.envsci.2015.02.011

Apergis N, Ben Ali MS (2020) Corruption, rentier states and economic growth: where do the GCC countries stand? In Miniaoui H (ed) Economic development in the Gulf Cooperation Council countries: from rentier states to diversified economies, Springer

Acikgoz S, Ben Ali MS (2019) Where does economic growth in the middle eastern and North African countries come from? Q Rev Econ Finance 73:172–183

AQUASTAT (2019) Main Database. http://www.fao.org/aquastat/en/. Accessed 20 May 2019

Ben Ali MS, Cockx L, Francken N (2016) The middle east and North Africa: cursed by natural resources? In: Ben Ali MS (ed) Economic development in the middle east and North Africa: challenges and prospects. Palgrave Macmillan US, New York, pp 71–93

Ben Mim S, Ben Ali MS (2020) Natural resources curse and economic diversification in GCC Countries. In: Miniaoui H (ed) Economic development in the Gulf Cooperation Council countries: from rentier states to diversified economies. Springer Singapore, Singapore

Borgomeo E, Fawzi NA-M, Hall JW, Jägerskog A, Nicol A, Sadoff CW, Salman M, Santos N, Talhami M (2020) Tackling the trickle: ensuring sustainable water management in the arab region. Earth's Future 8. https://doi.org/10.1029/2020EF001495

Brown J, Das P, Al-Saidi M (2018) Sustainable agriculture in the Arabian/Persian Gulf region utilizing marginal water resources: making the best of a bad Situation. Sustainability 10:1364. https://doi.org/10.3390/su10051364

Carr G, Potter RB, Nortcliff S (2011) Water reuse for irrigation in Jordan: perceptions of water quality among farmers. Agric Water Manag 98:847–854. https://doi.org/10.1016/j.agwat.2010. 12.011

D'Alisa G, Demaria F, Kallis G (2015) Degrowth: a vocabulary for a new era. Routledge Taylor & Francis Group, New York, London

Dare AE, Mohtar RH, Jafvert CT, Shomar B, Engel B, Boukchina R, Rabi A (2017) Opportunities and challenges for treated wastewater reuse in the West Bank, Tunisia, and Qatar. Trans. ASABE 60:1563–1574. https://doi.org/10.13031/trans.12109

El Bilali H, Ben Hassen T (2020) Food waste in the countries of the Gulf Cooperation Council: a systematic review. Foods 9. https://doi.org/10.3390/foods9040463

Engelmann J, Al-Saidi M (2019) Business-driven ecological innovations in green growth strategies. In: Bocken N, Ritala P, Albareda L, Verburg R (eds) Innovation for sustainability: business transformations towards a better world. Springer International Publishing, Cham, pp 97–113

Frija A, Chebil A, Speelman S, Faysse N (2013) A critical assessment of groundwater governance in Tunisia. Water Policy 16:358–373. https://doi.org/10.2166/wp.2013.038

GCC-STAT (2016) Water Statistics Report in the GCC Countries 2016. Musqat, Oman. https://www.gccstat.org/images/gccstat/docman/publications/205-WaterStatistics-En.pdf. Accessed 12 November 2019

Geissdoerfer M, Savaget P, Bocken NMP, Hultink EJ (2017) The circular economy–a new sustainability paradigm? J Clean Prod 143:757–768. https://doi.org/10.1016/j.jclepro.2016. 12.048

Geissdoerfer M, Morioka SN, de Carvalho MM, Evans S (2018) Business models and supply chains for the circular economy. J Clean Prod 190:712–721. https://doi.org/10.1016/j.jclepro. 2018.04.159

George DAR, Lin BC-a, Chen Y (2015) A circular economy model of economic growth. Environ Model Softw 73:60–63. https://doi.org/10.1016/j.envsoft.2015.06.014

GIZ (2016) Integrated wastewater management in the Mediterranean: Good practices in decentralised & centralised reuse-oriented approaches. https://www.adelphi.de/de/system/files/mediat hek/bilder/Integrated%20Waste%20Water%20Management%20in%20the%20Mediterranean% 20-%20Compendium%20-%20adelphi.pdf. Accessed 18 August 2020

Government of Jordan (2014) Jordan 2025 a National Vision and Strategy. Amman, Jordan. https://www.greengrowthknowledge.org/national-documents/jordan-2025-national-vis ion-and-strategy. Accessed 17 August 2020

Government of Jordan (2015) Jordan's way to sustainable development: First National Voluntary review on the implementation of the 2030 Agenda. https://sustainabledevelopment.un.org/con tent/documents/16289Jordan.pdf. Accessed 17 August 2020

Ibarrola-Rivas MJ, Granados-Ramírez R, Nonhebel S (2017) Is the available cropland and water enough for food demand? A global perspective of the Land-Water-Food nexus. Adv Water Resour 110:476–483. https://doi.org/10.1016/j.advwatres.2017.09.018

Jeuland M (2015) Challenges to wastewater reuse in the middle east and North Africa. Middle East Dev J 7:1–25. https://doi.org/10.1080/17938120.2015.1019293

Kalmykova Y, Sadagopan M, Rosado L (2018) Circular economy—from review of theories and practices to development of implementation tools. Resour Conserv Recycl 135:190–201. https://doi.org/10.1016/j.resconrec.2017.10.034

Khreisat A, Abu-Sharar TM (2018) Reuse of reclaimed wastewater in irrigation: review of Jordan's experience. Jordan J Agric Sci 14:91–103

Khraishy M (2015) Market Overview and Guide to Jordanian Market Requirements. https://apps.fas.usda.gov/newgainapi/api/report/downloadreportbyfilename?filename=Exporter%20G uide_Amman_Jordan_12-29-2015.pdf. Accessed 17 August 2020

Kirchherr J, Reike D, Hekkert M (2017) Conceptualizing the circular economy: an analysis of 114 definitions. Resour Conserv Recycl 127:221–232. https://doi.org/10.1016/j.resconrec.2017. 09.005

Kjaer LL, Pigosso DCA, Niero M, Bech NM, McAloone TC (2019) Product/service-systems for a circular economy: the route to decoupling economic growth from resource consumption? J Ind Ecol 23:22–35. https://doi.org/10.1111/jiec.12747

Korhonen J, Honkasalo A, Seppälä J (2018) Circular economy: the concept and its limitations. Ecol Econ 143:37–46. https://doi.org/10.1016/j.ecolecon.2017.06.041

Latouche S (2009) Farewell to growth. Polity, Cambridge

McDowall W, Geng Y, Huang B, Barteková E, Bleischwitz R, Türkeli S, Kemp R, Doménech T (2017) Circular economy policies in China and Europe. J Ind Ecol 21:651–661. https://doi.org/ 10.1111/jiec.12597

Ministry of Water & Irrigation (2009) Water for Life: Jordan's Water Strategy 2008-2022. Amman, Jordan. http://extwprlegs1.fao.org/docs/pdf/jor153874.pdf. Accessed 17 August 2020

Ministry of Environment (2015) Integrated investment framwork for sustainable land management in Jordan. https://www.undp.org/content/dam/jordan/docs/Publications/Enviro/UNDP%20IIF% 20Report.pdf. Accessed 15 August 2020

Ministry of Water & Irrigation (2016) Decentralized Wastewater Management Policy. http:// www.mwi.gov.jo/sites/en-us/Hot%20Issues/Strategic%20Documents%20of%20%20The% 20Water%20Sector/Decentralized%20Wastewater%20Management%20Policy%2025.2.2016. pdf. Accessed 15 August 2020

Murray A, Skene K, Haynes K (2017) The circular economy: an interdisciplinary exploration of the concept and application in a global context. J Bus Ethics 140:369–380. https://doi.org/10.1007/ s10551-015-2693-2

Pishchulov G, Richter K, Pakhomova NV, Tsenzharik MK (2018) A circular economy perspective on sustainable supply chain management: an updated survey. St Petersburg Univ J Econ Stud 34

Qureshi AS (2020) Challenges and prospects of using treated wastewater to manage water scarcity crises in the Gulf Cooperation Council (GCC) countries. Water 12:1971. https://doi.org/10.3390/ w12071971

Saif O, Mezher T, Arafat HA (2014) Water security in the GCC countries: challenges and opportunities. J Environ Stud Sci 4:329–346. https://doi.org/10.1007/s13412-014-0178-8

Seibert S, Henrich V, Frenken K, Burke J (2013) Update of the Digital Global Map of Irrigation Areas to Version 5. Rome, Italy. http://www.fao.org/3/I9261EN/i9261en.pdf. Accessed 20 November 2019

Schröder P, Bengtsson M, Cohen M, Dewick P, Hoffstetter J, Sarkis J (2019) Degrowth within— aligning circular economy and strong sustainability narratives. Resour Conserv Recycl 146:190– 191. https://doi.org/10.1016/j.resconrec.2019.03.038

Stahel WR (2016) The circular economy. Nature News 531:435. https://doi.org/10.1038/531435a

Tal A (2016) Rethinking the sustainability of Israel's irrigation practices in the drylands. Water Res 90:387–394. https://doi.org/10.1016/j.watres.2015.12.016

The Economist (2019) Global Food Security Index 2019. The Economist Intelligence Unit. Available online at https://foodsecurityindex.eiu.com/. Accessed on 9/17/2020

Tsai I-T (2018) Political economy of energy policy reforms in the gulf cooperation council: Implications of paradigm change in the rentier social contract. Energy Res Soc Sci 41:89–96. https:// doi.org/10.1016/j.erss.2018.04.028

UNU-FLORES (2017) The nexus approach and safe use of wastewater in agriculture: An international workshop on policy and implementation for Tunisia. https://collections.unu.edu/eserv/ UNU:6571/Proceedings_SUWA_Tunisia.pdf. Accessed 18 July 2020

Voulvoulis N (2018) Water reuse from a circular economy perspective and potential risks from an unregulated approach. Curr Opin Environ Sci Health 2:32–45. https://doi.org/10.1016/j.coesh. 2018.01.005

Woertz E (2013) Oil for food: the global food crisis and the middle east. Oxford University Press, Oxford

World Bank (2007) Making the Most of Scarcity: Accountability for Better Water Management Results in the Middle East and North Africa (MENA Development Report). Washington, D.C. https://openknowledge.worldbank.org/handle/10986/6845 Accessed 8 August 2020

World Bank (2020) World Bank Open Data. http://data.worldbank.org/. Accessed 20 June 2020

Zubari W, Al-Turbak A, Zahid W, Al-Ruwis K, Al-Tkhais A, Al-Mutaz I, Abdelwahab A, Murad A, Al-Harbi M, Al-Sulaymani Z (2017) An overview of the GCC unified water strategy (2016–2035). Desalin Water Treat 81. https://doi.org/10.5004/dwt.2017.20864

Chapter 10
Globalization and Environmental Pollution: Where Does the MENA Region Stand?

Muhammed Sehid Gorus and Mohamed Sami Ben Ali

Abstract This study conducts both descriptive and empirical analyses for environmental deterioration and globalization level in the MENA region. First, we give a snapshot of the current globalization level of MENA countries, including economic, social, and political aspects. Besides, we also discuss environmental issues in the region, such as forest area, internal freshwater resources, and environmental degradation level. Second, this study utilizes the Pearson's Correlation Coefficient analysis between ecological footprint and types of globalization indices. According to the findings, not only economic globalization but also social and political globalization have a major impact on the environmental problems in the MENA region. Several significant policy changes need to be tackled. A key policy priority should be to plan for the long-term care of environmental quality in the MENA countries. For this purpose, they should spend their oil and natural gas revenues on providing sustainable economic growth rather than plain economic growth.

Keywords Economic globalization · KOF globalization index · MENA countries · Political globalization · Social globalization

10.1 Introduction

The Middle East and North Africa (MENA) region represents a number of diverse countries representing diverse political, economic, and social features. Numerous MENA countries are witnessing a huge economic growth and high economic development paths fueled by their enormous oil reserves (Acikgoz and Ben Ali 2019; Acikgoz et al. 2016; Apergis and Ben Ali 2020; Ben Mim and Ben Ali 2020). A more sustainable economic growth is regarded as essential in the region. While the

M. S. Gorus (✉)
Ankara Yıldırım Beyazıt University, Ankara, Turkey
e-mail: msgorus@ybu.edu.tr

M. S. Ben Ali
Qatar University, Doha, Qatar
e-mail: msbenali@qu.edu.qa

© The Author(s), under exclusive license to Springer Nature Switzerland AG 2021   161
M. S. Ben Ali (ed.), *Economic Development in the MENA Region*, Perspectives on Development in the Middle East and North Africa (MENA) Region, https://doi.org/10.1007/978-3-030-66380-3_10

huge reserves provide vast financial resources to finance their ongoing projects and growth strategies, most of the countries in the region are exhausting their natural reserves and environment as well.

As MENA countries are growing at sustainable paths, they are becoming more and more open to international finance, trade, and investment both inward and outward.

Sustainable development strategies in the region require particular attention to what harms the globalization can cause. Indeed, it has been widely documented in the literature that openness and more widely globalization can obviously involve substantial environmental externalities to local economies. The pioneering study by Grossman and Krueger (1991) caught the attention of academicians and policymakers about the causal relationship between countries' economic globalization and the corresponding environmental effects. That is to say that the global increase in economic activity inevitably involves more production, more demand for goods and services, trade, and financial activities worldwide and, therefore, environmental problems.

From a more positive perspective, globalization can increase international direct investment between countries. Investment in the hosting countries can benefit, through Greenfield investments, joint ventures, or mergers and acquisitions, can involve a know-how and technology transfer that can mitigate the negative impact of globalization on the local economies. In the same line of thought, more globalized countries can involve, through social integration, including touristic visits, student movements, and cultural products, more awareness on the harmful effect of pollution. This may decrease the negative impact of globalization.

This is said, all countries inevitably bear the environmental cost of their globalization. However, they do not bear it the same way and intensity. Where do the MENA countries stand regarding this dilemma? What causal relationship the MENA region could display regarding the globalization-environmental pollution?

As said, the MENA region is not homogeneous. Diverse countries display different economic growth and development paths, and some countries present more sustainable economic strategies than others do. Therefore, they would display divergent paths related to the globalization-environmental pollution nexus. Moreover, when similarly globalized countries would not display the same outcomes as to the impact on the environment. Indeed, different economic structures and characteristics would yield different environmental outcomes. Discussing the effect of globalization on the ecological quality for the MENA region in a more general setting and from an individual perspective is of foremost importance.

This chapter sheds light on the globalization-environmental pollution nexus from a theoretical side and empirical one as well by discussing the relevant literature related to the relationship between globalization and pollution. It also discusses the case of the MENA region empirically by presenting different countries' situations.

10.2   An Overview for MENA Countries

In this section, we give a snapshot of the current globalization level of MENA countries, including economic, social, and political aspects. Besides, it is also discussed environmental issues in the region, such as forest area, internal freshwater resources, and environmental deterioration level.

10.2.1   Economic, Social, and Political Globalization

In the literature, various indicators are used to measure the globalization level in a given country: the composite globalization index, the KOF Globalization Index, the Maastricht Globalization Index, and the trade openness level (for economic globalization). In this study, we consider recent globalization data provided by the KOF Swiss Economic Institute; *Globalization Index* (or *composite index of globalization*). The merit of this dataset is that it measures the economic, social, and political aspects of globalization. The dataset was first introduced by Dreher (2006) and then developed by Gygli et al. (2019). The index does not only covers current activities on trade and finance but also includes regulations and policies (Yilanci and Gorus 2020). Moreover, this index evaluates the social aspect of globalization, including cultural activities and international movements of tourists and students. It also includes access to television, Internet, and telephone. In addition, the political aspect of this index is influenced by the ability to engage in global governance and the diffusion of public policies. The value of the index ranges between zero and one hundred. The globalization level of a country rises when the index value increases. In other words, a high level of index refers to a more globalized environment (economic, social, and political).

Figure 10.1 displays the composite globalization index level for 19 MENA countries in 2017. The composite index consists of economic (weight; 1/3), social (weight; 1/3), and political (weight; 1/3) globalization indices. The region's average for the globalization index is approximately 62.6. Besides, 12 countries are above average, while the remaining seven countries are below the average among the MENA countries. According to the figure, Israel has the highest index value with 77.1, while West Bank and Gaza (Palestine) have the lowest index value with 34.0. Also, Qatar (74.3), the UAE (74.1), Jordan (73.7), and Kuwait (71.2) are among the most globalized countries in the MENA region. In the next step, we consider economic, social, and political aspects of globalization to evaluate the globalization level differences across countries in the region (see Fig. 10.2).

Figure 10.2 provides an overview considering the economic, social, and political aspects of globalization for 19 MENA countries in 2017. First, we take into consideration the *Economic Globalization*. This index is affected by both trade and financial globalization. So, in addition to de facto measures (such as trade-in goods and services, trade partner diversity, FDI inflows, and portfolio investments), *de jure*

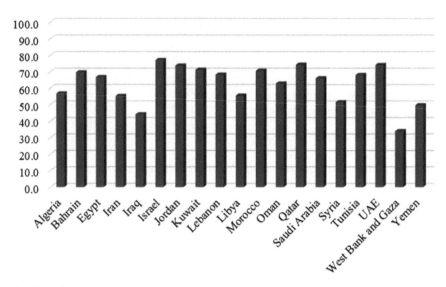

Fig. 10.1 Globalization level in MENA countries (2017). *Source* KOF Swiss Economic Institute, KOF Globalization Index dataset

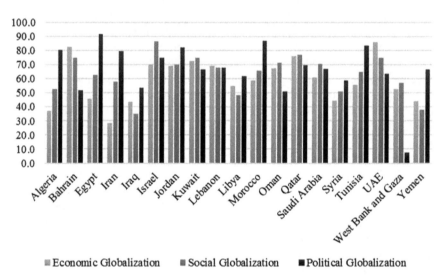

Fig. 10.2 Economic, social, and political globalization level in MENA countries (2017). *Source* KOF Swiss Economic Institute, KOF Globalization Index dataset

measures (such as policies and taxes on trade and financial activities) also shape the level of economic globalization in a country. The MENA region's average for economic globalization is 58.9. In detail, ten countries are above average, while nine countries are below the average. According to the data, the UAE (85.9) has a more global economy compared to other MENA countries. Moreover, Bahrain (82.5),

Qatar (76.1), Kuwait (72.5), and Israel (69.9) have a relatively high economic globalization level. All of these countries are high-income countries, according to World Bank classifications. They have diversified their economy for a few decades, and a significant amount of their income comes from non-oil sectors such as tourism, business services, finance, and manufacturing. For instance, 15.8 million tourists visit the UAE, while the economy receives 21-billion-dollar tourism revenue in 2017 (World Tourism Organization 2019). Besides, financial services and manufacturing were the largest non-oil sectors of Bahrain in 2019, and their shares in the total economy are 16.5% and 14.5%, respectively (MOFNE 2019). So, economic diversification causes a structural transformation of an economy. Then, trade-in goods and services, trade partner diversity, and trade agreements rise step by step. These improvements in economic activities provide a more globalized economy.

On the other hand, Iran has the lowest index value (28.2) among the MENA countries in 2017. This low level of economic globalization level can be attributed to economic sanctions on Iran by Western countries such as the United States and the European Union countries. These economic sanctions (a decrease in demand) decrease the supply of goods and services in Iran. They also lead to a decline in international trade and financial agreements.

Second, the index of *Social Globalization* can be divided into three main subcategories: interpersonal, informational, and cultural globalization. First, interpersonal globalization includes de facto measures such as the number of international telephone calls, tourism, migration, and international students. Besides, it also covers *de jure* measures such as telephone subscriptions, freedom of travel, and the number of international airports. Second, informational globalization consists of Internet bandwidth, the number of international patents, high-tech export, TV and Internet access, and press freedom. Lastly, the cultural globalization index includes several items, such as trade-in cultural goods and services, international brands, sexual equality, and human rights.

According to Fig. 10.2, the average value for social globalization is 63.2 in MENA countries in 2017. Eleven countries are above this threshold, while eight of them are below the average. Israel has the highest level of social globalization since they have a close relationship with Western countries. Thus, this relationship affects money transfers, tourism activities, student movements, and airports (and international flights) positively. This close relationship between Israel and the Western countries can be attributed, among others, to their similar social, political, and economic attributes. Also, high technology is one of the main drivers of the economic growth in Israel (Nathanson 2011), and it is one of the leading economies that reserve a significant share in research and development (R&D) activities. Therefore, these issues lead to an increase in high-technology export volume, international patents, and worldwide brands in Israel. However, Yemen (37.9) and Iraq (35.1) have low index values compared to the remaining MENA countries. The low level of social globalization in these countries can be attributed to a bunch of domestic conflicts and wars such as the Yemeni Crisis (since 2011) after the revolution against President Saleh, the Yemeni Civil War (since 2015), the Iraq War (2003–2011), Iraqi Civil War (2014–2017), and 2017 Iraqi–Kurdish conflict.

Third, the **Political Globalization** index measures the number of embassies, United Nations peacekeeping missions, non-governmental organizations, organizations, treaties, and treaty partner diversity in international settings. The region's average for the political globalization index is approximately 66.6. In detail, ten countries are above average, while nine countries are below the average. Figure 10.2 shows that Egypt (91.8), Morocco (87.1), Tunisia (83.7), Jordan (82.1), and Algeria (80.4) have a more global political environment compared to other MENA countries. The high index values of these countries can be identified with a high number of commitments in international political cooperation. On the other side, it is seen that West Bank and Gaza's political globalization level was 7.5 in 2017. Its low level of globalization can be attributed to political conflicts between Israel and Palestine. Moreover, the majority of Western countries do not recognize Palestine as a state. Therefore, its engagements in international political cooperation remain low.

Overall, one can say that both domestic and international conflicts and wars have an adverse effect on the globalization level in a country. These issues not only damage the composite globalization level but also affect its economic, social, and political dimensions. In this regard, Syria, Yemen, Iraq, and Palestine have very low globalization levels, mainly because of suffering from various political conflicts and wars.

10.2.2 Environmental Issues in the Region

Global Footprint Network (2020) defines the ecological footprint (on the demand side) as: "*ecological assets that a given population requires to produce the natural resources it consumes (including plant-based food and fiber products, livestock and fish products, timber and other forest products, space for urban infrastructure) and to absorb its waste, especially carbon emission.*" So, ecological footprint does not measure only air pollution or water pollution; it provides us with a more comprehensive environmental degradation indicator. Thus, in recent years, practitioners have utilized this dataset instead of specific pollution indicators like CO_2 emissions.[1]

Forests are one of the most significant natural assets in the environment. They shelter habitats, provide environmental services (disposal, productive, and consumption services), and store CO_2 emissions (World Bank 2008). However, forest areas in the world are not equally distributed. Figure 10.3 displays the forest area (% of land area) across different regions and income groups in 2016. According to the figure, on the one hand, the Latin America and Caribbean region has the largest share of the forest area to the total land area. On the other hand, the Middle East and North Africa and South Asia regions have the lowest shares regarding forest area as a percentage of the total land area. In detail, the South Asia region's percentage is around 17.5, while forests cover only 2.1% of the land area of the Middle East and

---

[1]The relationship between economic activities and the environmental quality (CO_2 or ecological footprint) will be discussed in Sect. 10.3.

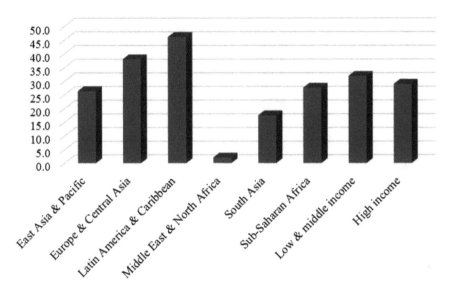

Fig. 10.3 Forest area, percentage of land area (2016). *Source* World Bank dataset (Accessed on 23.04.2020)

North Africa region. Thus, MENA countries suffer from a lack of forest coverage, and it is the primary source of environmental problems in the region, such as air pollution, erosion, flooding, and water scarcity (Smiet 1990).

Water scarcity and pollution cause various environmental issues such as water pollution and deforestation and health problems (such as diarrhea and cholera). Figure 10.4 exhibits internal freshwater resources per capita (cubic meters) across different regions and income groups in 2014. It is seen that water resources are abundant in the Latin America and Caribbean region with 22,510 cubic meters per capita. Besides, the remaining regions have limited water resources, especially the Middle East and North Africa (553.4 cubic meters) and the South Asia (1147.3 cubic meters) regions face water stress. These regions are under the water scarcity level, which equals to 2000 cubic meters per capita, according to the World Bank's (2008) Global Monitoring Report. The report had predicted that the water resources would fall below 500 cubic meters per capita by 2050. However, according to 2014 data, water resources in the region have fallen to this critical level earlier than expected. Therefore, countries in this region may face more challenging conditions on water availability in the following decades.

It is seen that these forest area and water resources shortages discussed above have caused various environmental problems such as air and water pollution. Figure 10.5 displays a historical overview of the per capita footprint in the region for the period 1984–2016. According to the graph, the world average per capita footprint is stable— between 2.5 and 3.0—in the period examined. However, it is seen that the MENA average is higher than the world average. Specifically, environmental degradation in the region has risen since the beginning of the 1990s. The demand for natural

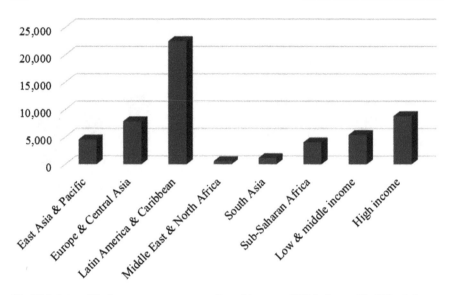

Fig. 10.4 Internal freshwater resources per capita, cubic meters (2014). *Source* World Bank dataset (Accessed on 23.04.2020)

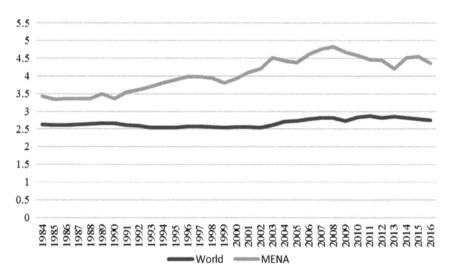

Fig. 10.5 Historical overview of per capita ecological footprint (1984–2016). *Source* Global Footprint Network dataset (Accessed on 23.04.2020)

resources has increased by around 30% in the period 1990–2016. The high level of environmental pollution in the region can be attributed to several factors such as oil extraction activities, high energy use per capita, deforestation, water scarcity, and industrial activities based on fossil-fuel combustion.

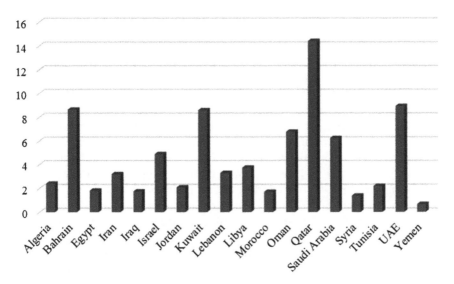

Fig. 10.6 Ecological footprint per capita in MENA Countries (2016). *Source* Global Footprint Network dataset (Accessed on 23.04.2020)

The country-specific pollution levels in the MENA region in 2016 are reported in Fig. 10.6. The region's average for per capita ecological footprint is 4.5 global hectares. The series shows that seven countries are above average, while 11 countries are below it. In detail, the demand for ecological assets (productive lands and sea areas) (Galli et al. 2014) is very high in Qatar (14.4 gha), UAE (8.9 gha), Bahrain (8.6 gha), and Kuwait (8.5 gha). Among these countries, Qatar, UAE, and Kuwait are the most energy-consuming (per capita) countries in the region. Besides, their consumption is mostly based on fossil fuels. Conversely, Yemen and Syria have better environmental quality compared to the remaining countries. Their per capita ecological footprint levels are very low, 0.6 gha and 1.3 gha, respectively.

10.3 Impacts of Globalization on Pollution Level

In this section, the study summarizes both theoretical and empirical literature on the impact of globalization on environmental degradation level. Also, we carry out Pearson's correlation coefficient analysis to detect the potential existence of a relationship between ecological footprint and types of globalization indices.

10.3.1 Theoretical Background

Originally, Grossman and Krueger (1991) examined the impact of economic activities on environmental quality. They report the existence of an inverted U-shaped relationship between pollution level and income. Then, Panayotou (1993) describes this connection as the *Environmental Kuznets Curve* (EKC) hypothesis. According to the EKC hypothesis, the scale effect increases environmental degradation, while technique effects lead to a decline in the environmental deterioration level (Liobikienė and Butkus 2019). Moreover, the impact of the composition effect on the pollution level can be either positive or negative based on the structure of the economy (Tsurumi and Managi 2010). We further discuss these concepts below.

The environmental effect of globalization can be divided into three subcategories, namely, the scale effect, the composition effect, and the technique effect (Grossman and Krueger 1991). Economic globalization triggers trade and financial activities in a country because people demand more goods and services in a more globalized economy. According to Copeland (2013), an increase in trade activities causes a rise in the overall production level. Then, the environment gets dirty since some parts of the production process depend on fossil fuel use. This type of pollution can be called as the *scale effect* of economic globalization. In addition, the *composition effect* is related to the structure of the economy. Its effect on the environment depends on the structure of the economy. If the production sector consists of dirty industries, an increase in the economic globalization level pollutes the environment. However, if the production sector consists of clean industries, its impacts on environmental quality become positive (Grossman and Krueger 1991; Tsurumi and Managi 2010). Besides, economic globalization leads to an increase in foreign direct investment inflows in the recipient countries. Thus, multinational companies invest in host countries through Greenfield investments, joint ventures, or mergers and acquisitions. If local firms get benefits and learn new and cleaner techniques from foreign companies, an increase in trade and financial globalization decreases pollution level in the host countries (Grossman and Krueger 1991). It is named as the *technique effect* in the environmental economics literature.

Table 10.1 presents an overview for the expected impact of different forms of globalization on environmental quality. As discussed above, economic globalization causes an environmental deterioration through the scale effect, while its impact

Table 10.1 The expected impact of globalization on environmental quality

Types of effects	Economic globalization	Social globalization	Political globalization
Scale effect	Negative	Ambiguous	Ambiguous
Composition effect	Ambiguous	Ambiguous	Ambiguous
Technique effect	Positive	Positive	Ambiguous
Total effect	Ambiguous	Ambiguous	Ambiguous

Note This table is constructed by authors based on the studies of Grossman and Krueger (1991) and Bu et al. (2016)

on environmental quality is positive through the technique effect. Furthermore, the composition effect has an ambiguous impact on the environment. Its effect can be either positive or negative, based on the structure of the economy. Besides, Bu et al. (2016) argue that public environmental awareness can be increased by social globalization since it helps to provide social integration between the developing countries and developed countries. This high degree of social integration (including touristic visits, student movements, and cultural products) may decrease environmental degradation through technique effect. The environmental degradation level can be affected by lifestyle changes owing to social globalization. Lastly, the impact of the political globalization on the environmental quality is ambiguous; its effect changes with respect to the effectiveness of the political globalization actions.

The above expectations are derived from Grossman and Krueger (1991) and Bu et al. (2016). The impacts of globalization on the environment may vary from one country to another according to their economic, social, and political characteristics.

10.3.2 Empirical Background

Initially, there has been a surge of interest in the impacts of trade openness on environmental pollution in the empirical literature. Among the studies, Halicioglu (2009) finds that foreign trade and emission levels move hand in hand in the long run for the Turkish economy. His results prove that an increase in foreign trade causes a decline in environmental quality for the period 1960–2005. Al-Mulali and Ozturk (2015) indicate that a rise in trade activities causes an increase in ecological footprint in 14 MENA countries covering the period 1996–2012. Moreover, Jamel and Maktouf's (2017) results suggest that an increase in trade activities pollute the environment in 40 European countries during the period 1985–2014. In a similar setting, Lv and Xu (2019) confirm the detrimental effect of trade openness on the environment in 55 middle-income countries of the period 1992–2012. Besides, Mahmood et al. (2019) examine the effect of trade openness on CO_2 emission for the Tunisian economy through linear and nonlinear cointegration tests for the period 1971–2014. According to their findings, trade openness increases environmental degradation in the long run. These studies mainly used the trade flows to gross domestic product ratio as a proxy for trade openness. Therefore, these studies fail to assess the effect of trade openness (globalization) on the environment accurately. Indeed, when dealing with globalization, other measurements, such as trade partner diversity, trade policies, and taxes on export and import activities should be considered. To overcome these shortcomings, the number of studies focusing on this issue has increased since the mid of the 2010s. The results emerging from these studies show that, in the long run, an increase in globalization level leads to a rise in CO_2 emissions (Shahbaz et al. 2015). This study was reported in India and covered the period 1970–2012. Moreover, Bu et al. (2016) examine the impacts of different types of globalization indices on the environmental quality through panel fixed effect and two stages least squares panel fixed methodologies. Their findings demonstrate that the composite index for globalization and its three main dimensions have an adverse effect on the environmental quality for 166 countries for the period 1990–2009. Moreover, their findings support that the EKC hypothesis is valid for the examined countries and for some model specifications. Besides, Shahbaz et al. (2016) investigate the relationship between CO_2 emissions, per capita income, energy intensity, and globalization level for a panel of African economies. For this purpose, they utilize the ARDL bounds and the Bayer-Hanck cointegration tests to determine the long-run relationship between variables. According to their results, the aforementioned variables move together in the long run for the majority of the countries except for Côte d'Ivoire, Egypt, and Gabon. The empirical findings of their study provide evidence for a negative relationship between globalization level and CO_2 emissions in 19 African countries covering the period 1971–2012. In detail, the impact of globalization on environmental degradation is negative in seven countries, while the coefficient is estimated positive in only five countries. Also, Haseeb et al. (2018) examine the impacts of globalization on CO_2 emissions in BRICS over the period between 1995 and 2014. According to the panel results, there is no statistically significant linkage between these variables. Nevertheless, country-specific results indicate that the impact of globalization on CO_2 emissions is positive in Russia and India. At the same time, the coefficient is negative in Brazil, China, and South Africa for the period of study.

You and Lv (2018) employ a spatial panel analysis to reveal the link between economic globalization and CO_2 emissions for 83 countries of the period 1985–2013. Their empirical findings support that economic globalization has a negative and statistically significant impact on emission levels. Also, their findings demonstrate that there is an inverted U-shaped relationship between income level and carbon emissions, which support the EKC hypothesis. In addition, Sabir and Gorus (2019) reveal that a rise in the KOF index leads to an increase in per capita ecological footprint in five South Asian countries for the period 1975–2017. They utilize the panel ARDL methodology and panel Granger causality analysis to find out the relationship between variables. Besides, their findings support the EKC hypothesis for South Asian countries; they estimated the threshold level of income as around 4500$. Moreover, the empirical results of the study reveal that there is a one-way causality running from globalization to ecological footprint. Besides, Bilgili et al. (2020) find that economic and social globalization indices have a negative impact on environmental quality, while political globalization decreases per capita ecological footprint level in Turkey during the period 1970–2014. More recently, Etokakpan et al. (2020) investigate the long-run impact of globalization on the ecological quality via various cointegration analyses in the Turkish economy during the period 1970–2017. They find that ecological footprint, energy consumption, globalization, and income level are cointegrated in the long run in Turkey. Their empirical findings support the pollutive impact of globalization in the long term. Besides, the Granger causality analysis results indicate that there is a bidirectional causal relationship between ecological footprint and globalization level. In a similar setting, Le and Ozturk (2020) investigate the link between carbon emissions, energy use, income level, government expenditures, institutional quality, financial development, and globalization level through recent panel cointegration techniques in 47 countries. They find that these variables move together in the long run. Their empirical findings support the idea that the level of globalization causes environmental degradation in 47 developing countries of the period 1990–2014. Moreover, the Dumitrescu-Hurlin panel causality test results show that there is a two-way causality between carbon emissions and globalization in the countries examined. In addition, Ulucak et al. (2020) examine the effect of the financial globalization index on per capita ecological footprint for 15 developing countries covering the period 1974–2016. For this aim, they conduct the Pedroni and Kao panel cointegration tests. They find that, according to PMG (Pooled Mean Group) and DOLS (Dynamic Ordinary Least Squares Estimator) estimation results, the financial globalization level leads to an improvement of environmental quality in the long run for this set of countries. However, MG (Mean Group) estimation results exhibit that there is not statistically significant relationship between these variables. Besides, Usman et al. (2020) study the impact of globalization on the environmental deterioration for the United States. They consider structural breaks both in unit root and cointegration analyses. In detail, they carried out the Zivot-Andrews unit root and Maki cointegration tests and utilized the ARDL bounds test approach. Their findings reveal that an increase in the globalization index causes a rise in environmental pollution level in the United States both in the short and long run for the period 1985–2014. Recently, Yilanci and Gorus (2020) find that ecological footprint Ganger causes both economic and trade globalization indices, while there is a bidirectional causal link between ecological footprint and financial globalization in 14 MENA countries in the panel setting. However, country-specific results provide mixed evidence for the causal relationship between the aforementioned variables.

Overall, there is no consensus on the effects of globalization level on demand for ecological assets in the literature. The empirical findings are profoundly affected by the methods and periods used, countries examined, and indicators measuring pollution level (such as ecological footprint, CO_2 emission, particulate matters) utilized. In addition, country-specific factors, including environmental policy stringency, taxes on fossil fuel combustion, and the structure of the economy may affect the impact of globalization on environmental quality.

10.3.3 Pearson's Correlation Coefficient Analysis

In this section, we conduct Pearson's correlation coefficient analysis for ecological footprint and types of globalization measures for a sample of 18 MENA countries, namely, Algeria, Jordan, Qatar, Bahrain, Kuwait, Saudi Arabia, Egypt, Lebanon, Syria, Iran, Libya, Tunisia, Iraq, Morocco, UAE, Israel, Oman, and Yemen. This correlation coefficient (r) shows the strength and direction of the relationship between two variables. The coefficient only considers the linear relationship, not nonlinear one. Specifically, if $r \geq (\pm) 0.70$, there exists a positive (negative) and strong relationship between variables. Besides, if r is around $(\pm) 0.50$, it shows a positive (negative) and moderate relationship between variables. Moreover, if r equals to zero, there is no linear relationship between the two series (Rumsey 2009). Table 10.2 presents the Pearson's correlation coefficient analysis' results for MENA countries.

According to Table 10.2, there is no statistically significant relationship between ecological footprint and different globalization indices in Bahrain and the UAE for the period considered. Also, it is reported that there is a positive and strong relationship between ecological footprint and composite index for globalization in Algeria, Egypt, Iran, Israel, Jordan, Libya, Morocco, Oman, Qatar, Saudi Arabia, and Tunisia. A similar relationship is found for eight countries regarding economic globalization, for 11 countries regarding social globalization, and for 11 economies regarding political globalization, respectively.

We can say that environmental degradation and globalization have a positive relationship (strong or moderate) in the majority of the MENA countries. These findings exhibit that expected changes in per capita ecological footprint and globalization indices seem to move in the same direction in most of the countries of our sample. Therefore, this study confirms the previous findings of the literature that there is a close relationship between these series.

Table 10.2 Pearson's correlation coefficients between ecological footprint and globalization indices in MENA countries

Country	Period	Ecological footprint and globalization	Ecological footprint and economic globalization	Ecological footprint and social globalization	Ecological footprint and political plobalization
Algeria	1970–2016	0.842^{***}	0.548^{***}	0.895^{***}	0.794^{***}
Bahrain	1980–2016	-0.114	0.028	-0.201	-0.131
Egypt	1970–2016	0.961^{***}	0.675^{***}	0.878^{***}	0.926^{***}
Iran	1979–2016	0.929^{***}	0.818^{***}	0.869^{***}	0.930^{***}
Iraq	1982–2016	-0.090	-0.609^{***}	0.155	0.484^{***}
Israel	1970–2016	0.826^{***}	0.797^{***}	0.817^{***}	0.774^{***}
Jordan	1970–2016	0.903^{***}	0.903^{***}	0.833^{***}	0.907^{***}
Kuwait	1999–2016	0.603^{***}	0.489^{**}	0.518^{**}	0.667^{***}
Lebanon	1970–2016	0.460^{***}	0.330^{**}	0.303^{**}	0.571^{***}
Libya	1981–2016	0.823^{***}	0.833^{***}	0.886^{***}	0.634^{***}
Morocco	1970–2016	0.915^{***}	0.892^{***}	0.917^{***}	0.854^{***}
Oman	1984–2016	0.939^{***}	0.880^{***}	0.939^{***}	0.929^{***}
Qatar	1980–2016	0.857^{***}	0.830^{***}	0.789^{***}	0.873^{***}
Saudi Arabia	1981–2016	0.801^{***}	0.094	0.778^{***}	0.741^{***}
Syria	1970–2016	0.545^{***}	0.503^{***}	0.296^{**}	0.700^{***}
Tunisia	1970–2016	0.939^{***}	0.880^{***}	0.850^{***}	0.903^{***}
UAE	1980–2016	-0.061	-0.130	-0.013	-0.038
Yemen	1970–2016	0.657^{***}	0.609^{***}	0.531^{***}	0.627^{***}

Note *** and ** display the significance level at 1% and 5%, respectively

The above empirical findings show that the economic globalization level of a country may affect environmental quality negatively. As we discussed before, economic globalization consists of both trade and financial globalization. First, trade activities, including export and import volume, increase in a more globalized economy. Then, the production level of an economy may rise when trade activities increase. These developments lead to environmental degradation in countries that have not completed the economic transformation because their production processes are heavily dependent on fossil fuel combustion. Second, FDI inflows play a significant role in building the financial globalization index. FDI inflows may cause environmental deterioration in the host country due to differences in environmental regulations between developed and developing countries (Copeland 2010). Particularly, multinational companies (especially in the developed Western world) choose to invest in countries that have lower environmental standards (such as MENA, African, and Asian countries) due to their cost benefits. So, they are eager to move their dirty industries to emerging economies because of incurring low (or zero) environmental costs. Indeed, even if host countries get an economic benefit from this kind of FDI inflow, their environmental quality is affected negatively because of an increase in dirty production. This harmful effect of FDI inflows on the environment is named in the literature as the *Pollution Haven Hypothesis*. Obviously, the correlation coefficient between ecological footprint and economic globalization is very high—around 0.90—in Jordan, Morocco, Oman, and Tunisia for the period examined. Thus, policymakers in these countries should take some precautions regarding environmental issues and design economic policies to prevent the pollutive impact of trade and financial activities.

The empirical results of Table 10.2 also suggest that the demand for ecological assets and social globalization (includes tourism activities and international airports) are highly correlated for most of the MENA countries. In addition to the positive effects of tourism development on economic growth, including employment effect, higher demand on goods and services, higher demand on the domestic currency, an inflow of foreign exchange (Solarin 2014), tourism development has harmful impacts on the environment. In the empirical literature, there is a bunch of studies supporting the detrimental effect of tourism activities on environmental quality. To name few, the nexus has been reported by Solarin (2014) for the Malaysian economy, Vita et al. (2015) for Turkey, Balogh and Jámbor (2017) for 168 countries, Paramati et al. (2017) for 26 developed and 18 emerging economies, Sharif et al. (2017) for Pakistan, and Koçak et al. (2020) for 10 most visited countries. The theoretical explanation of the pollutive impact of tourism on the environment shows that tourism activities cause fossil fuel combustion through international flights, domestic transportation, land alteration activities, cooking, heating, cooling, etc. (Gössling 2000). Notedly, the correlation coefficient between ecological footprint and social globalization is above 0.90 in Morocco and Oman for the period considered. In these countries, policymakers should take into consideration high fossil fuel usage originating from tourism activities. Besides, they should design encouragement policies on clean energy consumption.

The sixth column of Table 10.2 reports the correlation coefficient between ecological footprint and political globalization for the MENA countries. It is seen that there is a positive correlation between the aforementioned variables. According to the findings, the correlation coefficient is very high in Egypt, Iran, Jordan, Oman, and Tunisia. As discussed above, political globalization measures the number of embassies, peacekeeping missions, non-governmental organizations, organizations, treaties, and treaty partner diversity in international settings. However, being a part of international treaties always does not mean countries are responsible for all the commitments in the protocol or agreements. For example, developed countries are responsible for carbon reduction targets, while most of the developing countries do not have these goals in the Kyoto Protocol (Bu et al. 2016). Therefore, the positive correlation between these variables can be attributed to this issue. Thus, governments in the region should take active roles in international agreements and choose specific targets for increasing environmental standards in their countries.

Overall, our empirical results exhibit that not only economic globalization but also social and political globalization have a prominent impact on the environmental problems in the MENA region.

10.4   Conclusion and Policy Implications

We discussed in this chapter the current economic conditions, energy production and consumption level, globalization level, and environmental issues in the MENA region. According to the data, we reported that domestic and international conflicts and wars have negative impacts on the globalization level in the MENA countries. These issues not only damage the composite globalization level but also affect its economic, social, and political dimensions.

At the environmental level, water and forest resources are limited in the region. These scarcities cause various environmental problems such as air, land, and water pollution.

In our empirical part, we conducted Pearson's correlation coefficient analysis between ecological footprint and globalization (and its subcomponents) for a panel of MENA countries. Empirical results show that not only economic activities, but also social and political globalization have a significant impact on the environmental problems in the MENA region.

There are several important policy changes that need to be tackled. A key policy priority should be to plan for the long-term care of environmental quality in the MENA countries. There is, therefore, a definite need for environmental actions such as clean energy encouragement policies, taxes on emission levels and fossil fuel combustion, the introduction of public awareness policies on environmental issues. Besides, governments should take active roles in international non-governmental organizations for increasing environmental standards in their countries. Moreover, they should introduce tighter environmental policies in order to avoid becoming *pollution havens*. In conclusion, countries in the MENA region should spend their oil and natural gas revenues on providing *sustainable economic growth* rather than *plain economic growth*.

References

Acikgoz S, Ben Ali MS (2019) Where does economic growth in the Middle Eastern and North African countries come from? Quart Rev Econ Finan 73:172–183

Acikgoz S, Ben Ali MS, Mert M (2016) Sources of economic growth in MENA countries: technological progress, physical or human capital accumulations? economic development in the Middle East and North Africa. Springer/Palgrave Macmillan, New York, pp 27–69

Al-Mulali U, Ozturk I (2015) The effect of energy consumption, urbanization, trade openness, industrial output, and the political stability on the environmental degradation in the MENA (Middle East and North African) region. Energy 84:382–389

Apergis N, Ben Ali MS (2020) Corruption, rentier states and economic growth: where do the GCC countries stand? In: Miniaoui H (eds) Economic development in the gulf cooperation council countries: from rentier states to diversified economies. Springer

Balogh JM, Jámbor A (2017) Determinants of CO_2 emission: a global evidence. Int J Energ Econ Policy 7(5):217–226

Ben Mim S, Ben Ali MS (2020) Natural resources curse and economic diversification in GCC countries. In: Miniaoui H (eds) Economic development in the gulf cooperation council countries: from rentier states to diversified economies. Springer

Bilgili F, Ulucak R, Koçak E, İlkay SÇ (2020) Does globalization matter for environmental sustainability? Empirical investigation for Turkey by Markov regime switching models. Environ Sci Pollut Res 27(1):1087–1100

Bu M, Lin CT, Zhang B (2016) Globalization and climate change: new empirical panel data evidence. J Econ Surv 30(3):577–595

Common M, Stagl S (2005) Ecological economics: an introduction. Cambridge University Press

Copeland BR (2010) The pollution haven hypothesis. In: Gallagher K (ed) Handbook on trade and the environment. Edward Elgar Publishing

Copeland BR (2013) Trade and the environment. In: Palgrave handbook of international trade. Palgrave Macmillan, London, pp 423–496

De Vita G, Katircioglu S, Altinay L, Fethi S, Mercan M (2015) Revisiting the environmental Kuznets curve hypothesis in a tourism development context. Environ Sci Pollut Res 22(21):16652–16663

Dreher A (2006) Does globalization affect growth? Evidence from a new index of globalization. Appl Econ 38(10):1091–1110

Etokakpan MU, Adedoyin F, Vedat Y, Bekun FV (2020) Does globalization in Turkey induce increased energy consumption: insights into its environmental pros and cons. Environ Sci Pollut Res 1–16. https://doi.org/10.1007/s11356-020-08714-3

Galli A, Wackernagel M, Iha K, Lazarus E (2014) Ecological footprint: implications for biodiversity. Biol Cons 173:121–132

Global Footprint Network (2020) Ecological Footprint. https://www.footprintnetwork.org/our-work/ecological-footprint/. Accessed on 18.06.2020

Gössling S (2000) Sustainable tourism development in developing countries: some aspects of energy use. J Sustain Tourism 8(5):410–425

Grossman GM, Krueger AB (1991) Environmental impacts of a North American free trade agreement. Working paper No. 3914. National Bureau of Economic Research, Cambridge, MA

Gygli S, Haelg F, Potrafke N, Sturm JE (2019) The KOF globalisation index–revisited. Rev Int Organ 14:543–574

Halicioglu F (2009) An econometric study of CO2 emissions, energy consumption, income and foreign trade in Turkey. Energ Policy 37(3):1156–1164

Haseeb A, Xia E, Baloch MA, Abbas K (2018) Financial development, globalization, and CO_2 emission in the presence of EKC: evidence from BRICS countries. Environ Sci Pollut Res 25(31):31283–31296

Jamel L, Maktouf S (2017) The nexus between economic growth, financial development, trade openness, and CO_2 emissions in European countries. Cogent Econ Finan 5(1):1341456

Koçak E, Ulucak R, Ulucak ZŞ (2020) The impact of tourism developments on CO_2 emissions: an advanced panel data estimation. Tour Manag Perspect 33, Article 100611

Le HP, Ozturk I (2020) The impacts of globalization, financial development, government expenditures, and institutional quality on CO_2 emissions in the presence of environmental Kuznets curve. Environ Sci Pollut Res 27:22680–22697

Liobikienė G, Butkus M (2019) Scale, composition, and technique effects through which the economic growth, foreign direct investment, urbanization, and trade affect greenhouse gas emissions. Renew Energ 132:1310–1322

Lv Z, Xu T (2019) Trade openness, urbanization and CO_2 emissions: dynamic panel data analysis of middle-income countries. J Int Trade Econ Dev 28(3):317–330

Mahmood H, Maalel N, Zarrad O (2019) Trade openness and CO_2 emissions: evidence from Tunisia. Sustainability 11(12):3295

MOFNE (2019) Bahrain 2019 Economic Report. Bahrain Economic Quarterly-Q4. https://bahrai nedb.com/app/uploads/2017/06/Bh-Economic-Quarterly-end-of-2019-EN.pdf

Nathanson R (2011) Growth, economic policies and employment linkages: Israel. International Labor Office, Sector Employment Working Paper, No. 83

Panayotou T (1993) Empirical tests and policy analysis of environmental degradation at different stages of economic development (No. 292778). International Labour Organization

Paramati SR, Alam MS, Chen CF (2017) The effects of tourism on economic growth and CO_2 emissions: a comparison between developed and developing economies. J Travel Res 56(6):712–724

Rumsey DJ (2009) Statistics II for dummies. Wiley

Sabir S, Gorus MS (2019) The impact of globalization on ecological footprint: empirical evidence from the South Asian countries. Environ Sci Pollut Res 26(32):33387–33398

Shahbaz M, Mallick H, Mahalik MK, Loganathan N (2015) Does globalization impede environmental quality in India? Ecol Ind 52:379–393

Shahbaz M, Solarin SA, Ozturk I (2016) Environmental Kuznets curve hypothesis and the role of globalization in selected African countries. Ecol Ind 67:623–636

Sharif A, Afshan S, Nisha N (2017) Impact of tourism on CO_2 emission: evidence from Pakistan. Asia Pacific J Tourism Res 22(4):408–421

Smiet AC (1990) Forest ecology on Java: conversion and usage in a historical perspective. J Trop Forest Sci 2(4):286–302

Solarin SA (2014) Tourist arrivals and macroeconomic determinants of CO_2 emissions in Malaysia. Anatolia 25(2):228–241

Stern DI (2004) The rise and fall of the environmental Kuznets curve. World Dev 32(8):1419–1439

Tsurumi T, Managi S (2010) Decomposition of the environmental Kuznets curve: scale, technique, and composition effects. Environ Econ Policy Stud 11(1–4):19–36

Ulucak ZŞ, İlkay SÇ, Özcan B, Gedikli A (2020) Financial globalization and environmental degradation nexus: evidence from emerging economies. Resour Policy 67:101698

Usman O, Akadiri SS, Adeshola I (2020) Role of renewable energy and globalization on ecological footprint in the USA: implications for environmental sustainability. Environ Sci Pollut Res 1–13. https://doi.org/10.1007/s11356-020-09170-9

World Bank (2008) Global monitoring report 2008: MDGs and the environment: agenda for inclusive and sustainable development. World Bank

World Tourism Organization (2019) Tourism in the MENA region. UNWTO, Madrid. https://doi.org/10.18111/9789284420896

Yilanci V, Gorus MS (2020) Does economic globalization have predictive power for ecological footprint in MENA counties? A panel causality test with a Fourier function. Environ Sci Pollut Res 1–11. https://doi.org/10.1007/s11356-020-10092-9

You W, Lv Z (2018) Spillover effects of economic globalization on CO_2 emissions: a spatial panel approach. Energ Econ 73:248–257

Chapter 11
ICT and Growth in MENA Countries: What Are the Involved Transmission Channels?

Sami Ben Mim and Mounir Jeguirim

Abstract This study assesses the impact of information and communication technologies on growth for a sample composed of 14 MENA countries. We also investigate various transmission channels of this effect using the difference GMM estimator to control for endogeneity. Estimation results show that the Internet use contributes significantly to promote growth. Investment and human capital are the main involved transmission channels. The positive relationship between ICT and growth is however nonlinear. The intensity of this relationship is higher in countries investing massively in ICT infrastructure. The results also suggest that ICT substitute for control of corruption in the MENA countries.

Keywords ICT · Growth · MENA · Investment · Human capital

11.1 Introduction

Information and communication technologies (ICT) spread widely throughout the last decades. Beyond their economic impact, they influenced various and important aspects of our lives such as access to health and education (Ben Ali and Selmi 2020; Dutta et al. 2019). Some studies emphasized their role in curbing corruption and promoting democracy, mainly through enhancing transparency and access to information (Ben Ali 2020; Ben Ali and Sassi 2017). It has also been proved that ICT played a major role in promoting pro-environmental behavior (Pattinson 2017), overcoming cultural barriers, and promoting diversity.

On the economic side, ICT induced major transformations during the last decades. Much research has focused on the causal links between ICT and economic growth, highlighting multiple channels such as: productivity of production factors, the rate of

S. Ben Mim (✉)
University of Sousse, IHEC, LaREMFiQ, 40-4054 Sousse, Tunisia
e-mail: sbenmim@yahoo.fr

M. Jeguirim
Faculty of Economics and Management of Mahdia, University of Monastir, 5111 Mahdia, Tunisia

© The Author(s), under exclusive license to Springer Nature Switzerland AG 2021
M. S. Ben Ali (ed.), *Economic Development in the MENA Region*, Perspectives on Development in the Middle East and North Africa (MENA) Region,
https://doi.org/10.1007/978-3-030-66380-3_11

equipment in computer hardware, the territorial coverage by the broadband network, the development of telecommunications networks, the number of mobile phones, etc. Most contributions have shown that the impact of ICT on firms, industries, and international trade is considerable. However, the impact of ICT on economic growth differs considerably from one country to another and from one region to another. Indeed, the share of ICT in GDP ranged between 0.1 and 1% till the 1990s. This share increased dramatically from 1995 onward, as confirmed by Jorgenson (2001) for the US, Oulton (2002) for the UK, Colecchia and Schreyer (2002) for Europe and Jorgenson and Vu (2005) worldwide. Accordingly, Stiroh (2002) showed for a sample of 61 US firms that productivity gains are an increasing function of the industry's capital intensity, particularly after 1995. On the other hand, Van Ark et al. (2011) showed that between 1995 and 2004, the contribution of ICT to the economic growth of 10 European countries (Austria, Belgium, Denmark, Finland, France, Germany, Italy, the Netherlands, and the UK) was significantly lower than that achieved in the USA. Similarly, for a sample of 42 developed and developing countries over the 1985–1995 period, Pohjola (2002) found that the contribution of ICT in most countries was lower than that recorded in the USA. In the same vein, Dewan and Kraemer (2000), referring to data from 1985 to 1993, showed that the effect of ICT on economic growth is lower in developing countries than in developed countries.

Through a meta-analysis based on 150 studies, Cardona et al. (2013) showed that most of the empirical results confirmed the existence of a positive and significant effect of ICT on the productivity of the different production factors. Moreover, these effects tend to increase over time. However, the assertion that general-purpose technology (GPT) can affect an entire economy remains to be confirmed. In a recent study, Vu et al. (2020) assessed the impact of ICT on growth by emphasizing their impact on average labor productivity for 102 countries representing 95% of the global GDP in 2017. The authors divided the sample into two sub-periods: from 1977 to 1997 and from 1997 to 2017. They showed that the average annual growth rate increased by 0.75% between these sub-periods (from 2.95% during the 1977–1997 period to 3.70% over the 1997–2017 period). In parallel, the average annual growth rate of labor productivity increased by 1.38%, passing from 0.99 to 2.37%. The authors argued that growth recovery during the second sub-period is highly correlated with the increase in labor productivity, which is mainly due to an increasing use of ICT. Stiroh (2005) confirmed the productivity effect of ICT use but argued that the obtained results are very sensitive to the model specification and to the econometric approach.

In the same vein, Stanley et al. (2018), through a linear regression model, confirmed the positive ICT contribute to boost factors productivity. They showed that the impact of wireless technologies (Wi-Fi, Bluetooth, etc.) is double that of landline technology. Similarly, the impact of these technologies is higher in developed countries than in developing countries. However, the authors argued that the effects of the growing use of the Internet are limited.

Another strand of literature argued that the long-term effects of ICT on growth are higher than the short-term effects. In this respect, Brynjolfsson and Hitt (2003) showed that the long-run effects of ICT occur within 3 to 7 years and are higher than those recorded in the short run. Such a long gestation period is attributed to the fact that ICT investments imply important organizational changes. Hong (2017) confirmed these findings by examining the links between ICT investments in R&D and economic growth. Comparing public and private investments, he pointed out that the impact of ICT on economic growth is higher in the long term than in the short term for both categories of investment.

Various empirical studies have shown that the effect of ICT on economic growth accelerates above a certain threshold. Roller and Waverman (2001) examined the impact of investment in telecommunications infrastructure on economic growth in 21 OECD countries over the 1970–1990 period. They found that above a certain threshold, the contribution of ICT to economic growth is more significant. Similarly, Koutroumpis (2009) has shown that investments in broadband have increasing returns on scale, proving the existence of a critical threshold. Gruber et al. (2011) found that the correlation between mobile telecommunications and growth is significantly lower in countries with low geographic coverage than in countries with high coverage.

Literature dealing with transmission channels emphasized the impact of ICT on human capital, not only through the learning effect but also through promoting health care (Dutta et al. 2019). Furthermore, ICT contribute massively to facilitate and accelerate international trade. In this respect, Vu (2011) has shown that the use of the Internet has facilitated access to knowledge, technology, and global markets. The Internet is a major factor that has enabled many developing countries to boost their growth. Meijers (2014) argued that the use of the Internet has a significant effect on international trade, particularly in developing countries. International trade, in turn, will produce a positive effect on growth.

On the other hand, complementary investments, particularly of an organizational nature, are of paramount importance to enable ICT investments to improve productivity and stimulate economic growth. Brynjolfsson and Hitt (2000) and Dedrik et al. (2003) emphasized the importance of organizational investments. Such investments should allow firms to take full advantage of the benefits generated by ICT. Among these complementary investments, the authors highlighted investments in vocational training, improvement of working methods, decision-making decentralization, and relations with third parties such as suppliers and customers. The authors concluded that organizational change induced by ICT investments provides more productivity gains than the ICT investments themselves.

Some studies focused on specific transmission channels and highlighted that ICT may actively contribute to promote financial development and the efficiency of anti-corruption policies. Shamim (2007) proved that better connectivity enhances financial depth, which in turn leads to a higher growth performance. Accordingly, Claessens et al. (2002) argued that developing countries should massively invest in ICT to overcome the shallowness of their financial systems. At the institutional level, several studies showed that higher ICT investments are associated with lower corruption levels and higher governance standards (Ben Ali 2020; Backus 2001). In particular, the Internet helps curbing corruption by facilitating access to information and by favoring transparency and accountability. Promoting ICT is also a major prerequisite for developing countries to attract foreign direct investments (FDI).

Gholami et al. (2005) showed that causality runs from ICT to FDI in developed countries, which leads to higher growth perspectives.

Despite the strong evidence for a positive correlation between ICT use and economic growth, the intensity of this impact is still difficult to assess. Indeed, while the mainstream literature pointed out a positive link between ICT and economic growth, some empirical studies have shown that, in many cases, this relationship is ambivalent. In this respect, Meijers (2014) questioned the hypothesis of the positive impact of the Internet use on economic growth. Similarly, Brynjolfsson and Hit (1996) showed that the causal link between ICT and economic growth is ambiguous. This ambiguity stems mainly from the difficulty of quantifying the effects of these technologies on factor productivity, the difficulty of measuring and anticipating the indirect and "delayed" effects of ICT on economic growth, and finally the low profitability of ICT investments due to poor corporate governance.

This paper tries to contribute to this empirical debate by assessing the impact of ICT on economic growth in the MENA region over the 1990–2019 period. We also check for the nonlinearity of the relationship between ICT and growth, and explore six transmission channels expected to be involved in this relationship. We address the endogeneity issue by relying on the Arellano and Bond (1991) difference GMM estimator. The chapter is organized as follows. Section 11.2 discusses the econometric methodology and presents the main characteristics of the sample. The main empirical results are summarized and discussed in Sect. 11.3. The last section concludes and formulates some policy recommendations.

11.2 Sample and Methodology

11.2.1 The Econometric Approach

To gauge the impact of ICT on growth, we consider the following model where per capita GDP is explained by a set of control variables in addition to indicators reflecting a country's endowment of information and communication infrastructure:

$$\ln(\text{pcGDP}_{it}) = \alpha_0 + \alpha_t + \alpha_i + \lambda \ln(\text{pcGDP}_{it}) + \beta X_{it} + \theta \text{ICT}_{it} + \varepsilon_{it} \quad (1)$$

where α_i and α_t represent, respectively, country and period fixed effects, ICT_{it} an indicator relative to information and communication technologies and ε_{it} the error term. The set of control variables, X_{it}, includes the investment rate (*lninvestment*) and the population size (*lnpopulation*) as proxies for the main production factors, capital, and labor force. A higher investment rate should spur growth, while population growth deteriorates the standards of living according to the neoclassical growth theory (Solow 1956). We also control for human capital (*lnschool*), financial development (*lncredit*), and the degree of trade openness (*lntrade*). According to endogenous growth theory, human capital is one of the main drivers of economic growth

(Romer 1986). On the other hand, various studies highlighted the positive effects that financial development and trade openness may produce on growth (Levine 1997). Finally, we control for the effect of the inflation rate (*inflation*), foreign direct investment (*FDI*), and control of corruption (*COC*) on growth. A weak inflation rate often reflects a stable macroeconomic environment which favors growth, while an important strand of literature emphasized the economic benefits of a developed institutional framework (Acemoglu et al. 2005). As for FDIs, they contribute not only to foster growth but also to accelerate technology transfers (Blalock and Gertler 2008). Moreover, the communicational infrastructure became a major determinant of a country's attractiveness for foreign investors.

The ICT are proxied by four different indicators reflecting different aspects of the informational infrastructure in each country. In line with the literature, we introduce, respectively, the number of subscribers to mobile phones and the percentage of Internet users among the independent variables. High levels of these indicators reflect high access to information technologies in the considered country. However, the percentage of Internet users refers to the individuals having accessed to Internet at least once during the three last month. Therefore, it doesn't reflect neither the intensity of Internet use nor the connection quality, particularly the connection speed. To overcome this problem, we controlled for the number of subscribers to broadband connections, which refer to fixed subscriptions to high-speed access to Internet. Persons enjoying a high-speed connection are supposed to make a more intensive use of the Internet. Furthermore, firms using ICT are highly concerned by the security issue. Specific protocols were developed to protect sensitive communication and information transfers across the net. To account for the security aspect, we introduced the number of secure Internet servers among the ICT indicators. Table 11.1 provides the full definitions of the variables included in model (1).

Econometrically, some of the control variables are suspected to generate an endogeneity problem. Endogeneity often arises from reverse causality between some independent variables and the dependent variable. In our case, school enrollment as well as the trade volume is highly dependent on per capita GDP. Moreover, per capita income reflects the purchasing power of consumers and represents a major determinant of domestic and foreign investments. On the other hand, most macroeconomic variables often suffer from measurement errors which represent an additional source of endogeneity. Given these multiple sources of endogeneity, the OLS method is likely to provide biased estimates and misleading conclusions. We address the endogeneity problem by applying the difference GMM estimator developed by Arellano and Bond (1991). The first difference transformation is applied to the initial model which can be written as follows:

$$\Delta \ln(pcGDP_{it}) = \alpha_t + \lambda \Delta \ln(pcGDP_{it-1}) + \beta \Delta X_{it} + \theta \Delta ICT_{it} + \varepsilon_{it} \quad (2)$$

Model (2) assesses the determinants of per capita GDP growth rather than those of per capita GDP level, which is more consistent with the objective of the paper. We note, however, that the lagged difference of the dependent variable is now correlated

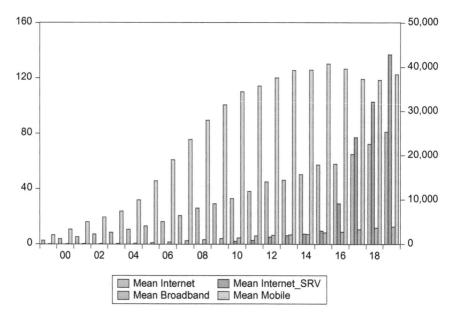

Fig. 11.1 ICT indicators dynamics, 1999–2019

with error term. An instrument variable procedure allows to correct for both endogeneity and first-order autocorrelation. In particular, if ε_{it} are serially uncorrelated and $E[\varepsilon_{it}/X_{is}] = 0$ for $t > S$, then second and higher lags of the independent variables are valid instruments. Nevertheless, if the sample includes a large number of periods, it is highly recommended to restrict the lag's depth. In fact, the instruments proliferation may lead to an overidentification of the endogenous variables and hence affect the robustness of the results. We perform the Sargan-Hansen overidentification test and the Arellano and Bond correlation tests to assess the validity of the used instruments.

11.2.2 The Sample Characteristics

We consider a sample composed of 14 MENA countries and covering the 1990–2019 period[1]. Figure 11.1 describes the dynamics of the ICT indicators over the sample period. The four indicators exhibit a clear increasing trend which reveals that MENA countries have been intensively developing their communicational infrastructure over the last decades. We can also notice that mobile phone users progressed more rapidly than Internet users, while security of networks increased significantly only during the last decade. Figure 11.2 suggests that the major part of ICT equip-

---

[1]The countries belonging to the sample are: Algeria, Bahrain, Egypt, Iran, Iraq, Jordan, Libya, Morocco, Oman, Palestine, Saudi Arabia, Tunisia, Turkey, and the United Arab Emirates.

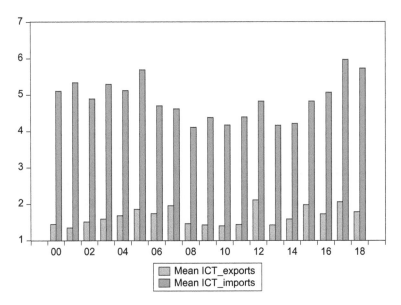

Fig. 11.2 ICT goods exports and imports, 2000–2018

ments in MENA countries is imported rather than produced domestically. In fact, ICT imports represent around 5% of total goods imports, while ICT exports barely exceed 1% of total goods exports. Disaggregated statistics reported in Table 11.2 reveal significant disparities between countries. Rich oil countries (Bahrain, Saudi Arabia, and the Emirates) and Turkey are much better equipped with ICT compared to Algeria, Libya, and Egypt.

The scatter graphs in Fig. 11.3 describe the joint evolution of ICT and some key macroeconomic indicators. We notice that higher percentages of Internet users are associated with higher per capita GDP levels and lower unemployment rates. However, the kernel fit suggests that these relationships are nonlinear. It seems that the percentage of Internet users should exceed a certain threshold to produce a significant effect on per capita GDP and unemployment. A similar result was evidenced by Roller and Waverman (2001) and Gruber et al. (2011). The two last graphs show that the share of industry in GDP is higher in countries highly endowed with ICT, while the opposite is true for the share of agriculture. Such results suggest that the diffusion of ICT contributes to transform the production structure by shifting it toward higher levels of industrial activities.

The descriptive statistics are summarized in Table 11.3 in the appendix. The high standard errors of the ICT indicators confirm that the adoption rate of these technologies differs dramatically across the sample countries. We also notice that the mean level of the control of corruption index is particularly low in the MENA region.

The correlation coefficients provided in Table 11.4 show that all ICT indicators are positively and significantly correlated to per capita GDP. The correlation matrix

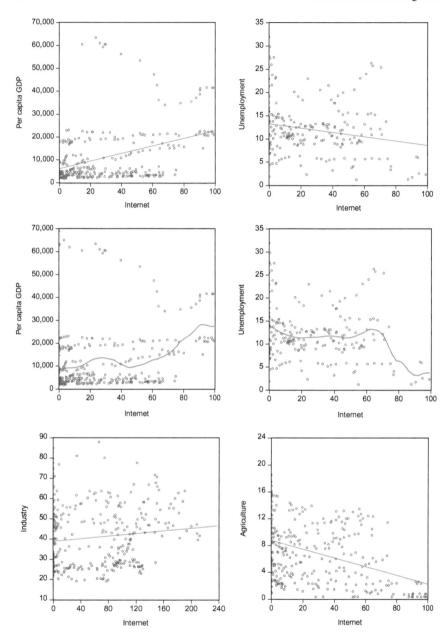

Fig. 11.3 ICT's impact on macroeconomic variables, full sample

provides also interesting insights into the relationship between these indicators and the remaining control variables. We mainly notice that all ICT proxies are positively and significantly correlated to school enrollment, credits provided by the banking sector and control of corruption. These variables are therefore suspected to act as transmission channels through which ICT may act on growth. Vu (2011) argued that ICT contribute to promote human capital, while Shamim (2007) pointed out that ICT foster financial development. Various studies highlighted the positive effects these technologies may produce on control of corruption (Ben Ali and Sassi 2017). However, the correlation analysis offers less clear evidence for some other explanatory variables. For the investment rate and FDI, all the correlation coefficients are positive, but only two of them are significant, while trade openness is positively and significantly correlated to three ICT indicators and negatively correlated to the number of secure Internet servers. Further support for the conclusions drawn from the correlation analysis is provided by the scatter plots in Fig. 11.4. It is therefore interesting to investigate which among these transmission channels is operational in the MENA countries.

11.3   Results and Discussion

Results relative to the difference GMM estimator are reported in Table 11.5. In each of the columns from 1 to 4, we associate one of the four ICT indicators with the set of control variables. The coefficient associated with the investment rate is positive, but significant only in two equations out of four. Oppositely, the volume of credits produces a negative and significant impact on growth in columns 1 and 4. The inefficiency of the banking system in MENA countries and its negative effect on growth have been proved by various empirical studies (Barajas et al. 2011). The coefficients associated with the school enrollment rate are all positive but non-significant, while results relative to the impact of control of corruption on growth are ambiguous.

As for the ICT proxies, we notice that the three indicators relative to the Internet use (percentage of users, broadband subscribers, and secured servers) contribute significantly to promote economic growth. Only the percentage of mobile phone users doesn't produce any significant effect on growth. It seems that mobile phones are mostly used for personal purposes in MENA countries. To explore the nonlinearity issue detected in the descriptive analysis, we divided the sample according to the mean value of Internet users[2]. Results relative to the two subsamples are reported in columns 5 and 6. We notice that the effect of the Internet use increases dramatically when we pass from countries with low percentages of users to countries showing high percentages of Internet users. The coefficient associated with "*Lninternet*" passes from 0.019 for the first subsample to 0.104 for the second one. Such results offer

---

[2]We retained this proxy because it provides the largest number of observations compared to the remaining ICT indicators. It allows therefore to obtain robust result for the subsamples.

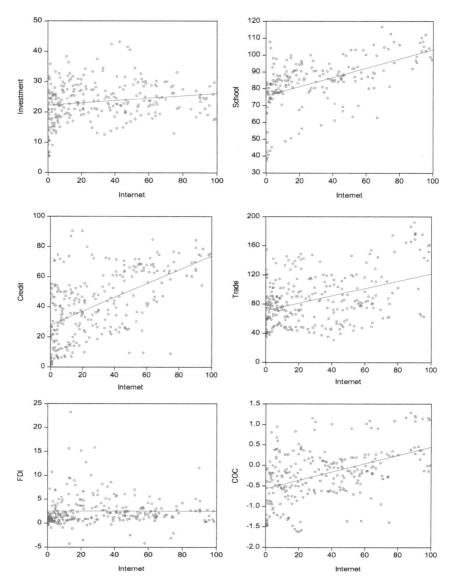

Fig. 11.4 ICT transmission channels, full sample

strong evidence for the nonlinearity hypothesis and reveal that the impact of ICT on growth increases as countries improve their communicational infrastructure.

To investigate the transmission channels through which ICT contribute to spur economic growth, we introduced six different interaction terms in the model. We tested, respectively, each of the following transmission channels: investment, human capital, financial development, trade openness, foreign investment, and institutional development. Results are summarized in Table 11.6.

Estimation results show that ICT contribute to promote growth in MENA countries by accelerating investment and by fostering human capital accumulation. The role of the investment channel was emphasized by Brynjolfsson and Hitt (2000) and Dedrik et al. (2003). The Human capital channel was also highlighted by Vu (2011). On the other hand, results suggest that financial development, trade openness, and FDI channels are not yet operational in the case of the MENA countries. Finally, the coefficient associated with the control of corruption index is negative and significant. This result indicates that ICT substitute for control of corruption in MENA countries. The descriptive statistics pointed out the weak level of the control of corruption index in the MENA region (the means value is −0.244 for the full sample period). In many of these countries, communication networks, and mainly social networks, became an effective tool to disclose and fight corruptive practices, in the absence of a clear political will to tackle corruption.

11.4 Conclusions and Recommendations

MENA countries are constantly upgrading their information and communication technologies. Such a strategy may contribute to foster growth through various channels. The major objective of this study is to assess the overall effect of ICT on growth and to highlight the involved transmission channels for the MENA region, over the last three decades.

Results show that a higher percentage of Internet users leads to higher growth rates. Access to high-speed connection and higher security standards contributes also to spur economic growth. However, mobile phone technology doesn't produce any significant effect on growth in MENA countries. Estimation outcomes suggest also that the relationship between ICT proxies and growth is nonlinear. The impact of ICT indicators on growth gains intensity as countries improve their communicational infrastructure.

Results relative to the transmission channels reveal that ICT foster investment and human capital accumulation which translates into higher growth rates. Moreover, ICT seem to substitute for inefficient anti-corruption policies. However, financial development, FDI, and trade channels are ineffective in the case of the MENA countries.

Three main recommendations can be drawn from these results. Firstly, MENA country should invest intensively in ICT to obtain the expected economic benefits from these investments. The existence of a nonlinear relationship suggests that low ICT investment levels will moderately contribute to enhance growth perspectives. Secondly, ICT can be part of an efficient anti-corruption policy in MENA countries, as they may help disclose corruptive practices. Finally, MENA countries should improve the intermediation role of their domestic financial systems in order to speed-up the growth process.

Appendix

See Tables 11.1, 11.3 and 11.4.

Table 11.1 Variables definitions

Variable	Abbreviation	Definition
Real per capita GDP	LnpcGDP	Log of per capita GDP in constant US dollars. Source: World Development Indicators, World Bank
Investment rate	LnInvestment	Log of fixed capital formation as a percentage of GDP. Source: World Development Indicators, World Bank
Population size	LnPopulation	Log of the midyear estimates of all residents (regardless of legal status or citizenship). Source: World Development Indicators, World Bank
Human capital	LnSchool	Log of secondary school gross enrollment ratio. Source: World Development Indicators, World Bank
Financial development	LnCredit	Log of domestic credits provided by the banking sector as a share of GDP. Source: World Development Indicators, World Bank
Trade openness	LnTrade	Log of exports plus imports of goods and services as a share of GDP
Inflation rate	Inflation	Annual rate of change in the consumer price index. Source: World Development Indicators, World Bank
Control of corruption	COC	Perceptions of the extent to which public power is exercised for private gain, including all forms of corruption, as well as "capture" of the state by elites and private interests. Source: The Worldwide Governance Indicators (WGI), World Bank
Foreign direct investment	FDI	Net total foreign direct investment inflows as a percentage of GDP. Source: World Bank Development Indicators; United Nations Conference on Trade and Development (UNCTAD)

(continued)

Table 11.1 (continued)

Variable	Abbreviation	Definition
Percentage of individuals using the Internet	LnInternet	Individuals (% of population) who have used the Internet (from any location) in the last 3 months. Source: World Development Indicators, World Bank
Secure internet servers	LnSecureSrv	The number of distinct, publicly trusted TLS/SSL certificates found in the Netcraft Secure Server Survey. Source: World Development Indicators, World Bank
Fixed broadband subscriptions	LnBroadband	Fixed subscriptions (per 100 people) to high-speed access to the public Internet (a TCP/IP connection). This includes cable modem, DSL, fiber-to-the-home/building, other fixed (wired)-broadband subscriptions, satellite broadband, and terrestrial fixed wireless broadband. Source: World Development Indicators, World Bank
Mobile subscriptions	LnMobile	Subscriptions (per 100 people) to a public mobile telephone service that provide access to the PSTN using cellular technology. Source: World Development Indicators, World Bank

Table 11.2 ICT indicators, Country mean values

Country	Internet	Broadband	Server	Mobile
ALG	16,466	3380	1.986921	68,406
BHR	55,266	11,198	27.23259	113,565
EGY	22,191	2513	1.567779	59,417
IRN	21,677	4243	18.45406	56,320
IRQ	13,752	3304	0.437146	60,729
JOR	26,722	2452	5.682851	73,105
LYB	9185	1555	32.52278	84,924
MAR	34,902	2092	10.03331	76,749
OMAN	35,737	3305	10.05643	98,395
PLS	33,387	4071	17.71289	45,465
SAR	41,123	7974	9.028604	107,842
TUN	29,527	3809	9.735393	79,418
TUR	34,749	8359	157.8129	73,234
UAE	62,652	9738	73.03391	131,338
All	31,754	5154	26.80697	81,131

Table 11.3 Descriptive statistics

	Mean	Median	Maximum	Minimum	Std. Dev.	Observations
LnpcGDP	8.801	8.457	11.139	7.267	0.993	404
LnInvestment	3.104	3.160	3.763	1.071	0.326	377
LnPopulation	16.354	16.439	18.425	13.114	1.364	420
LnSchool	4.319	4.386	4.758	3.553	0.270	283
LnCredit	3.446	3.586	4.504	0.236	0.732	388
LnTrade	4.252	4.356	5.348	−3.863	0.855	400
Inflation	11.945	3.857	448.500	−16.117	36.177	374
COC	−0.244	−0.192	1.281	−1.627	0.629	294
FDI	2.219	1.293	33.566	−5.288	3.394	384
LnInternet	1.926	2.803	4.602	−7.928	2.612	331
LnSecureSrv	6.466	6.247	13.025	0.000	2.321	140
LnBroadband	0.369	1.207	3.447	−9.265	2.494	231
LnMobile	2.438	3.997	5..360	−6.306	2.961	383

Table 11.4 Correlation matrix

	LnpcGDP	Investment	Population	School	Credit	Trade	Inflation	COC	FDI	Internet	Secure Srv	Broadband	Mobile
LnpcGDP	1.000												
Investment	−0.124**	1.000											
Population	−0.509***	0.094*	1.000										
School	0.517***	0.122**	−0.334***	1.000									
Credit	0.172***	0.244***	−0.265***	0.324***	1.000								
Trade	0.291***	−0.070	−0.383***	0.343***	0.315***	1.000							
Inflation	−0.153***	0.042	0.191***	−0.262***	−0.277***	−0.712***	1.000						
COC	0.606***	0.230***	−0.462***	0.424***	0.510***	0.324***	−0.221***	1.000					
FDI	−0.025	0.039	−0.210***	0.162***	0.297***	0.341***	−0.131***	0.094*	1.000				
Internet	0.336***	0.131**	−0.159***	0.594***	0.419***	0.366***	−0.304***	0.274***	0.139***	1.000			
Secure Srv	0.282***	0.033	0.278***	0.290***	0.471***	−0.130*	0.180**	0.262***	−0.018	0.592***	1.000		
Broadband	0.247***	0.231***	−0.072	0.410***	0.463***	0.195***	−0.164***	0.220***	0.094	0.887***	0.597***	1.000	
Mobile	0.360***	0.074	−0.091*	0.624***	0.293***	0.321***	−0.254***	0.198***	0.196***	0.934***	0.160**	0.745***	1.000

Table 11.5 The impact of ICT on growth, Difference GMM method

	Internet	Internet server	Broadband	Mobile	High internet	Low internet
$LnPCGDP_{t-1}$	0.4572*** (0.0891)	0.3711** (0.1628)	0.6481*** (0.0731)	0.5099*** (0.0713)	0.4633*** (0.1311)	0.4862*** (0.0833)
Lninvestment	0.0314 (0.0379)	0.0826*** (0.0287)	0.0676* (0.0394)	0.0014 (0.0296)	0.0834* (0.0448)	−0.0159 (0.0414)
Lnpopulation	−0.2580* (0.1311)	−0.242824 (0.1609)	0.0229 (0.1640)	−0.1723 (0.1237)	−0.2494 (0.2027)	−0.3116** (0.1249)
Lnschool	0.0353 (0.0685)	0.0313 (0.109)	0.0351 (0.0821)	0.0163 (0.0751)	0.2713*** (0.0999)	−0.0488 (0.0678)
Lncredit	−0.0558* (0.0293)	−0.021841 (0.048)	−0.0201 (0.0377)	−0.0524* (0.029)	−0.0556 (0.0437)	−0.0566** (0.0271)
Lntrade	0.0081 (0.0194)	0.0108 (0.0298)	−0.0358 (0.0662)	0.0388 (0.0347)	0.0340 (0.078)	0.0134 (0.0528)
Inflation	0.00067 (0.0007)	−0.0006 (0.0006)	−0.0004 (0.0006)	0.0003 (0.0007)	−0.0005 (0.0009)	0.0006 (0.0005)
COC	0.0367* (0.0186)	−0.0846** (0.0384)	−0.0019 (0.032)	0.0374* (0.0211)	−0.0334 (0.0445)	0.052** (0.0244)
FDI	−0.0526 (0.0919)	0.270 (0.1736)	0.1421 (0.1712)	−0.0003 (0.1117)	0.0445 (0.2133)	−0.0898 (0.0638)
Lninternet	0.0210*** (0.0071)				0.1048* (0.0623)	0.0193*** (0.0059)
LnSecureSrv		0.0291*** (0.0105)				
LnBroadband			0.0063* (0.0037)			
LnMobile				0.0051 (0.010)		
Nb. Obs.	156	60	129	158	67	86
Nb. Countries	14	12	12	14	11	12
Sargan Stat.	83.0720	12.4560	72.8326	98.1402	24.6238	50.0432
Sargan Prob.	0.1548	0.6442	0.3220	0.1946	0.2638	0.1572
AR(1)	0.0101	0.0669	0.0015	0.0023	0.2962	0.0274
AR(2)	0.3466	0.8706	0.2375	0.8108	0.3713	0.5337

Table 11.6 Transmission channels, Difference GMM method

	Investment	Human capital	Financial development	Degree of openness	Foreign investment	Institutional development
LnPCGDP(−1)	0.5091*** (0.0644)	0.5052*** (0.0744)	0.4566*** (0.0914)	0.4586*** (0.090)	0.4608*** (0.0907)	0.4657*** (0.0763)
Lninvestment	−0.0676 (0.0416)	0.0219 (0.0328)	0.0351 (0.0387)	0.0312 (0.0379)	0.0279 (0.0378)	0.0264 (0.0343)
Lnpopulation	−0.1879 (0.1233)	−0.2486* (0.1401)	−0.2609* (0.1359)	−0.2535* (0.1389)	−0.2492* (0.134)	−0.1877 (0.139)
Lnschool	−0.0162 (0.0602)	−0.0271 (0.0708)	0.0337 (0.0639)	0.0349 (0.0701)	0.0459 (0.0668)	−0.0047 (0.0736)
Lncredit	−0.070** (0.0329)	−0.0534 (0.0318)	−0.0584* (0.0304)	−0.055* (0.0298)	−0.0552* (0.029)	−0.0603** (0.0285)
Lntrade	0.017 (0.0383)	0.0221 (0.0383)	0.0101 (0.0212)	0.0114 (0.0263)	0.0071 (0.019)	0.0175 (0.0376)
Inflation	0.0002 (0.0007)	0.0003 (0.0006)	0.0005 (0.0007)	0.0006 (0.0007)	0.0006 (0.0007)	0.0003 (0.0006)
COC	0.0425** (0.0196)	0.0282 (0.0215)	0.0341* (0.0195)	0.0366* (0.0191)	0.0372* (0.0188)	0.0743*** (0.0219)
FDI	−0.0708 (0.1079)	0.0242 (0.0977)	−0.0632 (0.0963)	−0.0536 (0.0919)	−0.1092 (0.1065)	−0.037 (0.0958)
Lninternet	−0.1086 (0.0595)	−0.0569 (0.0388)	0.017** (0.0084)	0.0245 (0.0339)	0.0216*** (0.0073)	0.0122 (0.0103)
Internet× Investment	0.0393** (0.0177)					
Internet× School		0.0187** (0.0094)				
Internet× Credit			0.0020 (0.0027)			
Internet×Trade				−0.0008 (0.0079)		
Internet×FDI					0.0004 (0.0003)	
Internet×Coc						−0.0147** (0.0073)
Nb. Obs.	156	156	156	156	156	156
Nb. Countries	14	14	14	14	14	14
Sargan Stat.	92.4004	95.7243	82.4635	82.5827	82.1342	95.2177
Sargan Prob.	0.2991	0.2219	0.1660	0.1638	0.1723	0.2328
AR(1)	0.0030	0.0069	0.0112	0.0102	0.0095	0.0073
AR(2)	0.4311	0.2967	0.2925	0.3608	0.3420	0.5515

References

Acemoglu D, Johnson S, Robinson J (2005) Chapter 6 Institutions as a fundamental cause of long-run growth. In: Handbook of economic growth, vol 1, pp 385–472

Arellano M, Bond S (1991) Some tests of specification for panel data: monte carlo evidence and an application to employment equations. Rev Econ Stud 58(2):277–297

Backus M (2001) E-governance and developing countries. IICD Research (Report No. 3)

Barajas A, Chami R, Yousefi SR (2011) The impact of financial development on economic growth in Mena region. Finan Dev 48

Ben Ali MS, Selmi N (2020) ICT for education and health care systems: potentialities and discrepancies in low and high income countries. In: Lechman E, Popowska M (eds) Society and technology: opportunities and challenges, pp 95–107

Ben Ali MS (2020) Does ICT promote democracy similarly in developed and developing countries? A linear and nonlinear panel threshold framework. Telematics Inform 50

Ben Ali MS, Sassi S (2017) The role of ICT adoption in curbing corruption in developing countries. In: Kaur H, Lechman E, Marszk A (eds) Catalyzing development through ICT Adoption. Routledge, pp 36–50

Blalock G, Gertler PJ (2008) Welfare gains from foreign direct investment through technology transfer to local suppliers. J Int Econ 74(2)

Brynjolfsson E, Hitt L (1996) Paradox lost? Firm-level evidence on the returns to information systems spending. Manag Sci 42(4):541–558

Brynjolfsson E, Hitt L (2000) Beyond computation: information technology, organizational transformation and business performance. J Econ Perspect 14(4):23–48

Brynjolfsson E, Hitt L (2003) Computing productivity: firm-level evidence. Rev Econ Stat 85(4):793–808

Cardona M, Kretschmer T, Strobel T (2013) ICT and productivity: conclusions from the empirical literature. Inform Econ Policy 25(3):109–125

Claessens S, Glaessner T, Klingebiel D (2002) Electronic finance: a new approach to financial sector development. World Bank discussion paper No. 431. World Bank, Washington, DC

Colecchia A, Schreyer P (2002) ICT investment and economic growth in the 1990s: is the United States a unique case? Rev Econ Dyn 5(2):408–442

Dedrick J, Gurbaxani V, Kraemer KL (2003) Information technology and economic performance: acritical review of the empirical evidence. ACM Comput Surv 35(1):1–28

Dewan S, Kraemer KL (2000) Information technology and productivity: evidence from country-level data. Manag Sci 46(4):548–562

Dutta U, Gupta H, Sengupta P (2019) ICT and health outcome nexus in 30 selected Asian countries: fresh evidence from panel data analysis. Technol Soc 59

Gholami R, Lee S-Y, Heshmati A (2005) The causal relationship between ICT and FDI. Research Paper 2005/026. UNU-WIDER, Helsinki

Gruber H, Koutroumpis P, Mayer T, Nocke V (2011) Mobile telecommunications and the impact on economic development. Econ Policy 26(67):387–426

Hong J (2017) Causal relationship between ICT R&D investment and economic growth in Korea. Technol Forecast Soc Change 116:70–75

Jorgenson D (2001) Information technology and the G7 economies. World Econ 4(4):139–169

Jorgenson DW, Vu KM (2005) Information technology and the world economy. Scand J Econ 107(4):631–650

Koutroumpis P (2009) The economic impact of broadband on growth: a simultaneous approach. Telecommun Policy 33(9):471–485

Levine R (1997) Financial development and economic growth: views and agenda. J Econ Lit 35(2):688–726

Meijers H (2014) Does the internet generate economic growth, international trade, or both? Int Econ Econ Policy 11(1):137–163

Oulton N (2002) ICT and productivity growth in the United Kingdom. Oxford Rev Econ Policy 18(3):363–379

Pattinson Colin (2017) ICT and green sustainability research and teaching. IFAC-PapersOnLine 50(1):12938–12943

Pohjola M (2002) The new economy in growth and development. Oxford Rev Econ Policy 18(3):380–396

Roller L, Waverman L (2001) Telecommunications infrastructure and economic development: a simultaneous approach. Am Econ Rev 91(4):909–923

Romer P (1986) Increasing returns and long-run growth. J Polit Econ 1002–1037

Shamim F (2007) The ICT environment, financial sector and economic growth: a cross-country analysis. J Econ Stud 34(4):352–370

Solow RM (1956) A contribution to the theory of economic growth. Quart J Econ 70(1):65–94

Stanley TD, Doucouliagos H, Steel P (2018) Does ICT generate economic growth? A meta-regression analysis. J Econ Surv 32(3):705–726

Stiroh KJ (2002) Information technology and the U.S. productivity revival: what do the industry data say? Am Econ Rev 92(5):1559–1576

Stiroh KJ (2005) Reassessing the impact of IT in the production function: a meta-analysis and sensitivity tests. Annales d'Economie et de Statistique 79(80):529–561

Van Ark B, Timmer MP, O'Mahony M, Inklaar R (2011) Productivity and economic growth in Europe: A comparative industry perspective. Int Prod Monit 21(21):3–23

Vu K (2011) ICT as a source of economic growth in the information age: empirical evidence from the 1996–2005 period. Telecommun Policy 35(4):357–372

Vu K, Hanafizadeh P, Bohlin B (2020) ICT as a driver of economic growth: a survey of literature and directions for future research. Telecommun Policy 44

Author Index

Subject Index